P

A SPY IN THE ARCHIVES

'The vanished world of Brezhnev's Russia brought to life with unusual verve, a disarming candour and a shrewd eye for the telling detail.' — **Robert Dessaix**

'Sheila Fitzpatrick single-handedly set in motion the renewal of Soviet studies: instead of the Cold War Manichean reports on the horrors of Stalinism, she delivered vivid portrayals of what did it effectively mean to be an ordinary citizen of the Stalinist Russia. *A Spy in the Archives* is the insanely readable crowning achievement of her distinguished career, a book every historian should dream to write. Through the autobiographic report on her visits to Soviet Union, she tells a story of bureaucratic hassles but also of deep and lasting personal friendships. One gets a touching picture which renders the taste of everyday life and its small pleasures without obfuscating the nightmares of a totalitarian state. If *A Spy in the Archives* will not become a bestseller, then there is something seriously wrong with our culture!'— **Slavoj Zizek**

A SPY IN THE ARCHIVES

A MEMOIR OF COLD WAR RUSSIA

SHEILA FITZPATRICK

I.B.TAURIS
LONDON · NEW YORK

To Igor and Irina, in memoriam

New paperback edition published in 2015 by
I.B.Tauris & Co. Ltd
London • New York
www.ibtauris.com

First published in hardback in 2013 by I.B.Tauris & Co. Ltd

First published in 2013 in Australia and New Zealand by Melbourne University Press.

ISBN: 978 1 78453 295 6
eISBN: 978 0 85773 481 5

A full CIP record for this book is available from the British Library
A full CIP record is available from the Library of Congress

Library of Congress Catalog Card Number: available
Printed and bound by CPI Group (UK) Ltd, Croydon, CR0 4YY

FSC www.fsc.org MIX Paper from responsible sources FSC® C013604

Contents

1

At the 'Spy College'

I was a student at Oxford writing a doctoral dissertation in Soviet history when I was outed as a spy in a Soviet newspaper. Or at least the next thing to a spy. According to the newspaper, I was one of those scholars who pretend to be doing scholarly research but are actually putting out disinformation, the way intelligence agents do. My work was 'simply provocation, a dishonest game', whose purpose was to obscure the truth. My activities 'differed little from the ploys of bourgeois spies'; I was an 'ideological saboteur'.

I didn't intend to be an ideological saboteur, whatever that might mean. I was in Moscow in June 1968, near the end of my second stint as a British exchange student, and all I wanted to do was get on with my archival research and be able to come back to the Soviet Union in the future to do more. I was passionate about my research and fascinated, in a non-admiring way, by the Soviet Union. But this was the period of the Cold War, and relations between the Soviet Union and the West were full of tension and mutual accusations. Anybody who worked on the Soviet Union was at risk of being seen by the Soviets as a spy. But when they actually accused you, the consequences were likely to be serious.

The cause of offence was my first scholarly article, published the previous year in a sober academic journal called *Soviet Studies*. It required some imagination to see my article in such a light: it was bibliographical, with the prosaic title 'AV Lunacharsky: Recent soviet interpretations and republications'. Lunacharsky, the first Soviet People's Commissar of Enlightenment after the Bolshevik Revolution of 1917, was the subject of my dissertation. My article wasn't even anti-Soviet by the standards of the time. Almost certainly it was not the content of the article that upset the Soviets but the fact that the author's name was followed by my academic location, St Antony's College, Oxford. St Antony's was often referred to in the Soviet Union, and in the West, too, as a 'spy college', meaning that a number of the Fellows had worked for British intelligence in the past, and were presumed to retain some ties in the present. The college's Russian Centre, particularly my supervisor, Max Hayward, the translator of *Dr Zhivago*, was in Soviet bad books for publicising writers in trouble with the regime and associating too closely with the Congress for Cultural Freedom in London and its alleged CIA sponsors.

Being outed as the next thing to a spy would really have upset me if I had known about it. I would have expected to find the KGB on my doorstep in Moscow informing me of my expulsion from the country, with the British Embassy hovering nearby to make sure I got out quickly. But fortunately I didn't read the newspaper, a particularly conservative one, and neither did any of my Russian friends nor, apparently, anyone from the embassy, so it passed unnoticed. The Russian friends might not have picked it up anyway, because they knew me by my married name, Sheila Bruce. Also, of course, they knew me to be a woman, whereas the newspaper thought S Fitzpatrick was a man. Whether the KGB, which presumably inspired the newspaper article, knew that Sh Bruce of the British Council Exchange (Sh is one letter in Russian) and S Fitzpatrick of St Antony's were one and the same remains unclear—though, if they didn't, shame on them for professional sloppiness. St Antony's comes out better from this Cold War story, professionally speaking, than the KGB: at least they were reading the Soviet press carefully enough to notice the article and tell me about it when I got back to Oxford that summer. I don't remember who gave me the news; I just remember my reaction, which was horror.

From a St Antony's standpoint, it wasn't that big a deal to have the Soviets throwing spying accusations at the college; it happened so often. But it was different for me than for Max Hayward and the other Russian Centre Fellows. Most of them were already persona non grata with the Soviets and therefore didn't go to the Soviet Union, which during the Cold War was very touchy about letting foreigners behind the Iron Curtain. I was a historian at the beginning of my career, and I needed Soviet archives and libraries to keep on doing the kind of work I wanted to do. In addition, I had made very close friends in Moscow and didn't want to lose touch with them: these relationships were shaped, no doubt, by the political context but transcended them, becoming bonds for life.

I had been bitten by the Moscow bug, like a number of my contemporaries on the student exchanges. The Soviet Union might be the most uncomfortable, inconveniently organised place imaginable, xenophobic and even dangerous at times, with an obstructive and suspicious bureaucracy to drive you mad, but we had managed to get to this exotic country, and had the almost unique status among resident foreigners of living among Russians, not in special foreign enclaves. We felt like cosmonauts who had landed on the moon: the question of liking or disliking the place was irrelevant. Students bitten by the Moscow bug were not content with a single year on the exchange, but did their best to return, as I did in two successive years. I explained it in a letter to my mother as being like soldiers in wartime, desperate to get back to the front.

I probably had a better background knowledge of spying than I did of Russian history when I set off to England in 1964 to study Soviet history and politics. They didn't teach Russian history at the University of Melbourne in my day. They did teach Russian, however, in a department headed by my parents' friend Nina Christesen, and I took two years of it, which was enough to read the language, but not very well. I wouldn't have admitted myself to graduate school later, when I was a professor of Soviet history in America, but Oxford in the 1960s had no qualms. Oxford—which offered no courses in modern Russian history, and only Old Church Slavonic on the language side—was not really in the business of teaching its postgraduates anything. Cynically, one could say that it was a matter of hanging around to absorb the atmosphere and leaving with a brand-name degree in your resume. As one of the (lower-status) spies among my Oxford acquaintances remarked, 'Oxford is a fine place to have been because you can always come back, even if they don't like you'.

My background knowledge of spying came from growing up in a left-wing family in Melbourne in the Cold War. I was nine when Julius and Ethel Rosenberg were convicted in the United States of being spies who passed on the secrets of the atomic bomb to the Soviet Union, and eleven in February 1953 when, despite worldwide protests, they were executed. My father, Brian Fitzpatrick, a civil liberties activist, was active in the local campaign to save them from execution, and I had no doubt that this just cause, supported by so many of the great and good throughout the world, would be victorious. As the execution date neared, we listened regularly to the bulletins on the radio, and I was sure that, as in any good radio serial, there would be a last-minute reprieve. It was a big shock when the reprieve didn't come, and I had to adjust some assumptions about how the world works. I was left with a certain puzzlement about my father's professed conviction that the Rosenbergs were innocent. They were Communists, which according to my father was OK, though at school people thought otherwise. As Communists, they believed that the Soviet Union was a better country than the United States; and they—and my father, too—thought the world would be a safer place if both superpowers had the bomb. So why shouldn't they have passed over atomic secrets? And if this was spying, what was so terrible about being a spy?

The next spying lesson came from the Petrov case. Vladimir Petrov, cultural attaché with the Soviet Embassy in Canberra, defected in 1954, bringing with him information about Soviet espionage procedures which was of great interest to all Western intelligence agencies. British intelligence secretly flew Leonard Schapiro, a British Soviet expert (and future mentor of mine) to Australia to help in Petrov's debriefing. When the Soviets attempted a forcible repatriation of Petrov's wife, Eugenia, also an embassy staffer, there was a scuffle at Darwin airport that made headlines all over the world. But it was the domestic aspects of Petrov's information that mattered most in Australian politics. In light of the information Petrov gave on his various contacts as a Soviet spy, Prime Minister Robert Menzies appointed a Royal Commission on Espionage headed by Mr Justice Owen. The Petrov affair was a political gift, as Petrov's contacts included someone on the staff of the opposition leader, Dr Evatt. This enabled Menzies to make Communist subversion, particularly within the ALP, a key issue in the upcoming election, which he duly won. Various friends of my father's, including Clem Christesen, with whom he worked on the journal *Meanjin*, and Clem's wife, Nina, of the Melbourne University Russian Department, were called as witnesses, a summons seen on the left as a form of smearing. My father would, I'm sure, have been happy to have been called, having relished his jousting with the commissioners at a Victorian Royal Commission on Communism a few years earlier. Unfortunately, he didn't know the Petrovs, not having the social standing or Canberra residence that might have thrown him in their way, so Petrov didn't name him. But my father attended every session of the royal commission and reported it with gusto and mockery. Many on the left thought the Petrov case was a put-up job to blacken the Soviet Union and the ALP and denied that the Petrovs were spies at all. I don't think that was my father's position. He didn't exclude the possibility that the Petrovs could have been spies under diplomatic cover but also didn't find that surprising or specific to Soviet diplomatic missions. In any case, he was more interested in the subsequent smear campaign against the left than the original circumstances. By the time of the Petrov case, when I was going on thirteen, I was less of a true believer in my father's causes than earlier. It impressed me, not altogether favourably, that he was having such a good time making fun of the royal commission and being regularly consulted by the opposition leader, Dr HV Evatt, who in his hour of need turned to my father—whose political roles included that of informal liaison between ALP leaders and Communists—for support. But I couldn't help catching some of my father's exhilaration with this real-life exposure to the spying game. He didn't want to be a spy himself (as far as I know), and he didn't take the occupation seriously, but it added a spice to life. He had always enjoyed the thought of being watched by the Australian Security Intelligence Organisation (ASIO), and might have been a bit disappointed by the thinness (as I now know, having read it in the National Archives) of his file. My father enjoyed greeting Colonel Spry, the head of ASIO, with punctilious politeness when he met him on the street. Perhaps it was in something of the same spirit that I chose to go to St Antony's to study Soviet history.

Becoming a Soviet historian wasn't a foregone conclusion, even with a left-wing father and a bit of Russian. I can't say that as a child I was particularly drawn to things Russian, despite the twelve unread orange volumes of Lenin's *Works* on our shelves, a few Left Book Club editions and our 78 recordings of the Red Army Choir singing patriotic folk songs. I positively disliked my picture books of Russian folk tales, the frightening *Baba Yaga* and *Petrushka,* probably presents from Nina, as well as the lacquered spoons and Eastern eggs to be found at the Christesens', the large oil painting of Napoleon at the gates of Moscow dominating the sitting room of our Russian-speaking refugee neighbours, and an annoying dog called Timoshenko, named during the wartime alliance for the Soviet Marshal, at our Australian neighbours' next door. Apart from my violin teacher, Boris Stupel, locally regarded as Russian though actually a Lithuanian Jewish survivor of the Kaunas ghetto, the only Russian element of my childhood that I really liked was Marjorie Fischer's *Palaces on Monday.* One of those Puffin books published by Penguin in the 1940s and 1950s to mould a generation of progressive children, *Palaces* was set in the Soviet Union of the 1930s, as seen through the eyes of two American children whose father, an engineer thrown out of work by the Depression, takes them to the USSR. The trip brings them undreamt-of independence from family control, apparently a characteristic of the Soviet Union, as the children ride a model railway built and run by children (I remember thinking how much better that was than Puffing Billy at Belgrave), participate in a film directed by an Eisenstein-like figure and spend a glorious summer at the Artek Children's Camp. Despite these wonders, Marjorie Fischer's children notice that in many respects the Soviet Union is still a mess, with crowded trams, few amenities and lots of crumbling buildings. But they learn to look at this in a future-oriented Soviet way: it's a construction site now, and necessarily a mess, but in a few years there will be a People's Palace of Culture. Years later, I borrowed the title of *Palaces on Monday* for a chapter in my book *Everyday Stalinism.*

The Russian Department at the University of Melbourne made me even less of a Russophile because of my objections to the sentimental-nationalist tone of most of the teaching (no Communist influence here that I could detect, despite the royal commission's concerns). What hooked me on Soviet history was researching and writing my fourth-year history honours thesis, 'Music and the People in the USSR'. Despite its title, which must have been partly tongue in cheek, this belonged neither to the fellow-travelling genre of the 1930s nor the genre of Cold War critique that was replacing it. My question was whether state pressure on Soviet composers like Shostakovich and Prokofiev to write simple, accessible 'music for the people' had in fact produced music that Soviet audiences (not just highbrows) wanted to hear; and my conclusion was that, since Soviet concert audiences still apparently preferred Tchaikovsky and the nineteenth-century classics, they hadn't pulled it off. Fifty years on, that conclusion seems a bit pessimistic, given the prominent place of Shostakovich's and Prokofiev's works in concert programs all over the world. But I was justly proud of my thesis and had a wonderful time doing the research in as many Russian-language sources as I could find, as well as cocking a snook at the existing scholarship by assuming that censorship, however annoying for the artists concerned, could conceivably have positive outcomes. After producing my first piece of independent historical research, I couldn't imagine that there was anything else in the world I would rather do. I particularly liked the thought of working on the Soviet Union, because so little was reliably known about it.

The custom in those days was for first-class honours graduates of the University of Melbourne to go off to Britain, preferably Oxford or Cambridge, for the postgraduate degree. I applied for a Commonwealth Scholarship to study

Soviet history and politics either at Oxford, where the literary scholar Max Hayward of St Antony's specialised in Soviet literary politics, or the London School of Economics, where the Sovietologist Leonard Schapiro taught political science. There were few Soviet historians around at this point, because the historical profession had not yet accepted the Soviet period as a proper subject of historical enquiry, but EH Carr, whose work I admired, was at Cambridge and I don't know why I didn't think of going to study with him. When both St Antony's and the LSE accepted me, I chose St Antony's. I have always said that the reason for this was that London seemed too intimidating for a young woman who had never been outside Australia, and Oxford more manageable. Perhaps, but why not the even more manageable Cambridge? I can't help feeling that at some level I wanted to stick my face into the lions' den.

An innocent from abroad landing in a spy college is the story I told over the years. But that can't be quite right. I knew a lot about St Antony's and the world of English Cold War Sovietology before I left. In my last months in Melbourne, I had written an article for the journal *Dissent* that analysed Soviet literary politics and the Cold War parameters of the field, and one of my key texts was the conference volume recently edited by Max Hayward and Leo Labedz, *Literature and Revolution in Soviet Russia*. While I couldn't then have known for sure that the conference, held under the auspices of St Antony's and the London Sovietological journal, *Survey*, was CIA funded, I certainly knew of the possibility. I knew that *Survey*, edited by Leo Labedz, was an organ of the Congress for Cultural Freedom in London, and that it was thought to have CIA funding, along with other Congress for Cultural Freedom–sponsored journals like *Encounter*. One of my first questions to Max Hayward after arriving at St Antony's was whether some kind of formal relationship existed between *Survey* and the college's Russian Centre (I remember this because of my embarrassment when he quoted the question, though without identifying me, on introducing Labedz as a speaker at the college; the answer was no.)

Everyone on the left in Melbourne had heard allegations about the Congress for Cultural Freedom and the CIA. They were a special preoccupation of Clem Christesen, for whom I worked one summer when I was at the University; Clem's suspicions were directed particularly at *Meanjin*'s anti-Communist competitor, *Quadrant*. In fact, as it later turned out, not only were *Encounter, Survey* and *Quadrant* in receipt of CIA money via the Congress, but so was *Dissent*, the journal (one of whose editors was a good friend of mine) in which my article appeared. It's hard to reconstruct attitudes after fifty years, but it looks as if I was less indignant about CIA funding of anti-Communist publications than Clem and my father were.

Literature and Revolution was state-of-the-art in the cultural branch of Sovietology that was of particular interest to me, and its analysis of current literary politics in the Soviet Union focused squarely on a Soviet journal that was to have great importance in my life, *Novy mir*. *Novy mir* (New World) was presented as the standard bearer of the 'liberal' camp in Soviet literature, dedicated to greater openness and less oppressive censorship in the spirit of the Thaw. Its chief opponent was the journal *Oktyabr'*, representing Stalinist 'dogmatists' and 'die-hards'. Hayward's sympathies, and those of all Western Sovietologists writing on the subject, were with *Novy mir*. I had no difficulty in recognising the ideologically based conflict of the literary journals described because it had its Australian analogue in the battles of *Meanjin*, regarded by its opponents as soft on Communism, and *Quadrant*. For my father, it would have been obvious that *Meanjin* was the *Novy mir* equivalent—that is, 'progressive' and on the side of the angels—while the right-wing *Quadrant* was the bad guy. This was one of my father's political assumptions that I don't seem to have got round to questioning, as of 1964. It's only now that it strikes me that, for Hayward and the Sovietological world I was entering, the analogy would have worked the other way.

I went to Oxford in 1964 ready to be disappointed. That was my general attitude to life, combined with a strong hope that the fabled places that were bound to fall below expectations would also be of consuming interest. Oxford disappointed me even in this: I found it intellectually substandard (at least in my area) and full of self-regard and snobbery; I never developed an affection for the place or even a deep interest in it. A particular source of disappointment was that the St Antony's people seemed to think that Soviet history could be written on the basis of diplomatic and intelligence gossip, without any kind of decent source work, and they were shameless in their displays of what I took to be political bias, though a more sympathetic observer might have called it exercise of moral judgement. From my letters to my mother, it appears that Max Hayward was more or less a default choice of supervisor, and that I looked around a bit before settling for him. That's odd, given his expertise in the area I was planning to work in. Perhaps I was put off by the college gossip about his being an alcoholic, recently forced to go on the wagon by his doctor and thus even more depressed and unsociable than usual, or perhaps it was just because he was a literary scholar and translator, not a historian. In his mid forties when I met him, a bachelor living above the St Antony's Russian Centre library in Church Walk, Max had been one of the young Russianists seconded to the British Embassy in Moscow in the postwar years, where he immersed himself in Russian literary life as well as bars. Back for a second posting in 1955, he was kicked out and was subsequently persona non grata, somebody who would always be refused a visa and was periodically attacked for his 'anti-Soviet activities' in the Soviet press. When he spoke of the Russia he had known in the 1950s, I had the impression, for all his anti-Communism, of a lost Eden. Oxford, where he landed after his expulsion, seemed a place of dreary travail by comparison, as well as a source of social insecurity (he was a scholarship boy, propelled out of a lower-class background by his great gift for languages).

I will sometimes call him 'Max', because that's what he ended up as for me, but in the Oxford period I always addressed him as 'Mr Hayward', which was standard practice at Oxford at the time, and he identified himself in this way when he rang me to make an appointment, which was not. The fact that he made such calls is evidence that, despite college gossip to the contrary, he was trying to be a good supervisor, but it was an agonising process. Eleven o'clock in the morning was the normal hour of our meetings and he would invariably offer me a glass of sherry, which I felt obliged to drink, although he, of course, had nothing. Not knowing what to say to me or ask, he usually fell back on monologues. He had a keen, almost obsessive sense of the tragedy of the Russian intelligentsia and of deluded international leftists who had believed in the

Soviet Union. As I wrote to my mother, this was so much the Hayward I had conjured up for myself in researching the *Dissent* article that I almost felt I had invented him. After attending (I can't think why) the funeral of a deluded American leftist, Joe Freeman, in the autumn of 1965, Max came back full of emotional reactions about the pathos of it, to which I listened in rigid silence in case I started to cry. I didn't tell him that another deluded leftist, my father, had died a few weeks after Freeman and I hadn't gone home for the funeral.

None of the students or (to my observation) Fellows at St Antony's seemed to be close to Hayward. The only close friend I knew him to have was Patricia Blake, a glamorous journalist with Soviet interests who lived in New York but quite often visited in connection with their literary collaborations. When she was around, or one of the visiting quasi-dissident Russian poets like Andrey Voznesensky, Hayward was a bit more lively; otherwise, shambling around like a bear away from his natural haunts, he conveyed an impression of mute suffering. His suffering seemed to be both personal and on behalf of Russian literature under the Soviet boot: in Patricia's words, quoted in his obituary by Leonard Schapiro, 'Max acted as the custodian of Russian literature in the West until such time as it could be restored to Russia'. He had wonderful Russian, although he spoke so slowly—in English, too—that he managed to sound simultaneously like a native speaker and totally unlike any real-life Russian ever sounded.

While I had my reservations about Max, I found him a more interesting character than anyone else around at St Antony's. I had rather an aversion to the Warden of St Antony's, Bill Deakin, famous for his wartime feat of being parachuted into Yugoslavia to make contact with Tito's partisans, though I can't locate its origins. Perhaps it was that he didn't like having women around the college (mine was the first year women had been admitted, and there were only six of us), or that I didn't like his wartime orderly, whom he had brought to serve (servilely, I thought) as Bursar of the College. The perpetual rumours about his intelligence connections—'Mr FW Deakin is running a school for spies in Oxford, disguised as St Antony's College', the *Saturday Evening Post* reported in 1967—didn't endear him to me either.

Not that I disliked everyone rumoured to have intelligence connections. In fact, the only Fellow I really warmed to was Sergey Utechin, said to be active in the *émigré* organisation NTS (the initials standing for People's Labour Union in Russian), which reputedly practised all sorts of 'sabotage' activity in the Soviet Union, and not just ideological either. Utechin (I never called him Sergey) was the friendliest of the Fellows, perhaps because he was only a junior one, and told me a lot about his life. A good Soviet Communist until the war, he found himself in German-occupied territory during the war, ending up afterwards in Berlin, and somewhere along the line married an Englishwoman and came to Oxford. There he wrote a doctoral thesis on the new elite in Russia, which EH Carr—notorious for his toughness as an outside examiner, especially if he thought the work was anti-Soviet—tried to fail. Despite the NTS connection, I found Utechin less stridently anti-Soviet than the other St Antony's Sovietologists. I saw him as a kind of Professor Pnin from the Nabokov stories, and, as I wrote to my mother, 'began to feel a great sympathy for him, looking at his bald head and his beard, and his arms of unequal length and his tennis shoes'. It was surely 'some Nabokovian accident' that he found himself 'in an impossible situation of a liberal, Marxist *émigré* who is not a Communist or a Fascist or an Orthodox Believer [of whom there was a thriving community in Oxford] and above all is not an English gentleman'.

My father was still alive when I was working out my dissertation topic, and I wrote things to him that I might not have written to my mother. I wanted to do a 'grand project', I told him, something difficult and creative that nobody else had done. That was my understanding of what my father himself had done with his early economic histories of Australia, written outside academia and as a conscious challenge to it. It was an interesting twist that I was trying to bring this off while travelling—with my father's blessing—the most conventional of academic paths and going to Oxford.

I didn't tell my father of another plan I had for my dissertation, although to be fair, this may be because he was dead by the time I formulated it. Critical of the preference of Hayward and other Sovietologists for focusing on victims of the regime and holding them up as heroes of a morality play, I decided I would like to write about one of the unheroic compromisers of Soviet history. 'O to have known, to have loved/Too many Davids and Judiths', wrote the American Robert Lowell in a poem about martyred tyrannicides; his message was that it was time to look at things from the tyrant-monster's point of view. I discovered Lowell and read him obsessively in the year after my father's death, which clearly provided a subtext for my reading of this poem. My father, a perpetual critic of government, seemed a natural David or Judith, and I certainly felt I might have loved him too much. At the same time, he played the political game with such gusto that I saw him more as a realist and compromiser (a potential monster?) than an idealist. In any case, out of this turmoil of hidden emotions, as well as for more respectable academic reasons, the subject I chose for my dissertation was one of the greatest of all Soviet compromisers: Anatoly Lunacharsky, People's Commissar of Enlightenment in the first Bolshevik government.

Lunacharsky, known as 'a Bolshevik among intellectuals and intellectual among Bolsheviks', was not deeply respected by either side, though he was regarded as someone who did as much good as he could, particularly in getting artists and intellectuals out of political trouble, while averting his gaze from other bad things going on around him. Before the Revolution, he had been a literary journalist living in European emigration, active in Russian Marxist philosophical controversies and sometimes at odds, as a result, with Lenin. My dissertation topic, approved in June 1965 on my admission to D.Phil. (the Oxford equivalent of PhD) candidacy, was 'Lunacharsky as Philosopher and Administrator of the Arts'. The 'philosopher' part was what I could work on in Oxford and the British Museum, which had good holdings of Lunacharsky's pre-revolutionary publications. 'Administrator' covered his activities as People's Commissar (the revolutionary term for minister) for education and the arts from October 1917 to his resignation in 1929, and would have to be researched in the Soviet Union, preferably from archives. After immersing myself for more than a year in Lunacharsky's pre-revolutionary philosophy writing, I came away with the sense that he was a nice, well-meaning man, but a worse than second-rate thinker. This was the attitude underlying my first scholarly paper on Lunacharsky, delivered first at St Antony's and then in Schapiro's seminar at the LSE. I was 'out-Oxfording Oxford', as one of my friends put it, in this paper. In other words, it was in the great Oxbridge tradition of witty one-upmanship, delivered with the right intonation of *de haut en bas* mockery of all things Soviet. I was good at this sort of thing, although it was not the quality in myself I most admired. 'Elegant writing in the well-turned-paradox style', was how I described it to my mother, adding that 'I know the dangers, but it seemed the only way to cope with the subject'. I suppose that by 'coping with the subject' I meant getting away with (privately) pitying the monsters, or at any rate their compromised associates, while addressing an audience that loved only the Davids and Judiths. But you would have had to know me well to pick up anything like pity.

'Perhaps there is a place in the writing of contemporary history not only for the crimes but for the follies of mankind', was how I led off the paper. 'Lunacharsky, who once called himself the poet of revolution, turns out to be its Mrs Malaprop, and his monumental building a folly instead of a temple.' I went on to describe him as 'the patron saint of fellow-travellers', with little political influence at home. Introducing the (comparatively bold) notion that most of the first generation of Bolshevik leaders regarded themselves as men of culture, I disarmed negative reactions by the gratuitously unkind comment that 'if private culture was an admissible part of the early Bolshevik image, there was always the possibility of a reduction ad absurdum. This, even before the revolution, was Lunacharsky's role'.

Bearing in mind that I was to be denounced in the Soviet press a few years later for an article on Lunacharsky, you might think on the basis of these quotations that I had it coming to me, being so disrespectful about a Soviet icon. So I should make it clear in advance that this first paper of mine was *not* my first published article. It would have been, but I pulled it at the last minute when I was already living in Moscow as an exchange student. From that vantage point, it looked completely different to me: not witty and urbane, but just bitchily anti-Soviet. At St Antony's and the LSE, my paper was a great success. Hayward, Schapiro, Walter Laqueur (of *Encounter* and the Congress for Cultural Freedom) and the rest were full of admiration. Laqueur wanted the original Oxford paper for the *Journal of Contemporary History*; Utechin wanted the LSE paper (somewhat different in content, but similar in tone) for *Soviet Studies*. I was on the way to being launched as a rising star in British Sovietology.

To my mother, informed of my successes in my weekly letters, it sounded as if I had gone over to the enemy. This reaction astonished me when I re-read our correspondence in the course of researching this memoir. Was I really being attacked from the left, as a Cold Warrior, by my *mother*? It was my father, much more overtly left wing in my childhood, with whom I had quarrelled about politics in my teens and early twenties. I had no memory of my mother taking my father's side in these arguments—in fact, I thought she, too, had been critical of my father's political activities, along with his drinking and lack of income and most other things about him. I knew that in the 1930s, when she first knew my father, she had been active on the left in her own right, but towards the end of her life she swung so far to the right, in her distaste for immigrants and innovation, that it seemed like ancient history. Here, however, was evidence that, at least in the years immediately after my father's death in 1965, she was as left wing as he was.

Our conflict started with my mother wondering whether the 'ideological history' I was doing in my dissertation might not look rather old hat by the time I was ready to publish, if Soviet conditions continued to liberalise. 'Ideological history' could be understood either as history of ideology or history informed by ideological bias. I evidently assumed the second—indeed, I seem to have misread her handwriting (although I realised this only on re-reading the letter almost fifty years later) and thought she was accusing me of 'ideological warfare'. I must have been feeling very uneasy about my new St Antony's–appropriate persona to have made such a mistake. In any case, I shot back that she had got it all wrong, and was being not only 'silly' but also 'insulting', an overreaction that clearly puzzled her. We never sorted out this misunderstanding, which was the sort of thing that happened in the days before cheap international telephone calls, when communication took place via exchange of blue aerogrammes, covered with tiny writing, that took five days to arrive.

Strangely enough, I thought of myself as a Young Turk in British Sovietology, despite writing the kind of thing the Old Turks loved. As I explained to my mother shortly after the 'ideological warfare' incident, I and one of the other St Antony's students were planning a revisionist volume that would attempt a kind of 'agnostic' or non-political approach to Soviet history, in contrast to Hayward's focus on heroic dissenters and Schapiro's on political opposition. At the same time, I cautiously noted, we would obviously need Hayward's approval to get it published—all the more since he was one of the editors of the St Antony's Papers, an obvious series in which to publish such a book. Our non-political stance would consist of avoiding Schapiro-like topics such as the growth of the totalitarian state, the Cheka (political police), and opposition factions within the Bolshevik Party, on the grounds that although such things existed, 'enough tears have been shed over them'. 'The more that is written [about such topics]', I concluded resentfully, 'the more people like you accuse innocent people like me of ideological warfare'.

I regarded myself as totally apolitical in these years, which meant that I was paying almost no attention to international politics but was sceptical of whatever seemed to be the dominant opinion on what I thought of as the woolly left. My indifference extended to the Vietnam War and the involvement of American and Australian troops. I signed a protest against Australian participation, though without particular enthusiasm, but I considered the arguments there to be 'much simpler' (as I wrote to my mother) than on American participation, presumably because I thought there was no need for Australia to follow America's footsteps without due calculation of its national interests. I believed 'there was strong support for Australian and American action in Vietnam among Australians', or so I told Radio Kiev in the spring of 1966, and 'supposed the Australian motive was fear and the need to keep America happy'. That seemed at least a realistic basis for foreign policy, although I thought the Australian government had 'overestimated the price that had to be paid for American defence'. This anti-anti-Vietnam formulation was no doubt influenced by the fact that Radio Kiev was fishing for an outright condemnation of Australian and American involvement, which got my back up. Still, the arguments against American involvement, as well as Australian, seemed pretty simple and straightforward to many people at the time (and to me in retrospect). My mother, now teaching history at Monash University in Melbourne and surrounded by young anti-Vietnam activists, was one of those who opposed it.

My rather self-satisfied report of my comments to Radio Kiev annoyed my mother to the point that she abandoned her usual indecisiveness, self-distrust and suspicion of unqualified statements and came back swinging. She must have been having a similar argument with my younger brother, then a student at Trinity College, Melbourne, and evidently in the throes of his own revolt against the family politics. Summarising the views of Vietnam that my brother and I 'found so distasteful', she pressed me on those Kiev comments on Australian support for the war.

> Have you been following the Australian press on this? At first, even when the sending of conscripts to Vietnam was announced, there was remarkably little feeling on it, but at least since the actual call ups have started the feeling has spread fairly extensively. Can you really see America's action as much short of inadequately called for aggression? Can you really accept, as we are required to do as axiomatic, that China is the aggressor there? Do you really accept the reasonableness of sending out people who have not volunteered to fight so completely offensive a war there?

She felt a 'steady hatred of the Vietnam policy' that was part of a general anti-Americanism which, although common on the Australian left, I hadn't associated with her before. 'I just feel that Pax Americana is a sort of perpetual but unavoidable defeat which at the same time is an intolerable insult to the intellect, that one should be expected to accept such phoney propaganda', she wrote in high irritation, adding that she found phoney propaganda and insults to the intellect 'much more excusable in the Communists, though I know you don't, if only because of its lack of surface attraction'. That makes me smile when I re-read it now; the sting in the tail was so typical of her. Reading it the first time round, I probably refused to be amused.

In her next letter, my mother recalled wistfully that 'there had been a time when the USSR seemed to offer a prospect of a society in which the intellectual need not be alienated'. Trampling roughshod over this excursion into nostalgia, I proceeded to read her some lessons on Soviet politics, or rather the mistaken readings of Soviet politics prevalent among Western leftists. My first text was a postwar libel action brought by Soviet defector Victor Kravchenko (author of *I Chose Freedom*, a bestselling bugbear of the left) against French critics, who said he had been bought by American money and made up all his Soviet horror stories. Reading the transcript, I had been appalled by the dishonesty of the French left in the trial. 'Well, maybe the Left was right about American money', I wrote to my mother,

> but their defence was absolutely unscrupulous. They had witnesses sent from the USSR (what about Soviet money?) including Kravchenko's wife, and they all lied on just about every point, naturally because they were going back; but what was worse was the utter credulous ignorance of the left-wing character witnesses for the USSR, and the fact that the defence lied intentionally on a number of points and flung mud when they were challenged.

Reading the Kravchenko trial had made me think I'd better have another look at another bestseller hated on the left, Arthur Koestler's *Darkness at Noon*, about the Soviet show trials of Nikolay Bukharin and other opponents of Stalin in the late 1930s. I had hitherto regarded Koestler in the orthodox left-wing way as an 'unpleasant paranoiac', I wrote to my mother.

> On re-reading this seemed impossible to defend. He was certainly a bit of a fool to have stayed in the Comintern so long ... with a great capacity for self-deception and rather unstable, almost artificial enthusiasms. But even *Darkness at Noon* is not a bad book, a bit romantic but not romanticised, and based extremely closely on Alex Weissberg's account of Soviet prisons (which is good of its kind) and even more on the verbatim reports of the 1937–8 show trials published in Moscow. The main character is quite a fair realisation of the speeches made by Bukharin and [Karl] Radek at those trials—of course the stenographic report may have been tampered with, but not by Koestler.

As I re-read all this, I'm torn between congratulating myself on the capacity for unbiased critical appraisal and reproaching myself for being so mean to my mother. Oddly enough, in the same letter I identified myself as a Soviet historian 'nearer to a fellow-travelling position' than a Cold War one, but it's not hard to see why my mother might have doubted it and thought that St Antony's had really done a job on me. In what was perhaps meant to be a reassuring conclusion, I noted that I wasn't going to publish my critique of the fellow-travelling reading of Kravchenko and Koestler, so as not to get into a political fight. No doubt feeling caught between two fires, I complained 'that you can say what you like about America, or Nazi Germany, or the English Establishment, or even General de Gaulle, or Vichy, and people will agree or disagree, but if you write about Russia, or China, or European Communism, everyone including yourself suspects your motives'. *Including yourself* surely came from the heart, and so it should have done. Looking back, my motives look pretty murky.

My Christmas present to my mother was a subscription to *Encounter.* She found it quite interesting until an open letter from Leonard Schapiro to Soviet Prime Minister Kosygin (calling on him to show respect for law and rein in the KGB) aroused her ire: 'I thought [it] was a pity if Schapiro is one of your Russian sponsors and would feel very annoyed and insulted if I were Mr Kosygin, even if I thought that Schapiro's views were reasonable'. I had disliked Schapiro's letter myself (though this was a slightly conflictual situation, as I liked the man, and he had gone out of his way to be kind to me), and agreed that the letter was 'pretty awful'—but then completely spoiled the effect by adding that its condescending tone and rather arch men-of-the-world-together approach 'seemed a bit like Brian's [my father's] in an off moment'. This was accurate but unforgivable, not only because my father was recently dead, but also because a subtext of the whole exchange was my mother's suspicion (and my own) that by becoming an Oxford-style anti-Communist Sovietologist, I was betraying him.

A spate of spy stories came out around this time, including allegations in the mainstream press that the CIA had funded the Congress for Cultural Freedom and the publications associated with it, including *Encounter* and *Survey*. I wrote to my mother in July 1966 that

> the latest *Encounter* is very defensive since the *New York Times* said they got money from the CIA (as is always said of money from American foundations, like the £1 million St Antony's is getting if they can match it from British sources; it might be true, but so what?) ... I remember Brian also applied for Rockefeller grant. Anyone can be smeared if you try. Why not switch your indignation from Vietnam and *Encounter* to the International Court decision on South Africa? Or to the Nobel Prize being given to ['official' Soviet novelist Mikhail] Sholokhov, and Sholokhov's remarks on [Andrey] Sinyavsky [convicted on charges of anti-Soviet activity after publishing literary work abroad]? I must say [Australian Prime Minister Harold] Holt was very disgusting on Vietnam (all the way with LBJ), which is not to say that the war could be ended if you and the *New Statesman* were in control. What happens to the 'sluggish Australian economy' if American money were withdrawn? ... Did you know, by the way, that mail going across Iron Curtain is read on *both* sides?

The tone was harsh, even in the context of our recent exchanges, and my politics had taken such a rightward turn, at least for purposes of family argument, that I might have been writing for *Encounter* myself.

All through my time at Oxford, I was desperate to go to the Soviet Union for a year of dissertation research. I tried to get on the British exchange, run by the British Council, but the problem was that I was an Australian without a British passport. The British Council was sympathetic and sent the case up to be adjudicated by the Foreign and Commonwealth Offices, but they ruled against me. Then I thought I had managed it, with Nina Christesen's help, and could go on a newly negotiated Australian exchange. But it fell through at the last moment and I had to spend a second year at St Antony's. The SS *Baltika*, on which I was to have sailed to Leningrad, departed without me on 3 September 1965. That was also the day my father died, without warning, in Australia. We had quarrelled a few months earlier and not made it up. The telegram announcing his death didn't reach me until too late for me to get back to the funeral. Both my mother and I were depressed and guilt-ridden after the death—I knew this about her from our correspondence, and she knew it about me—but we were unable to comfort each other and mainly pretended not to notice. I felt my life had become unmoored. I hated England but believed, for no rational reason, that my father's death had made return to Australia impossible.

Sometime during that miserable winter, I tentatively re-established contact with my Melbourne boyfriend, Alex Bruce, who had since my departure become a Japanologist and was currently living in Tokyo. We had broken up before I left Australia, but my letter was a cautious signal that that might be open for reconsideration, and Alex responded to it. This crystallised at some point into a plan to get married in Japan the next summer, but I didn't tell my mother or anyone else for some months; as I explained later, I was 'embarrassed to seem to be exploiting Alex and also extremely secretive about the whole thing'. The idea of possible exploitation came partly from the fact that

Alex was more or less the only man left standing in my world (another boyfriend from the Melbourne days having died a few months before my father) and partly because, being British born, he held British citizenship as well as Australian. If I had a British passport, to which marrying him would entitle me, I could go to the Soviet Union on the British exchange. I kept trying not to think about that when I thought about marrying Alex, but it was hopeless: it wouldn't be disregarded. I had, of course, non-instrumental reasons for marrying him, but I could never straighten out how the two sets balanced. The thought that this was an instrumental move on my part to get a British passport bothered both of us, and no doubt ensured the ultimate failure of the marriage. At the time, however, Alex had no objection to my going off to spend a year in the Soviet Union immediately after our marriage, since he himself wanted to spend another unencumbered year in Japan. The plan was that we should marry in Tokyo in the summer, I would go off to the Soviet Union if the British Council would send me, Alex would apply to do a D.Phil. in Japanese history at St Antony's, and then, if all went well, we would meet up in Oxford and start married life together in the summer of 1967.

I let the January deadline for applications to the 1966–67 British exchange go by, but once the marriage plan was settled, I flung myself into action. The British Council people, remembering my heroic efforts and last-minute disappointment the previous year, decided to interview me anyway early in June, on the basis that, since I was planning to marry a British citizen, I was a presumed future British passport holder. 'I thought the whole marriage issue was going to be embarrassing', I wrote to my mother, 'but it was not, since they seemed rather sympathetic to the idea and even pleased that I should be pleased'. (I winced a little re-reading this; clearly I was in a state of mind to be surprised that someone in England, or anywhere, might be interested in my happiness.) The problem was that they had already selected the list for the ten-month British Council scholarships, but decided to put me on the reserve list and hope one of the chosen twenty dropped out.

When I finally wrote to my mother, telling her simultaneously of the marriage plans and the possibility I would be going to the Soviet Union the next year, she responded with immediate and deep disapproval. Perhaps she would have been against my marrying in any circumstances, as she considered that her own marriage, with the consequent resignation from her job as a tutor in Politics at the University of Melbourne, had been a disastrous misstep, which, I inferred, was only compounded by my arrival in the world a year or so later. (I resented this view and had questioned her in the past about whether the university had formally banned employment of married women or if this was just her timid understanding of the prevailing conventions; in any case, I thought she should have put up a fight and shouldn't blame her blighted life on me.) Her opposition to my marriage was nothing to do with Alex, a former colleague of hers at Monash whom she liked, but she was very uneasy about the cloudy circumstances, and who can blame her. When she referred to my proposed 'passport marriage', I duly squirmed, but persisted. 'Don't throw too much cold water on these plans', I wrote firmly (her automatic naysaying and pessimism were a family joke, as well as a perennial source of resentment). 'You may think that the best thing for me to do is to stay in Oxford for another year but I don't.' About that, I was certainly right.

Perhaps it was the prospect of finally encountering the Soviet Union at first hand, or perhaps it was that I had got tired of out-Oxfording Oxford, but my Lunacharsky work had taken a new tack. I noticed that a lot of new books by and about Lunacharsky had been published in the Soviet Union recently, and was sufficiently intrigued by their contents to write to Utechin, now editing the journal *Soviet Studies*, to offer him an article on the phenomenon. This was to be in place of the written-up version of my LSE talk of the previous year that I had already promised him, so evidently I was having second thoughts about putting that in print. (I don't now remember if leaving my other article, based on the St Antony's paper, with the *Journal of Contemporary History* was an oversight, or because I still liked it.) In the spring of 1966, unsure if I would get to the Soviet Union on the British exchange, but hopeful, I went off on a student tourist trip (of which more later) that included five days in Moscow. Quite unexpectedly, this turned out to be a goldmine as far as my Lunacharsky study was concerned. It started when our young tour guide, the intellectual and free-thinking Alyosha, launched into an enthusiastic speech about the liberating implications of Lunacharsky's early philosophical work when he heard what my dissertation topic was; he and all his semi-alienated young intellectual friends were keenly interested in him, he said. Well versed in the subtleties of current Soviet literary politics, he told me that all sorts of interesting Lunacharskiana was being published and eagerly read by the intelligentsia, and that big fights were going on among scholars, editors and censors about what could be published and with what omissions.

Then, by remarkable accident, I met another Lunacharsky admirer in Moscow. (I think it really *was* an accident, although conspiracy-minded Russians might disagree; if, on the other hand, the KGB—tipped off by a double agent at *Soviet Studies*?—sent him and Alyosha to me, I can only thank them.) I was in a second-hand bookshop looking for Lunacharsky books when a man started talking to me about the latest Soviet Lunacharsky scholarship. We went off for a walk to continue the conversation. He was a graduate student at the Gorky Institute of Literature in Moscow, he said, and a friend of a scholar called Anatoly Elkin, who had written a biography of Lunacharsky. (This was true, and so was his judgement that the biography wasn't much good.) Elkin, however, was working on another biography, his friend said, to be published in the series Lives of Remarkable Men (as in due course it was), which would be much more interesting because he had put in material from the Party Archives about Lunacharsky's policy conflicts with Stalin in his last years. My new acquaintance, who didn't give his name, also filled me in on what was likely to be included in the forthcoming volumes of Lunacharsky's *Collected Works*, and what left out. 'It will be interesting to see if he is right', I remarked to my mother, but as I have forgotten exactly what he told me, I will never know. Before we parted, he promised to try and get hold of one of the interesting new Lunacharsky publications and, if he was successful, bring it to the bookshop the next day; I went back, but he didn't show up. Still, I could hardly have had more dramatic confirmation of my own suspicions, and Alyosha's claim, that Lunacharsky had become a hot and contested topic in the Soviet Union.

Utechin accepted my suggestion, and that's how, in the summer before my first year in Moscow, I came to write the article that *Sovetskaya Rossiya* would later denounce. It was written in a notably different tone than my earlier ones, more sympathetic to its subject and less mocking and belittling. Why were Soviet intellectuals suddenly so interested in Lunacharsky, more than thirty years after his death, I wondered. Some of his recent interpreters were representing him as a liberal and praising him for advocating a position of state 'neutrality' in the arts. That obviously had contemporary relevance to the intelligentsia's struggle, starting in the mid 1950s with the Thaw, to get the regime off its back. The interesting twist, however, was that, on my reading of the materials on the 1920s, Lunacharsky *wasn't* a liberal, though he was tolerant of divergent artistic currents and temperamentally disinclined to repression. Nor was he in favour of state or Party neutrality in the arts and scholarship; he just disliked using coercive means. Another set of editors and interpreters, notably the editors of the (still incomplete) eight-volume *Collected Works* that was in the process of publication, rejected the liberal argument but glossed over most of the contradictions in Lunacharsky's positions, making him much less interesting and complex than, in my view, he actually was. I didn't pay much attention to them in my article, which is no doubt why I omitted to memorise a name that would soon become important in my life: Alexander Ovcharenko, the deputy chief editor of the *Works*, who was to be my official supervisor in Moscow.

It was the third set of commentators, headed by a certain IA Sats, that impressed me most, both on grounds of scholarly integrity and objectivity and, in Sats's case, because there was a slightly off-beat quality to his way of arguing that appealed to me. Sats—the best of Lunacharsky's editors, I said in my article—had edited and published some really interesting materials on the philosophical explorations that had got Lunacharsky into trouble with Lenin before the Revolution. In addition, he had somehow managed to get back into print Lunacharsky's pen portraits of Soviet leaders from the 1920s—not the fully unmentionable, like oppositionists Lev Trotsky and Grigory Zinoviev, but an array of candid pictures of others, along with a lively revolutionary memoir. Since Sats wasn't trying to portray Lunacharsky as a liberal, I assumed that his agenda must be to demythologise, including both Stalinist and liberal myth as his targets. I knew from memoirs that Igor Sats, Lunacharsky's much younger brother-in-law, had been his literary secretary for the last ten years of his life, and Max Hayward had pointed out to me that an IA Sats currently sat on the editorial board of the revered 'liberal' journal *Novy mir*: could it be the same man? A name that occasionally came up with Sats's as editor was IA Lunacharskaya—a woman, judging from the form of the last name, perhaps Lunacharsky's daughter. Interesting people to try to meet, should I ever get to Moscow. This thought was sufficiently well formed for me to wonder if Alyosha's father, a journalist in Moscow, might help to make the contact.

At the end of June, the British Council came through with a ten-month fellowship to the Soviet Union. Remarkably, it was awarded unreservedly, without any stipulation that I must have acquired a British passport before departure—though I'm sure that if the British had presented an Australian passport to the Soviets there would have been endless visa complications. 'You can imagine the relief of being under the protection of the British Council', I wrote to my mother after the news came. 'Now all I have to do is be approved by the Russians, go to Japan, get married, get a British passport if I can', and finally get a visa to the Soviet Union. It should be 'relatively without problems', I wrote unrealistically, adding untruthfully that because of my spring trip in Russia, it all 'seems familiar and pleasant; I am not worried by it at all'.

In fact, those last-minute arrangements were a nightmare. I was scheduled to leave Oxford, with my luggage for a year in the Soviet Union, on 30 July. The bags I was proposing to take to the Soviet Union would be stored with friends in London, the Suttons, whom I had known in Melbourne; my other belongings went into storage in Oxford, where my St Antony's friend and fellow Australian Ross McKibbin had access to my bank account and was generally deputed as local handler of my affairs. To accomplish the marriage, which required Alex and myself to be in the same place, I was to leave England on 1 August with a student tour group travelling across the Soviet Union to Japan, arriving in Japan on 14 August. After two weeks in Japan, during which time Alex and I would presumably get married, I would leave Tokyo, arriving in London on 4 September. The boat to Leningrad on which the British Council had booked us left on 9 September. In those five days I should get my British passport, assuming that the Soviets had in the meantime accepted my nomination and issued a visa (how this was to be done in the absence of a passport was unclear, but, as I wrote to my mother, that was a problem for the British Council, thank God, not for me). As a practical matter, I noted, it was possible that I would miss the boat because of complications with visa and passport, but that 'wouldn't be very important anyway' as I would just wait a week and get the next one. I assume a lot of this was bravado, because any sane person would have been worried to death.

'Everyone asks after you and all are rather taken with the romance of your marriage', Ross wrote from St Antony's. 'I had no idea so many people had secret longings to fly across Asia to Japan to be married ... You have passed into College folkway myth.' But the reality wasn't romantic. As I never had time to write a long letter to my mother describing the trip, I have to rely on my memory for the appalling set of mishaps that followed. Once my student tour group got to Moscow, the Soviets tried to prevent us proceeding further, because we were on some cut-price arrangement involving Czech crowns that the Soviets wanted to cancel. As the only Russian speaker, I had to negotiate for several days with the Russians as well as with the British Embassy, while the group was kept uncomfortably confined in a boarding school on the outskirts of Moscow with only one (unreliable) telephone on the premises. Finally, we got permission to continue on our trip, but no sooner were we on the plane to Khabarovsk, in the Soviet Far East, than one of our group fell ill with pneumonia and had to be left in Omsk after an unscheduled landing. Khabarovsk and Nakhodka are a blur, though I do remember that in the former we saw *Some Like It Hot* in Russian at a local cinema (*There Are Only Girls in Jazz* was the Russian title). We went by train from Khabarovsk to Nakhodka, the windows covered for security reasons, and finally by boat to Yokohama.

I assume that Alex was waiting for me at Yokohama, though I couldn't swear to that; at any rate, we somehow made contact and went on up to Tokyo, where it was stiflingly hot and humid, very bad weather for my asthma. Alex and I eyed each other warily. It was two years since we had seen each other, and more than three since we had broken up. I had put on weight in the last miserable year and felt fat and ugly, as well as asthmatic. The only reserves I had to draw on were my new-found organisational abilities, but it was clear that Alex had reservations about this unfamiliar businesslike, career-oriented persona. I had the awful feeling everything was going wrong, and so, no doubt, did Alex. But we got married anyway, since that was the purpose of the visit. The marriage took place in a Japanese registry office, with various documents and stamps from the Australian and British Embassies. Ironically, under the circumstances, it turned out that Alex had to get married as an Australian citizen, not a British one, as that was how he was registered in Japan. As we tottered out of the registry office, sweating and harassed, the precious paper fell from our hands and nearly got swept away down a stormwater drain, but we just managed to retrieve it. I have no memory of the trip back to England after I rejoined my tour group, except that they had kindly clubbed together to buy me a Hiroshige etching as a wedding present, which I still have. Whether the person left behind in Omsk was ever found and repatriated, I can't say.

Back in London, I immediately fell sick with exhaustion and the worst attack of asthma I had ever had. My friends the Suttons, with whom I was staying outside London, had to call the doctor out twice in the one night to give me adrenaline injections (he came!—though I don't know why he didn't just tell me to go to the hospital casualty ward). I was, of course, tremendously on edge about getting the marriage certificate translated, Alex's British citizenship vouched for, the British passport and Soviet visa obtained, and coordinating all this with the British Council. In fact, all of these things wouldn't have got done if Gill Sutton hadn't turned out to be a virtuoso of the telephone, capable of tracking any bureaucrat to his lair. Having obtained, with great difficulty, a huge bottle of asthma tablets to last me for a year in Russia, I managed to leave this behind in Oxford, so Ross had to come rushing up to London with it as my personal courier. I went along to the British passport office with my passport application and handed in the various documents, along with my Australian passport. After a while they called me to the window and handed over a new British passport. My relief was substantially tempered by the fact that it lay there alone on the counter, a visual image that is preserved in my memory. 'Where's my Australian passport?' I asked in dismay. 'You won't see that again', the man said with (as I thought) relish. 'We have to send them back to the Australians.' It hadn't occurred to me that, by taking British citizenship, I would be losing Australian—after all, Alex had kept his British citizenship when he got an Australian passport, but it turned out that what was sauce for the gander wasn't sauce for the goose. I could have wept with frustration and a sense of dissolving identity. Sheila Mary Bruce, British citizen, was what it said on the new passport, but I had no idea who she was. The person I had always been, Sheila Fitzpatrick, Australian, apparently no longer existed.

2

Moscow in 1966

When I was young, I felt that the moment I came on the scene, the great times were over. The origins of this are a bit obscure, though it's possible that in my childish imagination the war and even the Depression were great times, or at least times for the history books. But it's true that I managed to miss the Thaw in the Soviet Union, and 1968 in London and Paris, and the whole 'sixties' in the US, arriving only in time to pick up their echoes.

The Thaw was that utopian moment in post-Stalinist Soviet history when it seemed as if the horrors and rigours of Stalinism were going to have a happy ending. Of course, not everybody in a society pays attention to utopian moments. In this case, it belonged peculiarly to the intelligentsia and the urban young, as well as to Nikita Khrushchev, the country's leader, and his advisors. The conventional starting point of the Thaw is 1956, with Khrushchev's Secret Speech condemning the evils of the Stalin period, though not Stalinism *in toto*. For some, to condemn anything was a terrible shock; for others, the condemnation didn't go far enough, but people were excited and started talking and arguing in a way they hadn't done for decades. The Thaw lasted into the early 1960s, though with some wobbles in the cultural field caused by Khrushchev's personal dislike of modern art; and was definitively ended with the ouster of Khrushchev in October 1964 and the advent of the greyer, more cautious Leonid Brezhnev. If you were young and reform-minded during the Thaw, a 'sixties person' (*shestidesiatnik*) as they came to be called, it was something you never forgot. One of the curiosities of Gorbachev's *perestroika* a quarter of a century later was to see the new utopian moment embraced by greying survivors of the old one.

For the sixties people, utopia was still socialist, just cleansed of the distortions and lethal violence of 'socialist construction' in the Stalin period. In 1961, Khrushchev said full Communism—the final stage, one up from socialism—would be reached within twenty years, and people believed him, according to the opinion polls. Who knew exactly what full Communism meant, but one thing it implied was abundance, the end of shortages of consumer goods and housing. The Soviet Union was soon going to catch up with the West in standards of living and quality of life, Khrushchev said. That was quite a claim, considering that life was still hard, though better than everyone but children remembered it being in the past. But for a relatively brief moment it seemed that anything might be possible. I'm telling this story, of course, not from the standpoint of a participant, since I came too late. This is how people told it to me, and how it's been preserved in Russian mythology.

Although utopia was socialist, it involved reaching across the borders—strictly closed under Stalin—to embrace the rest of the world and usher in the era of global peace. It started with the World Youth Festival in Moscow in 1957, which introduced a whole cohort of Soviet youth to their counterparts from abroad in a love fest that defied the KGB's attempts to control it. Then came the opportunity—first for a chosen few elite tourists, then for larger numbers—to see the fabled West at first hand. The travel accounts of the favoured few were read with passionate attention by the rest. This reaching to the West was not dissident but officially sponsored: cultural exchange was one of its products. Khrushchev himself got a great kick out of his travels to the US and Europe, and he wasn't a man to keep things to himself.

The British student exchange that took me to the Soviet Union in the autumn of 1966 was a product of the Thaw. So was the emergence of critically minded journals like *Novy mir* and the attentive educated Soviet public that followed them. Without the Thaw, we wouldn't have had the violinist David Oistrakh in Melbourne (my father dragged me backstage as a teenager to have my program autographed). The charismatic poet Andrey Voznesensky wouldn't have visited St Antony's (for all that it was supposed to be a nest of spies) a few months before I left, or the equally charismatic Yevgeny Yevtushenko have read poems to huge audiences in Moscow's Luzhniki stadium and made friends in Australia with Frank Hardy and Geoffrey Dutton. There wouldn't have been the sound of Beatles tapes wafting out of the Moscow University dormitory when the windows opened in spring.

The Thaw was more or less an era of détente in the international sphere, but one doesn't want to take this idea too far, because détente was always precarious. If 1956 was the year of Khrushchev's de-Stalinisation speech, it was also the year of the Soviet invasion of Hungary when it looked as if it might be going to slip out of the Communist bloc. The Berlin wall went up in 1961 on Soviet initiative, to stop the flood of refugees from East to West. In 1963, the world came as near as it ever was to a third world war over the Cuban Missile Crisis. From 1965, the US and Australia were increasing their support for South Vietnam while the USSR was upping its military assistance to the North, and that hot war through surrogates lasted until the early 1970s. Cultural exchanges with 'capitalist' countries coexisted with Soviet fears that their exchangees might be seduced in the West and ours might bring corrupt capitalist habits with them.

Spy scandals filled the newspapers, especially in Britain, in the 1960s. The names of Oleg Penkovsky and George Blake, famous in the early '60s as spies respectively for the Western and Soviet side who got caught, may now be forgotten, but surely not those of the Cambridge group of well-born English recruits to British intelligence who, on the basis of ideological sympathy, became double agents for the Soviets before being exposed. Guy Burgess and Donald Maclean had fled to the Soviet Union earlier, but Anthony Blunt, an art historian, continued to work as Surveyor of the Queen's Pictures for years, despite the persistent rumours of a third, fourth, or even a fifth man. In January 1963, Kim Philby, one of the top officials in British intelligence, disappeared from Beirut; in July, he turned up in Moscow.

Diplomats, journalists and businessmen could be spies, or accused of being so, leading to expulsion and, in rarer cases, arrest. So could scholars and students, for the exchanges offered too tempting a cover for infiltrating agents for either side to overlook it. The Soviet press often carried lively stories about the unmasking of such people—it was a kind of Soviet equivalent of yellow journalism, with spying instead of sex as the hook—but reading them you were never absolutely sure if the subjects had actually been spying or just looked suspicious to the Soviet authorities. Perhaps the American musicologist and double bass player Stanley Krebs really was a spy for the CIA during his stay on the American exchange (but why would the CIA want to know about the Moscow Conservatorium?). On the other hand, you had to wonder if the exchange student accused of 'infiltrating' Soviet trade unions under the guise of writing his dissertation on them was, in fact, just writing his dissertation.

The case of American Frederick Barghoorn, a professor of political science and Sovietologist at Yale, caused an international scandal in 1963. He was arrested on the street in front of the Metropole Hotel after a stranger walked up and shoved some papers in his hand. We students would have known better than to take them, but no doubt this was wisdom after the fact. Barghoorn was apparently bewildered, enabling KGB men to spring out, put him in handcuffs and take him off to the Lubyanka. He was released only after President Kennedy protested and said he was not a spy. Such government denials were routine, regardless of the facts of the case, but they were not usually made at presidential level; I remember wondering at the time if Kennedy was denying the accusation because Barghoorn wasn't a spy, or because, as a spy, he was really important. (Another possibility that didn't occur to me then is that Ivy League universities have good Washington connections and look after their own.) It turns out, according to David Engerman's recent study of Cold War Sovietology, that, while Barghoorn, like many of his American colleagues, was a longtime consultant to the CIA as well as the State Department, he was not working with any US government agency, even as a consultant, at the time of his trip. In other words, he wasn't on a spying mission, so the KGB had obviously overreached itself by clapping handcuffs on him. Nevertheless, by normal Soviet standards the mere fact of contact with the CIA, however intermittent, was enough to make you a spy.

The US president hadn't intervened in 1961 in the case of Edward Keenan, but it was of particular interest to exchange students because Keenan was one of us. He was close to the end of his second year on the American exchange, based in Leningrad, when he was caught wandering around closed areas in Central Asia and the Caucasus ('closed' cities or districts were those officially off-limits not only to foreigners but also to non-resident Soviet citizens, unless they had special permission). After his expulsion from the Soviet Union, he told the *New York Times* that he had neither been working for nor debriefed by the CIA; a Soviet commentator's reaction was, 'It's true, he denies it. What else is he going to say?' In one sense, the Keenan case might have served as encouragement to other exchange students; after all, he ended up with a job at Harvard, even if, being persona non grata with the Soviets and therefore unable to return for further research, he had to change his field from Central Asia to seventeenth-century Muscovy. On the other hand, some of the materials published by the Leningrad KGB blackening Keenan's name were such as to strike fear into our hearts. Under interrogation by the KGB, Russian friends of his claimed he had 'tried with all his might to show the superiority of the American way of life and capitalist system, to discredit socialism'. Agents who had followed him around Leningrad during the year reported that he didn't spend much time in libraries or archives, but could often be found 'at the theatre, clubs, the market, in church, the synagogue or other places far from scholarly activity', indicating that his real object was 'the collection of political information'. If this was all that was needed to show you were a spy, we were all vulnerable. Which of us wasn't interested in 'gathering information' about Soviet society? Who had never let drop an 'anti-Soviet' remark involving some favourable comparison between life at home and life in the Soviet Union?

A British student from the LSE, Peter Reddaway, one of my first friends in the field, had been expelled from Moscow in 1965. He was supposed to have had NTS connections. Worst of all, from the standpoint of someone planning to go to the Soviet Union on the British exchange, was the case of Gerald Brooke, a British teacher of Russian arrested on a tourist trip and accused of smuggling leaflets. This happened in April 1966, just a few weeks after my first visit. Brooke was sentenced to five years in a labour camp for anti-Soviet activity. He was released in 1969, at which point he told the British press that he had, in fact, been working for NTS. A five-year prison sentence, even if reduced in practice to three, was obviously in a different league of awfulness from simply being expelled, like Ned Keenan and Peter Reddaway. Whether Gerald Brooke and the others had, in fact, been spying was unknown to us. But we hoped they had, as that made our own situation (assuming we were not spies) less precarious.

I knew all about another pitfall for exchange students, the marriage trap, because of Mervyn Matthews, a Junior Fellow at St Antony's in my years there. In the late Stalin period, it had been made illegal for Soviet citizens to marry foreigners, and those who had previously married them (including the Russian wife of a young American diplomat, Robert C Tucker, who later became a Sovietologist and biographer of Stalin) were forbidden from leaving the Soviet

Union to join their spouses. By the 1960s, marriage between Soviet citizens and foreigners was no longer illegal, but it remained full of bureaucratic complications. Matthews had fallen in love with a Soviet woman during his stay in Moscow but was not allowed to marry her. He returned to Oxford, she remaining in the Soviet Union, and waged an obsessive battle for years to get her out (he finally succeeded in 1969, as part of the same spy swap that released Gerald Brooke; their son Owen Matthews recently wrote a book about it called *Stalin's Children*). I remember looking at Matthews, a gloomy Welshman at the best of times, and thinking that the case had eaten him up; there was no room in his life for anything else. I vowed never to let myself be put in such a position.

It was, of course, not unusual for exchange students to have affairs with Russians, or even to want to marry them. The view among students in my time was that, while it was extremely difficult for a male foreign student to export a Soviet woman, it was next to impossible for a female student to export a Soviet man. The exception was the British art historian Camilla Gray, whom I met in London in connection with my Lunacharsky work while I was at St Antony's (she was discouraging, perhaps seeing me as competition). She finally managed to marry the composer Sergey Prokofiev's son Oleg, as well as publish her own excellent book on Russian avant-garde art in the 1920s, only to catch typhoid fever and die on vacation in the Caucasus a few years later. In the 1960s, most of the women on the exchange who fell in love with a Soviet man didn't even try to marry them. Though, to be sure, the people they fell in love with—often poets, painters and sculptors—were not necessarily available for marriage, let alone export.

If you survived all this, there was still the possibility of having your scholarly work held up to scorn and mockery in the Soviet press as an example of 'bourgeois falsification' of Soviet history. In a perverse version of the spirit of cultural exchange, Institutes of History were acquiring new sectors of 'bourgeois historiography', whose purpose was to offer critical assessments of Western scholarship from a Soviet Marxist–Leninist perspective. Critical, in the sense of disapproving and admonitory, was what they had to be, though one young woman who had published a critique of EH Carr (admittedly, guilty only of 'bourgeois objectivism' rather than outright falsification) confided to me privately how much she admired him. Such criticisms were likely to appear in the daily press as well as specialised journals. The American historian Richard Pipes (later National Security Advisor under President Reagan) was the subject of a whole book to himself: *Mr Pipes Falsifies History*, published in Leningrad in 1966. By comparison, the attack on me in *Sovetskaya Rossiya* was small beer—except that I was actually in the Soviet Union on the exchange when it came out and I was attacked in a national newspaper instead of a scholarly publication. But I wasn't the only one to be attacked *in situ*. The Marxist philosopher Eugene Kamenka, in Moscow on the ANU exchange the year before I arrived, was branded a 'cheap anti-Communist scribbler' for writing critically about Soviet philosophy in a British journal before he came to Moscow. (Apparently the author, unlike my critic, knew Kamenka and continued to maintain normal professional and even social relations with him at the Moscow Philosophy Institute.)

Finally, you could be catapulted into attention as a bit player in one of the periodic scandals that characterised Soviet literary life, such as those involving Boris Pasternak, Joseph Brodsky, Andrey Sinyavsky and Alexander Solzhenitsyn. Foreign contacts and the sending of manuscripts for publication abroad were almost a staple of these scandals, which could result in the author's public humiliation (Pasternak was forced to renounce the Nobel Prize for Literature), criminal conviction (Brodsky and Sinyavsky) or expulsion from the Soviet Union (Solzhenitsyn). Almost always, some luckless Westerner who had become a friend and go-between for these writers became a casualty as well, accused (usually correctly) of smuggling their manuscripts to the West. Proscribed manuscripts were widely circulated informally in *samizdat* (literally, self-publication, that is, reproduction of manuscripts without the censor's approval), reproduced by hundreds of devoted women with typewriters, since such copying machines as the Soviet Union possessed were firmly locked up. *Samizdat* was more or less tolerated, but *tamizdat*—getting manuscripts published *there* (*tam*), in the anti-Soviet West—was strictly off-limits. Throughout the 1960s, the KGB was vigilant, though not always successful, in trying to prevent the smuggling out of manuscripts that couldn't get by the Soviet censor. Sometimes these went by diplomatic pouch, but at other times in someone's suitcase—and as there weren't too many foreigners to do the job, apart from a few businessmen and journalists, 'someone' was often an exchange student.

No wonder we went off to the Soviet Union expecting adventure, even danger. It was a cause of apprehension but also of excitement. You might end up as the next Peter Reddaway—or, God forbid, Gerald Brooke. Or you might make it through to the end of the year and come back with a fund of 'war' stories to astonish your friends. Even if you weren't a spy, there was the exhilarating sense of being parachuted into enemy territory and left to fend for yourself.

I'd had a foretaste of the Soviet Union in the three-week trip I made in the spring of 1966. That trip took us by train to Warsaw, the Baltics, Moscow, Leningrad, Kiev, Prague and Berlin, with five days in Moscow. I was a tourist then, but I was reasonably hopeful of getting back in the autumn as a ten-month exchange student. My mood was fairly buoyant, as it hadn't been since my first months in Oxford, much cheered by the thought that, because of Alex and the marriage plans, I wasn't alone in the world. I made friends with other people in the student group right at the start, and then I made friends with our tour guide, Alexey (Alyosha) Mikhalyov, and kept in touch after the trip. I was full of curiosity about what we saw in the Soviet Union and communicated easily enough with the young Russians we met (though I still complained of shyness and uneasiness with the language). The long, chatty description I wrote to my mother is alert and uncharacteristically light-hearted. The trip was the best thing that had happened to me for years.

Alyosha, I wrote, was 'really the highlight of the trip'. Aged twenty-one, of mixed Polish, Russian and gypsy descent, he was the son of a former ballerina and an editor of the literary journal *Oktyabr'*, which as I explained to my mother was 'the great rival to the more liberal *Novy mir*, in a *Quadrant/Meanjin* opposition' (note that despite my St Antony's conditioning I still instinctively put the anti-Communist *Quadrant* as the *Oktyabr'* analogue, that is, in the camp of reaction). Alyosha was in his final year at the Moscow School of Oriental Languages, specialising in Persian and Arabic, and was about to go to Afghanistan as an interpreter; being a guide for Sputnik, the student travel organisation, was just a part-time job for him in which he could practise his English. I liked Alyosha and found him very engaging as a person, but I was even more fascinated by him as a type: the critically minded Soviet intellectual who still had Soviet values.

Max Hayward and other Western Sovietologists, deeply interested in and sympathetic to intellectuals who got into trouble with the system, were inclined to assume that the whole Russian intelligentsia, except for a few 'Party hacks', were dissidents at heart. I remember Peter Reddaway explaining to me how Soviet Russians seemed orthodox on first meeting but then, as you got to know them better, inevitably revealed the dissident within that was their true self; and I remember doubting him. My own experience suggested that the self was always divided. I could imagine Russians who were friends of Peter's picking up his way of thinking the way I picked up Max Hayward's, but I didn't see that that meant they were showing their 'true' self.

I had a professional and personal stake in seeing the Soviet Union as something more complicated than a repressive society in which people mouthed Soviet orthodoxies simply because they were forced to. Until I met Alyosha, I wrote to my mother, I had suspected that the dissident Russian intelligentsia was a creature of Max Hayward's imagination: 'I almost believed, and certainly wanted to believe that'. That 'wanted to believe' is interesting, but at this distance I find it hard to interpret. Was it out of resistance to the Cold War model prevalent at St Antony's that I wanted to believe this? Out of loyalty to my parents' left-wing sympathy with the Soviet Union? Am I telling my mother, as in my Koestler letter, that I would have stuck to the verities of the left if I could, but the evidence was against them? Or am I admitting that my supposedly objective analysis of Soviet society was influenced by emotion?

Alyosha, in any case, was my first real-life example of semi-alienated Soviet intellectual: sophisticated, knowledgeable about the West, capable of mocking Soviet clichés and bureaucratic stupidity. But on close examination, I believed he proved my point as much as he did Max Hayward's. In the first place, he was not politically dissident. While there was 'some intellectual hauteur in his attitude to Party men, especially those like Khrushchev who talk peasant Russian', as I wrote to my mother, he took offence when one of our group scoffed at the embalmed Lenin at the Mausoleum, and it wasn't just for show: this was evidently sacred ground for him. But politics didn't really interest Alyosha. Trained as a solo dancer at the Kirov school until an injury ended his ballet career at seventeen, he was passionate about ballet, literature, theatre and music. He admired Lunacharsky, though not uncritically, and shared his vision of a socialist society in which culture was available for the masses. He hoped he would learn to write about high art, especially ballet, in a way that would help people understand it, as the French writer Romain Rolland (much admired in the Soviet Union) did in his study of Beethoven.

I have never been a ballet aficionado, but Alyosha managed to turn me into one, if only temporarily. We went to see *Legend About Love*, a ballet by Yury Grigorovich, a charismatic Leningrad choreographer, much admired by Alyosha, who had recently moved from the Kirov company to the

Bolshoi. 'Magnificent; I have never seen anything like it', I wrote to my mother, in one of the few statements of unqualified admiration in our entire correspondence. One of the reasons I liked it so much was that Alyosha had given me an intensive private briefing before we went, dancing some parts—I remember my astonishment when he suddenly started whirling and leaping in the small hotel room—and explaining the symbolism. It was a story of love renounced, inspired by a text of the Turkish poet Nazim Hikmet with music by the Azerbaijan composer Arif Melikov, which in Grigorovich's choreography carried a high erotic as well as philosophical charge. The ballet ended with a proper Soviet statement of optimistic belief in the future, with the male lead (a builder) renouncing love for the collective good and striking the familiar pose of a Soviet Hero of Socialist Labour, hammer in hand. But, as I explained to my mother on the basis of Alyosha's analysis, 'It is clear that life affirmation is not a total but a selective act, just as heroism which is sacrifice (the soviet cliché) is also irreparable loss ... This kind of exegesis is not Sovietology ... it is how the Russians understand art', I concluded.

It was certainly unlike my normal style, as I tended to shy away from symbolic analysis and even make fun of it. But Alyosha had 'the marvellous Russian enthusiasm which turns intellectual sympathy into a real thing ... the Russian high seriousness in art', as I told my mother, and it was 'very good for me not to mock for once'. Even Alyosha's dreams fitted the artistic pattern: in a group discussion on the subject, 'it emerged that whereas I dream in documentary style with explanatory subtitles, Alyosha dreams in symbolic images, so like the dreams Freud analysed that it seems to me that (although he knows something about Freud) they belong to a pre-Freudian generation. It is a thing I like about the Russians, that even when they are sophisticated they are not self-conscious'.

Between Alyosha's high seriousness about aesthetics and the realities of Soviet life there was, of course, a gulf. I didn't admire Moscow as a city on first encounter, although clearly it interested me in a way Oxford and London had never done. It had 'suffered a lot from Stalinist planned architecture', I reported to my mother; 'great big blocks of flats, each with its own peculiar ornamentation of small ornate balconies on alternate storeys, or appliquéd pillars'. The prize for ugliest architectural complex went to the Exhibition of Economic Achievements near our hotel, a collection of monstrous buildings with a recurring ornamental motif which I interpreted as an urn or a pineapple but others thought was a sheaf of corn. Loudspeakers at the Exhibition played light classical music, interspersed with little talks about the Twenty-Third Party Congress, which was then in session in Moscow (I complained to my mother about all the 'pseudo-information' that was forced on you in the USSR). The Moscow University building on Lenin Hills, one of the city's seven skyscrapers, built in the late Stalin period in a wedding-cake style that was despised by Soviet intellectuals like Alyosha, struck me as 'a monstrous prison with about ten thousand small windows and two small doors, where an official inspects your pass; it includes residential quarters, which adds to the claustrophobic horror of it'.

Leningrad was our next stop. Alyosha, who had trained there, loved the city and, like many Russian intellectuals, thought its classical perfection immeasurably superior to anything Moscow could offer. I, too, was 'taken aback that it was so beautiful'. But what we saw—wandering around on our own, against the rules, as Alyosha was off seeing his old ballet friends—was not just classical beauty. We had already encountered Russia's flourishing black market in Moscow, but it was worse in Leningrad. The main street, Nevsky prospect, had 'a charm that survives the shock of finding that every third Russian in it wants to sell roubles or buy clothes, chewing-gum, ball-point pens (1 rouble is the market price, i.e. a dollar at the official exchange) or Beatles records', as I told my mother. 'Perhaps we struck a bad day, but we were really pestered by these people.'

A youth counter-culture had been emerging in the Soviet Union over the past decade, a subject of great interest in the West and concern to the Soviet authorities. This trip was not just my first close encounter with the Soviet counter-culture but more or less my last, since I moved in different social circles once I got there as a student. I have since read many lively accounts of such encounters by young Western tourists, but I had completely forgotten that I had written one of my own until I re-read the letter to my mother. Martin, a Mexican student from Glasgow who was one of my friends in the tour group, struck up an acquaintance on the street with Vic (they all went by English-sounding nicknames),

> twenty-seven, divorced, a student of something like geology. He wears rather English clothes—tweed jacket, V-neck cashmere sweater—which he must have got from tourists or in some other devious way. He speaks very good English with an American accent, like almost all young Russians; has never been out of Russia and said that it would be impossible for him to go even to Eastern Europe, meaning he had been in some kind of trouble which he wouldn't explain.

Vic invited us out to his place, which he seemed to share just with a twenty-something male flatmate (I didn't realise at the time how unusual that was in Soviet terms, since the housing shortage meant that almost all young people, even when married, had to live with their parents or in-laws). Compared to Alyosha, Vic was a cultural lightweight, though he too probably thought of himself as a member of the intelligentsia. He listened to Voice of America (for the music, not the politics) and played the guitar, with a Russian, folk and Western pop repertoire, rather well. He drank quite a lot but, in my summary, 'said very little of importance' even when tipsy, either from a habit of caution or because he had nothing much to say.

When we arrived at the one-room flat, Vic's flatmate, Valery, was in bed with his girlfriend. She emerged unabashed, 'wearing a woollen hat with earflaps, as if to compensate for having been caught in bed', and immediately began giving us a run-down on current literary politics. She was something of a name-dropper, talking about Andrey Sinyavsky, the writer recently convicted of anti-Soviet activity for publishing work abroad (but calling him 'Sinkovsky') and claiming to have seen the poet Joseph Brodsky, convicted a year or so earlier for 'social parasitism' on the streets of Leningrad when he was supposed to be in Gulag. I saw her as a literary fashionista rather than somebody genuinely interested in culture. She dismissed Yevtushenko and Voznesensky as 'Party poets' and called the ballad singer Bulat Okudzhava ('the latest Sovietologist discovery in dissident popular literature', as I explained to my mother) passé.

There wasn't too much high seriousness about art in Vic's ménage, or any real interest in politics, though he told a few stories of the Great Purges of the late 1930s, 'perhaps because [he] felt it was expected'. I made a similar comment on Vic's present to Martin of an icon; evidently I felt he was playing to a script for dealing with foreigners, though the script could well have been his own. He felt strongly about the drabness of Soviet life and had fantasies about the glamour of urban America. I noted the contradictions of his statements about police surveillance: when we first took a taxi to his place,

> he said we must be careful not to be followed; later he said things had changed and there was no danger of that anymore; later still, while we were walking along deserted and frozen Leningrad streets trying to get a taxi home, a police car stopped and asked Vic where we were coming from and took his name, and then he got frightened and tried to get away (though by that time it seemed a bit late) but changed his mind when we objected to being stranded.

'I would fairly happily spend a year in Russia now, if I could, and all other things being equal', I wrote to my mother after my return to Oxford. 'If I could' indicates that I was not allowing myself to be too hopeful about getting on the British exchange, even though it was now a real possibility. From the spring trip, I came away with a very negative impression of Moscow University as a place to live. Some Leningrad students we met told us living conditions there were pretty bad, but I still thought it would be hard to imagine anything more lowering to the spirit than Moscow. That may be the reason that, when I had to name a preferred destination, I chose Leningrad, even though all the major Lunacharsky archives were in Moscow. When the Soviets decided to send me to Moscow instead of Leningrad, I thought it typical Soviet perversity, an instinctive desire to deprive you of your first choice. But it could have been just commonsense.

I was still apprehensive about Moscow when I set off for the Soviet Union in September, writing to my mother from the boat that I had been warned that living in the Moscow University dormitory had a 'depressing effect'. On the other hand, the letter continued, 'I want to live in Russia, and it can hardly *not* compare favourably with last year's Oxford', the worst year of my life to date.

As it turned out, I quickly switched my allegiance to Moscow after arriving there as an exchange scholar in late September 1966. Nevertheless, at first I was quite miserable. The depression that had plagued me in Oxford years came back, though in milder form. I was irritable, prone to insomnia, wary, preoccupied with my bad spoken Russian and more than normally shy. I could manage the obligatory official interactions, but for the first month or so anything else was beyond me. I was exhausted by the sheer effort of getting myself on the exchange and off to Moscow. Without Martin and the rest of the student tour group to encourage me, I wasn't willing to make the kind of street contacts we had made in the spring; in any case, I was now deeply conscious of the danger involved in contacts with people like Vic, who sought out foreigners and probably had black-market connections. Having finally made it to the Soviet Union, the last thing I wanted was to be thrown out for some trivial and avoidable offence.

I corresponded with Alyosha through the summer, and if he had been in Moscow when I arrived, my early experiences there would no doubt have been different. But he was off in Afghanistan by the time I arrived, working as an interpreter, and remained there for several years. He sent messages to me in Moscow, and I visited his mother fairly regularly for a while, but contact lapsed after a few months. Surfing the web recently, I found a fully recognisable photo of Alyosha at about the age he was when I knew him, smiling happily against a snowy background; according to Wikipedia, he was an outstanding success as an interpreter, becoming a friend of the Shah of Iran and favourite translator of Leonid Brezhnev's before an untimely death from leukaemia at forty-nine. We should have kept in touch.

Fortunately, my aversion to human contact didn't prevent my getting out and about in the city, about which I was extremely curious. For a month or so, perhaps even a couple of months, I lived an intensely private inner life, observing the city and its inhabitants during the day as a non-speaking presence, as nearly invisible as I could manage. In my memory of this period, it's as if I had suddenly had a stroke, retaining the ability to use my eyes but unable to communicate with anything human. In the daytime, I spent whatever free time I had tramping around the city on foot and on public transport, preferably above ground, by bus, trolley-bus or tram, exploring. In the evenings I studied maps and guidebooks, read whatever newspapers and periodicals I had managed to pick up during the day, and wrote up my impressions in my diary. It was one of the few times in my life that I kept a diary, and I did it because I felt that the experience of living in the Soviet Union was so remarkable that it needed to be recorded.

Getting the materials necessary for my exploration of Moscow was not easy. Detailed maps were considered high-security items and there were no street directories available, just as there were no telephone books. If you wanted to find out where someone lived or get any other information about the city, you were supposed to go to one of the information bureaux scattered around, and they would give you the answer for a few kopeks. Peasants in from the provinces did this, but foreign students generally didn't, on the assumption that too much interest in the city would seem like spying, and asking for some Muscovite's telephone number would be likely to get that person into trouble. When Wolfgang Leonhard, child of a German Communist, arrived in Moscow with his mother in the mid 1930s, all they could find was a map of the city as it *would be*, according to the Plan, in 1945. Things had improved a little from then, but still, all you could get by way of city maps were schematic plans showing theatres and monuments in the centre. But I discovered PV Sytin's wonderful *History of Moscow Streets* in a second-hand bookshop, and it explained the layout of the city and showed changes in street names (of which there were many, often serial, as revolutionary heroes were first honoured and then fell out of favour). With Sytin in hand, it was possible to reconstruct the history of the urban landscape, building by building.

My Moscow was not empty of inhabitants, only free of communication between me and them. I was in 'I am a camera' mode, with most of my shots being taken on public transport or on the street. I recorded one such vignette of Moscow mores in my diary a few weeks after arriving:

> Came home on bus c. 9 o'clock. Drunk on bus with oldish woman (mother?), baby, small girl. Group of 15–16 year olds got on, v rowdy, esp ringleader reciting, singing off-key,

> hedging about paying fare etc. Bus-driver announced '*sleduiushchaia* [= next stop]—Leninskii prospect' and ring-leader made a mock-serious speech on subject of Lenin or Leninsky which I couldn't follow—final word '*vystreliat* [= shoot].' This, or something else, enraged drunken worker who attacked either his mother or someone else (hidden from me by crowd of kids). Front of bus became chaotic, people pushed to and fro, all shouting. Finally bus stopped (not at bus-stop) and drunk, mother and kids got out, drunk attempting to get back in and hitting mother who was trying to restrain him. One of kids was carrying the baby. Public indignation in bus seemed to be directed against kids, who had been quite obstreperous ... Kids looked very chastened ... and pushed off rather quickly. Mother pushing drunk along street; small girl marching ahead with baby about her own size, as bus moved off.

Intellectual that I was, the first thing I learned about Moscow was where the bookshops and the newspaper kiosks were. Not that you could rely on a kiosk to have the paper or magazine you wanted: I almost never found a copy of *Novy mir* in one, as its print run was kept artificially low and all the copies allocated to Moscow kiosks were quickly snapped up, though I sometimes snagged an *Oktyabr'*. There were special shops for foreigners and people with foreign-currency certificates, but I stayed away from them almost entirely, trying to repudiate my special privileged status. One of the few times I broke this rule was trying to buy a winter coat, having discovered my English one was hopeless for Moscow, but I couldn't find anything to buy, in the foreign-currency shops or anywhere else: all the coats were much too big for me.

I was doing my best not to look or behave like a foreigner. That meant looking drab, with mud-coloured clothes and sensible boots. Looking drab was not in itself a problem for me: the 'quiet and respectable' clothes I had brought with me, as listed for my mother's benefit, were not going to set the Moscow River on fire:

> I have a black coat and my old black and white one. I have a brown knitted dress, and two reasonably good sets of matching cardigan and skirt, olive-green and mauve respectively. I have a brown-black fur hat, and a blue and pink mohair scarf and a red woollen cap (or scarf) which you gave me.

I remember that cap/scarf, a rather bizarre item with a pom-pom, which looked odd in England, let alone Moscow; I never wore it. The mohair scarf, too, was unsuitable, being too skimpy for serious cold. All that autumn and winter, I was plaintively asking my mother to send me a warm woollen shawl, which was standard Moscow wear, but she never did. Perhaps she couldn't find any in Australia.

Though drab, I doubt that I achieved the exact look of *Soviet* drab. For one thing, I didn't have a Soviet winter coat (coarse wool, black or dark blue, close-fitting at the wrists, with a huge fur collar that could be turned up to shield your face from the cold; the whole thing weighing about as much as I did); I didn't have one of the obligatory thick shawls to wrap round my shoulders and head. I also didn't get my hair done and my hands manicured, which is how Soviet women tried to compensate for their clothes. In those days, below knee-length woollen skirts with woollen tights were standard Soviet garb; and I more or less followed this rule, even though mini-skirts were already coming into fashion in England. When the weather warmed up in the spring, Ann, another British Council student, took to wearing mini-skirts with patterned tights, but she was frequently loudly rebuked on buses by old ladies. I had one pair of trousers with me, probably ski pants, and I remember getting rebuked myself on one of my tram trips in non-tourist Moscow: 'Sports woman!' (*sportsmenka!*) was what he said, and it wasn't meant as a compliment. After that, I just wore them at home.

In dress, as in so many other things in the Soviet Union, you couldn't win, or at any rate, you couldn't win them all. The standard seductive foreign spy in the propaganda pieces is immediately recognisable because of her Paris fashions, exotic silks and jewellery (almost unknown in the Soviet Union in those years). On the other hand, dressing down might be a giveaway. Among the pen portraits of exchange-student spies in the Leningrad KGB publication is one of the American who went overboard trying to look like a Russian, buying a moth-eaten overcoat with a crumbling fur collar and hat with earflaps from *émigrés* in Chicago, confident that 'nobody could tell him from an ordinary Soviet lad'—but that, of course, was a spy's ploy.

Drabness was a hallmark of life in the Soviet Union in the Brezhnev age, later called the era of stagnation. Even Moscow, capital of the socialist bloc, was not exempt, its dingy greyness only occasionally enlivened with patriotic parades and fireworks displays. There was no graffiti and no advertising, unless you count the lone neon sign in the centre of the city that announced, without further elaboration, 'State Insurance', or the posters about World War II casualties claiming starkly 'Nothing is forgotten. No-one is forgotten'. On the street, people were poorly dressed; and, as the cliché has it, they didn't smile, although it must be said that smiling is difficult at twenty below. People on the street often asked you the way, especially the peasants in felt boots and headscarves who had come to town to buy sausage. There was a fine modern Metro, but almost any trip outside the centre required an additional ride on a rickety bus crowded to bursting point with Muscovites with large shopping bags in each hand—almost everyone had to take a bus journey for their regular grocery shopping, since neighbourhood shops had been done away with (petty capitalism!) in the early 1930s. In winter, drunks were often to be seen lying in the snow outside the Metro station; many were veterans missing a leg or so (the supply of Soviet artificial limbs had not caught up with demand, even twenty years after the war). There were hardly any public drinking places, so it was common for two or three men to buy a bottle of vodka and retreat to a stairwell in an apartment block to drink it, making the stairwells filthy and foul smelling (there were no public toilets either).

Shopping was a nightmare, with crowded shops, half-empty shelves, jostling queues and slovenly, hostile saleswomen: to buy anything, you had to fight your way through to the counter and see what they had and for what price, then fight your way back to the end of the queue for the cashier, pay, and finally get in a third queue to present your receipt and get your purchase (minimally wrapped, with butter or slices of sausage just slapped down on a small square of butcher paper, potatoes shoved into a twist of newspaper). 'I too am a human being' was a frequent riposte from the women who worked in shops (I heard it for the first time, and noted it in my diary, on the very day of my arrival), but that only reminded me how irritating human beings can be. If you were rash enough to buy food before going to the library or archive, the cloakroom attendant was likely to refuse to take your bag; if you waited until after the library closed, the shops were either closed or empty of goods. A handwritten sign I once saw at the university buffet, 'No milk. And won't be', captured the spirit of Soviet service perfectly. It was incredible that everyday life could be made so uncomfortable and inconvenient.

My new home was in the wedding-cake building of Moscow State University (MGU). I had hated it in the spring, but even on my first day as a resident I was changing my mind. 'It doesn't make me claustrophobic', I noted in my diary; 'I almost like it'. By the next day, in a letter to my mother written at 3 a.m., I was even more positive.

> I think I am going to like MGU. It is an incredible confusion—different blocks in same building ... Lifts not working and stopping only on certain parts of certain floors. Great Staircases leading almost nowhere. Huge empty corridors and lifts packed with people. Shops and stalls without enough goods in them. Restaurants with too many people. Women on duty everywhere—some *babushka* [Russian grandmother] type, others very aggressive. Necessary to show a pass to get into building, sometimes twice. Man on duty questioned mine out of sheer boredom, said the photograph was not like me.

My room was in a block of two, consisting of a small vestibule with a wooden outer door, locked with an old-fashioned key; shower and washbasin off to the left and lavatory to the right, then two smoked-glass doors, also lockable with old-fashioned keys, leading to two identical single rooms, of which mine was one. I made an inventory of the room late on my first day:

> 1 window, 4 feet high? No curtain but white material over bottom couple of feet. 1 desk lamp—2 globes, 1 now dead; thick white plastic shade, slightly mushroomlike in shape, v unattractive and not v efficient. 1 small carpet, patterned dark red, reasonable. 1 narrow bed, cover of indeterminate design. 2 glasses; 1 pale pink glass water jug, hideous, and fairly hideous kettle, both standing on sickly creamish oilcloth until all 3 put out of sight by me. 1 bookcase/cupboard with 3 glassed-in shelves, just too narrow or too low for foolscap folders or big sheets of music, but quite a lot of room for domestic oddments in bottom shelves. 1 old radio which *dezhurnaia* [woman on duty in the corridor] worked but I can't. 3 wooden chairs and a wobbly desk. 1 hanging cupboard and mirror. 3 high shelves out of reach. 3 other shelves, deep and impractical as clothes must be put in great piles. I have added a cabin trunk (containing my 3 other cases, like Russian dolls) uncovered with violin on top; transistor; Klee (*They're biting*); small Buddhist bell, 2 shelves of books, typewriter.

That small Buddhist bell strikes no chord in my memory; perhaps I got it in Japan during my late-summer trip to get married. 'I can live with everything', I concluded, 'except that pseudo-curtain and the oilcloth and water jug'.

Making those curtains was my first project—extraordinary, given my generally non-domestic habits, but I told myself that I wanted to find out what life was like for the Soviet consumer. My diary for my second day in Moscow reports a visit to GUM, the biggest state department store in the centre, where I bought three metres of some dark-green material. Since I couldn't find suitable curtain rings, I ended up attaching the material to an elastic cord someone in England had given me to use as a washing line. (These were the days before washing machines became common in Moscow, and Muscovites in regular flats usually still washed by hand and hung the clothes, and even the sheets, on lines they had tacked up in the bathroom over the bath. But we had no bath, only a shower, and dried everything on the towel rail.)

I needed nails and hooks to put up my curtain, but these were extraordinarily difficult to find in Moscow. Shops were open unpredictably, unless you actually visited in advance to check their hours; they had lunch breaks at odd times; and finally, like all Soviet institutions, they had monthly 'sanitation days' when they were simply closed, supposedly for cleaning. The dreaded notice 'Under repair' was common, and no end date was ever given. Do it yourself was an unknown concept in 1960s Moscow. I finally tracked down one of the very few hardware shops in Moscow (the Shop of Carpentry and Metal-Working Instruments on Kirov Street), bought two nails for one kopek each, and strung up my curtains. The whole thing took about a week, but at least it improved my knowledge of Moscow and I had a sense of accomplishment at the end. I was pleased with my curtain. Once it was up, and the plastic water jug out of sight, I felt the room had become mine.

I was run-down, insomniac (all those 3 a.m. letters to my mother!) and worried about my health in the first weeks in Moscow, and decided that swimming was the solution. This was strange, as I don't remember ever swimming at Oxford, but MGU had a pool, and I signed up to swim in it within a week of my arrival. The pool turned out to be buried in the bowels of the earth under those many layers of wedding cake, dark and hard to find. As I soon discovered, in the Soviet Union you didn't just go and have a swim. You were allocated a particular 45-minute time slot twice a week, and instead of peacefully swimming lengths, a coach standing on the side shouted instructions at you. I didn't notice the coach on my first session, being short-sighted and nervous, and was startled to hear a stentorian voice bellowing, evidently at me, 'Work with your legs! Work with your legs!' At least it was an addition to my Russian vocabulary (so *that*'s how you say 'kick'). I put a good face on this regimentation to my mother, saying the collective coaching was probably a good thing, 'making it more energetic and more sociable'. But I don't remember ever speaking to anyone and soon stopped going.

With similar lack of success, I tried out the famous 'Moscow' swimming pool built on the site of the Cathedral of Christ the Redeemer, which had been blown up in 1930 in a mixture of atheist fervour and enthusiasm for building the new Moscow. A Palace of Soviets topped by a statue of Lenin was meant to be built in its place but somehow never got started; all sorts of rumours floated around Moscow that the site was jinxed and inhabited by demons. So finally under Khrushchev the open-air swimming pool was built, remarkable for being usable in winter, when the warmth was kept in by a thick cloud of condensation. But then, after the collapse of the Soviet Union, that too was demolished, to be replaced by a rebuilt cathedral which for years was only a hollow shell with gold cupolas, but still completely changed the look of the city skyline; I suddenly understood how angry people must have been when it disappeared. But who knew in the 1960s that the days of the 'Moscow' swimming pool were numbered, let alone those of the Soviet Union.

It was still autumn when I made my one and only trip there—on my own, as was my habit, though anyone else would surely have roped in one of the other exchange students for company. You had to have a shower before swimming, so I undressed and put on my swimsuit and went to the showers, only to have the woman on duty shout at me: *No swimsuits in the shower!* I went back to the locker, got out of the wet swimsuit, returned naked to the showers, and was shouted at again: where were the rubber flip-flops on my feet that were compulsory for showering? When we had finally gone through all that, it was time to get into the pool, which in my memory (can it really have been so?) involved diving through a small, round aperture perhaps two feet in diameter and two feet long, with just an inch or so of air in the opening. I did it, overcoming intense inner objections, and came up gasping on the other side, where there was a small layer of warm air underneath a thick cloud of steam. The whole process sparked an acute attack of asthma, so I had to get myself through the horrible tunnel again immediately. In one of those typical contradictions of Soviet life, the women on duty who had earlier seemed so hostile suddenly became motherly types who, when I abruptly re-emerged, gasping and choking, fussed over me kindly and sat me down on a bench to recover.

My early health problems were exacerbated by eating troubles. Getting food was a problem for everyone, given the shortage of goods in the shops, their inconvenient location and awkward opening hours, and the fact that everything had to be lugged home in bulging string bags on public transport. Neighbourhood cafes and corner shops had been eliminated as part of a policy of centralisation and moving beyond capitalism in the early 1930s, so there was no question of dropping into the local Indian restaurant for supper. We exchange students at Moscow University were really comparatively well off, as we had access to the British Embassy's shop, which sold food as well as the otherwise unprocurable toilet paper, as well as MGU's cafeteria, which was open until 9 p.m. Still, I found it terribly difficult. This was initially connected with my dislike of being in public places with lots of other people whom I might have to speak to, and the fact that my gorge rose (literally) at the sight of meat, miserably grey and sinewy, as it arrived on Soviet plates in cafeterias. Later, once I started working in the evenings at the Lenin Library, there was the added complication that it was hard to get back to the university in time to get a meal. Plus, of course, I was too shy to use the communal kitchen on my floor of the dormitory.

Giving a sanitised version of this to my mother, I wrote that

> it is very boring queuing for meals, which aren't very pleasant when you get them, and so I simply don't; I have rye bread and tomato juice for breakfast, if anything; pick up something for lunch, like apples, or *pirozhki* (pies), that can be bought at stalls and eaten in the street in the Russian manner; come home and have rye bread and *kefir* (sour milk) and cheese or soup for supper.

Cheap and local, I commented,

> except for the tomato juice, which comes from British Embassy Commissariat, and peanut butter. I could cook meals—there is a communal kitchen—but I am always

> coming home terribly hungry and eating rye-bread so as to sustain myself, and then not wanting anything else enough to cook it.

That was all very well, but it produced a bout of painful constipation that drove me a few weeks later to the Moscow University polyclinic. On 26 October, I told my mother that I had changed my eating habits (no mention of the constipation or the polyclinic visit), dropping bread altogether (that didn't last long) and buying lots of tinned fruit and veg at the embassy shop. Lima beans eaten cold out of the tin became one of my staples for supper.

My initial explorations of Moscow were conducted in a spirit of autumnal melancholy. My diary entry on 25 September, my third day in Moscow, set the tone: 'Moscow in autumn in the rain ... Yellow leaves or few or none. Russian trees (birches?) seem to drop their leaves quite easily'. The streets were full of men in belted plastic raincoats imported from Italy, a new fashion item on the Moscow scene, and I imagined their wearers as black-marketeers, like the conman Ostap Bender from Ilf and Petrov's satirical classics of the 1930s. At a more exalted level, Lunacharsky and Stalin were also on my mind, Lunacharsky as the humanist who managed to glimpse an ideal future through the messy reality of Soviet life, Stalin as the destroyer with grandiose plans for rebuilding which, like the Moscow University wedding cake, didn't quite come off. 'All this grand manner and poverty of furnishings and genteel atrocities of taste', I wrote in my diary the day of my arrival, obviously under the influence of my first close encounter with MGU on Lenin Hills. 'What a place to work on Lunacharsky.' It was the gulf between pretensions and accomplishments in Soviet life that struck me, yet I was sentimentally inclined to take the Lunacharskian view that 'an imperfect likeness of human dignity comes out of the attempt'.

The oddly configured open spaces around the Kremlin caught my attention, and I found out by reading Sytin that this was because whole swaths of streets and buildings had been pulled down. 'What a time it must have been (1935–41 mainly) when they were pulling down the slums and the little lanes', I wrote to my mother. 'There are a few survivals, but I don't believe a Muscovite of 1917 would recognize the place, except for the Kremlin and Novo-Devichy monastery, both complexes still intact and remarkable.' The oddest effect was near the Kremlin, where the old merchants' quarter (Kitay Gorod) had been pulled down, leaving 'a sort of shapeless sea of asphalt breaking on the Kremlin Wall and St Basil's, which is like a fantastic island all on its own'. Various parts of the sea had been given new names, like Sverdlov Square and Square of the Revolution, but it was hard to distinguish one from the other 'because their shapes were determined by things which aren't there anymore'. The whole thing was unsuccessful, I concluded in my diary, 'because no new forms emerged from destruction of old. As if the Great Destroyer became suddenly helpless when told to rebuild'. There was a 'poverty of imagination' that reminded me of Australia.

What particularly fascinated me in Moscow was the palimpsest effect, layer upon layer. Having started with Stalinist monumental architecture and the rare remnants of 1920s modernism, I soon found my attention and sympathies drawn to eighteenth-century classical buildings in side streets, seventeenth-century churches tucked away in odd corners, now used for storage. There were other echoes. 'Walked through Gorky Park more or less dismantled for winter', I wrote in my diary. 'Sympathetic thoughts about people's palaces ... Notice that I am more and more slipping into a *Palaces on Monday* frame of mind. How unexpected—and no doubt impermanent. Result of going to parks and swimming pools.' To my mother, I expanded on that as a 'weakness for the Lunacharskian aspects [of Moscow]—the People's Palaces and Pioneers' Playgrounds with coloured lights and statues and notices saying "Art belongs to the people" ... chandeliers in the metro stations: it is all in that Puffin book called *Palaces on Monday*'.

My diaries and letters to my mother are full of theatre and music criticism, a reminder of how seriously I took high culture, and the idea of myself as a high-culture person, at this point, but also that this all happened so long ago that people still wrote letters of this kind. On my second week in Moscow, having mastered the complexity of buying tickets without Intourist's help, I went to a Sunday matinee at the Bolshoi opera and saw Tchaikovsky's *Evgenii Onegin*, based on Pushkin's poem. It was a disappointment, particularly compared to the ballet *Legend About Love* that had so impressed me six months earlier. Tatiana, the heroine, played by Bolshoi veteran Maslennikova, was middle-aged, plump and plain, quite unlike the eager, pretty young girl who falls in love with Onegin in Pushkin's story. In the first two acts, her 'hopeless dowdiness' made the story seem like the tragedy of an unattractive girl. It was the 736th performance of a 1944 production, I noted in my diary. I wonder if they usually keep them so long. 'Perhaps Maslennikova played

Tatiana in 1944.' The fabled Moscow Arts Theatre was no better. They played Mikhail Bulgakov's Civil War play *Days of the Turbins* for laughs, I noted in my diary in November, as if it were a slapstick comedy. I found the Arts Theatre style overblown and rather vulgar; it reminded me of one of the conclusions from my fourth-year thesis that in practice the Soviet concept of 'accessible' and 'popular' art teetered on the edge of kitsch. There was a lot of kitsch (*poshlost*) around in the Soviet Union, I noticed, starting with that plastic water jug in my room, as well as a certain amount of high-cultural anxiety about succumbing to it.

There was a bit of kitsch in Andrey Volkonsky's Monteverdi, in my opinion. That was a heretical reaction to a high-class musical event I stumbled on at the Moscow University House of Culture. I went because I happened to see it advertised and liked Monteverdi, but it was clear from the packed and enthusiastic audience that the newly rediscovered music of the baroque, especially in Volkonsky's rendition, was highly valued by Moscow's cognoscenti. I noted the presence in the audience not only of students but also of 'a number of oldish women who looked as if they might have been cherishing Art Nouveau and Ars Antiqua through the long hard winter' since the Revolution. Volkonsky himself was an exotic figure, a returned *émigré* of aristocratic lineage who was both an avant-garde composer *au courant* with developments in Paris and an admired interpreter of early music trained by Nadia Boulanger. His baroque style, however, had a different quality from Boulanger's: the music was staged in a highly theatrical way, with overtones of religious celebration (a reliably exciting element in an officially atheist state) and Russia's early-twentieth-century Silver Age.

The stage was bathed in red and yellow light, with two brackets of candles; the singers, all women, were in black, except for one with titian hair in dramatic red velvet. Musically, it was all very professional, I recorded in my diary, but

> tremendously emphatic: women moving gracefully, rolling their eyes, sighing, imploring with pathetic gestures (they all had little books of words, or perhaps music, bound in black leather) or *Merry, merry, merry month of maying* with great clarity of articulation ... All *molto affetuoso,* which is quite right historically, and yet the atmosphere was Blok's [Alexander Blok, the Silver Age poet, currently making a comeback among Soviet intellectuals] and not Monteverdi's.

I found the total impact quite odd, and was a little inclined to giggle. Volkonsky, who accompanied at the keyboard, had his hair cut very short in the style of a French student or the German avant-garde composer Karlheinz Stockhausen. 'He is tall, holds head high, throws out chest and, to some extent, backside, and ends up looking not quite as distinguished as one feels he should.' 'Began to wonder what Volkonsky's avant-garde music sounds like', I wrote in the diary: 'Scriabin?' From me, that wasn't a compliment.

By mid-November, my Moscow landscape was becoming more populated. My spirits were recovering, along with my confidence; my command of Russian was improving. The left-hand pages of my diary were no longer used for elementary Russian language exercises (*Can I leave my coat? Where can I leave my coat? Did anyone leave a book for me? How does one get money? We are going (by transport) into the centre of Moscow for lectures. We are going (on foot) to the University*

Metro. The professor has gone home. When will they be back?). I remember the linguistic breakthrough quite clearly. It occurred when I read a newspaper article on common mistakes in colloquial Russian and suddenly saw what must be the underlying grammar (not admitted by the grammarians, of course) of the spoken language.

I went off twice a week to Russian-for-foreigners classes run by the university, conducted entirely in Russian with a polyglot student group. Our lively young teacher, Nina Abramovna, had recently made an eye-opening trip to Cuba, the most exotic destination in the 'fraternal' bloc, and often talked about it. She also helpfully provided the Russian phrases appropriate for discouraging men who were trying to pick you up or just groping you on the bus. As in all oral language classes, we were sometimes asked to make an impromptu speech about something that had interested us in the past week, and I chose to talk about spies. I had noticed a lecture advertised in the evening paper on the famous spy Richard Sorge, whose information from Tokyo on the date of the imminent German attack of June 1941 was disregarded by Stalin. Sorge interested me partly because he was the subject of a recent book co-authored by the St Antony's warden, William Deakin. This was a more dramatic version, read by an actor from a text from a popular book of docu-fiction with piano accompaniment. I enjoyed the slightly over-the-top heroics, as when Sorge under questioning by the Japanese said defiantly, 'I have never been a spy. I am a Soviet citizen doing my patriotic duty.' 'Just like Biggles', I noted in my diary. Biggles was the pilot and adventurer hero of a series of popular children's books by WE Johns, originally with World War I settings. As a child, I had been struck by the fact that the one about

Biggles as a spy (published in 1940) was euphemistically called *Biggles—Secret Agent*. As a minor provocation, I used the term 'spy' (*shpion*) rather than 'secret agent' (*tainyi agent*) in my report on Sorge, and Nina A duly corrected me: our men are secret agents, their men are spies.

The descriptions of Moscow life I was sending back to my mother were becoming less high-flown and more immediate. Public transport was an early preoccupation. It was forty minutes, usually on two forms of transport, from Lenin Hills to the university in the centre or the Lenin Library, and I often had to do this round trip twice:

> impossible to get a seat unless you get on at the terminus, which means extra minutes' walk. I counted thirty people standing in a bus that seats about twenty-five this morning, and there were quite a few people of my size jammed underneath elbows and crouched over the ticket machines. Carrying a violin in these circumstances is quite frightening.

My size was five foot nothing, which in the Soviet Union of the 1960s was not out of the normal range. It was only in the 1980s that the height of the younger generation suddenly shot up, so that I became a short person again, much to my disgust, just as I was in the West.

I gradually mastered the various rituals of bus travel. You passed your five-kopek fare hand over hand (the appropriate phrase was 'pass it on, please'—*peredaite pozhaluista*) until it got to the person squashed against the ticket machine, who had to put in the five kopeks, obtain the ticket and pass it back through five or seven intermediaries. As soon as you got on, especially on a short trip, you had to start squeezing your way forward through the mass of bodies, because the back door was only for entrance and the front one only for exit. 'You're not getting off at the next one, are you?' was the polite form of words indicating that you were about to thrust your elbows into whomever stood between you and the door. By December, I clearly felt I had the hang of it.

> I came home with a Japanese girl, Tomiko, and English John today; Tomiko got on the bus, because I gave her a great shove in proper Moscow manner, and I had one foot on when they closed the doors; everyone shouted at the bus-driver and he opened the door for one second, in which I flung the rest of myself after my foot; but John was left behind.

I mastered these habits of aggressive self-preservation so well that, back in Oxford the next year, I found myself shamelessly elbowing aside little old ladies in Sainsbury's.

Life in the Soviet Union is 'a sort of obstacle race cum marathon which one habitually approaches in a spirit of stubborn and virtuous perseverance, not a spiritual or mental strain but rather a physical one', I wrote to my mother in October. I took the image of a race seriously, keeping a wary eye on the competition, that is, the British student group. When my mother expressed concern that I seemed socially isolated, I took this as a suggestion that I was lagging behind in the race—as, in terms of social interaction, I surely was—and quickly corrected her: with regard to 'achievements' in Moscow (a concept I left undefined, though I may have meant language proficiency), I thought I was coming out pretty well in comparison with the others. Noticing that this sounded 'all rather competitive', I said everyone was like that: in a foreign country, there was a compulsion to measure your success against that of other foreigners. Even Alex was like that in Japan, I claimed implausibly (Alex was the least competitive of men and in any case didn't mix much with other foreigners in Tokyo). The fact was, I was always competitive, almost regardless of context, as my mother obviously knew; and, I think, approved. I then added a rather disarming postscript: 'I suppose my main success is being quite happy here. Moscow has made me optimistic, whereas Oxford depressed me'.

Winter was a challenge, but on the whole I weathered it, despite having an inadequate coat (the warmest I could find at Fenwick's in Bond Street) and very little previous experience of the cold. 'MGU is a shelter from the icy blast', I wrote to my mother in December.

> The hot water is hot and the rooms are warm. One can see the point of building in one huge mass. I had to walk from the Lenin Library to the Zoological Museum where we have Russian lessons at lunchtime today, and suffered greatly. Everyone on the street was covering their pink and anguished faces with scarves, but mine isn't big enough. But anyway they still look anguished, even with scarves.

Snow first fell on 30 October, and in those days it was expected to remain on the ground in Moscow until spring, and duly did so that year. I followed the general example and shut up my outer windows with modelling clay (obtained from the Children's World department store: child consumers seemed to be better served than adults in the Soviet Union) to keep out the draughts. 'The space between the two windows serves as a refrigerator', I explained.

'I saw the first casualty of winter today', I wrote to my mother in November: 'a man lying outside a Metro Station surrounded by a great crowd of people shouting: someone said he was alive, and he may just have been drunk'. The streets became perilous not only for drunks but also for limbless men on crutches, a quite substantial population with a big overlap with the drunks. It was hard to imagine how they survived on their crutches even when sober, since snow and frosts made the ground very slippery, and the buses had to be entered via a step that was two feet off the ground. I was amused by the look of Russians in winter dress, just the way the English caricaturist David Low used to draw them.

> The men mainly have hats with earflaps which tie on top, or can be pulled down and tied under the chin, but it is absolutely not done to tie the flaps under the chin unless it is thirty below so they go round with the flaps down and flapping—it makes them look like dogs. The women wear extraordinary heavy coats with great big collars above which emerges the top quarter of a tiny head like a nut, wrapped in a scarf. The children who are old enough to face the winter (babies and the very young stay at home all winter) have fur coats tied round the middle with string usually; collars turned up and tied round the neck with a thin woollen scarf which is also used to hold the child; fur bonnet; woollen tights; felt boots called *valenki*. They are so loaded with clothes that they can hardly sit down.

I had a bad winter moment on an excursion organised for the British student group to Suzdal. The temperature had dropped to more than thirty below and the wind howled at us as we staggered over what seemed like several kilometres of snowy wastes to reach Suzdal's seventeenth-century churches. The inadequacy of my winter clothes, especially my lack of a good scarf, made itself painfully felt: I have never been so cold in my life, and my nose even started to freeze and lose colour, the first stage of frostbite. The others, perhaps more warmly dressed, seemed in slightly better shape. When we got to the churches, there was some kind of hut with a peasant stove on which, thank God, they laid me down to thaw. '*Perezhili*', said the guides sympathetically, meaning 'You've had a bad time'. But with my still bookish Russian I misunderstood and thought they were using the word in another sense: 'You've survived', meaning you don't have much to complain about. I looked resentful and they looked puzzled. But the sentiment was not inappropriate to my own feelings of the time. I had survived the emotional crash after my father's death; I was surviving Moscow; I was even not going to lose my nose to frostbite.

I'm glad I kept a diary in those first months in Moscow. Otherwise the texture of that people-less life would have been overlaid by later experiences. I would never again be in Moscow like a traveller to the moon, exploring the terrain alone, fascinated but all the time with a slight feeling that I might never get back home. The analogy only partly holds, because at this point in my life I didn't know where home was, or if I had one. But you can know you're away from home without knowing where home is, and my remembered Moscow has that quality. Even now that Moscow has been tarted up for post-Soviet capitalism, I can still find glimpses of those vistas and corners of the city I first discovered then and made my own—or, sometimes, their absences. When I see the No. 119 bus, running from Lenin (now Sparrow) Hills to the centre of Moscow, I mentally salute the small person in an unsuitable coat flinging herself against the closing doors. When I see the pretty little seventeenth-century church squashed in a modern street near the 'Arbat' Metro, I remember the thrill of discovering it, and with it the charm of incongruous juxtaposition which is so characteristic of Moscow. I look at the rebuilt church of Christ the Redeemer on Volkhonka and remember the plume of steam from the 'Moscow' swimming pool that once occupied that spot, after the old church was blown up in 1930; I remember, too, how back then I would look at the swimming pool and imagine the old church that was once there and the Palace of Soviets that never was. When I walk on certain streets, the echoes of music wafting out—Mozart, perhaps, or Tchaikovsky—come back to me, and with it that wistful sense of a life there inside, my kind of life, while I'm outside looking in, like a little ghost.

Gradually, in these first months, human figures started emerging in the Moscow landscape. I reacted to them with all the wary joy of a traveller in the steppe, scrutinising approaching riders, wondering about their intentions. Of course they were scrutinising me, too: for many of them, it was their job. Taking the broadest view of KGB surveillance, you might say I was an object of anthropological study for them; certainly they were objects of anthropological study for me. But that doesn't quite cover my reaction to the figures approaching on the steppe, unless we assume that anthropologists tend to be looking for the perfect informant, like a young girl searching for Mr Right. What I was looking for was someone with a key to this strange society who would open the door and let me in.

3

Foreign Student

The Foreign Office briefed us before we went off to Moscow on the British Council exchange. Or rather, I suppose, MI6 briefed us, for the speaker was never introduced by name. The setting was a dark-panelled windowless basement in the Foreign Office building, and the subject was the dangers facing foreign students in Moscow. Everybody we met in the Soviet Union would be a spy, we were told. It would be impossible to make friends with Russians because, in the first place, they were all spies, and, in the second, they would make the same assumption about us. As students, we would be particularly vulnerable to Soviet attempts to compromise us because, unlike other foreigners resident in Moscow and Leningrad, we would actually live side by side with Russians instead of in a foreigners' compound. Detailed instructions were offered about how to avoid getting into trouble with the KGB. We should be particularly careful not to be entrapped into sexual liaisons which would result in blackmail (from the Soviet side) and swift forcible return to Britain (from the British). If any untoward approach was made to us, or if we knew of such an approach to someone else in the group, we should immediately inform the embassy.

Our group of twenty listened respectfully, but few availed themselves of the chance to ask questions. There must have been quite a lot of silent scepticism in the room about the briefer's claim that it would be impossible to make friends with Russians, as most of the group, like me, had surely been before on tourist trips and met their own Alyoshas, not to mention Vics. I certainly thought the briefer was out of date, and was a bit surprised at the strength of the Cold War message. At the same time, it was hard not to shiver at the cloak-and-dagger atmosphere and the speaker's emphasis that if you got into trouble in the Soviet Union, it could be *real* trouble. In Stalin's time, the Soviet assumption had been that foreigners, particularly from capitalist countries, were likely to be spies. That wasn't exactly the dominant view in the post-Stalin Soviet Union, but it hadn't wholly disappeared either. Exchanges like ours existed, but it was presumed that both sides would use them to send a few spies, or spies in training, along with the regular students. I found out when I was doing some research on the exchanges that one of the Soviet students sent to Britain in the mid 1960s—our counterparts—was an up-and-coming intelligence agent who by 1971 was KGB resident in Norway and thirty years later had risen to No. 3 in the KGB hierarchy. I doubt that the intelligence man in our group, whoever he was, had such a brilliant later career, but he was surely there.

Certainly the Soviets frequently protested about spies on the student exchanges. The Leningrad KGB put out a booklet based on its files of such cases from the 1960s entitled *Scholarly Exchange and Ideological Diversion*. Since the beginning of the exchanges in the late 1950s, the booklet noted, 'the sinister shadow of the CIA', and by the same token

MI6 and all the European intelligence agencies, had hung over them. The exchange was frequently used as a cover for spying and 'anti-Soviet activity', which meant expressing opinions the Soviet authorities didn't like or spreading information they regarded as harmful; 'anti-Soviet activity' was actually an offence punishable by imprisonment under the Soviet Criminal Code, although in practice they didn't usually prosecute foreigners for it but just expelled them from the country. In one of the Leningrad cases, a Belgian exchange student caught in anti-Soviet activity had confessed to his KGB interrogators that 'he had been given detailed instructions about how to act so as not to attract the attention of the Soviet security forces'—in other words, he had had a briefing just like ours. His interrogators smiled at such naivety (this observation is included in the report), but it didn't give us exchange students much to smile about if even attending the Foreign Office's mandatory advance briefing put us in the wrong with the KGB.

Spying was an obsession with everyone on the exchange. Our conversations throughout the year were full of speculation about whether such and such a Russian was a spy. There was gossip about the American exchange group, which seemed to have trouble keeping the CIA as well as the KGB at bay. We assumed that at least one of our number was a real spy, since in that Iron Curtain divided world the chance of smuggling someone in would obviously be irresistible to both sides. We also assumed, based on the experience of previous years, that at least one of us, who might be a real spy but probably wasn't, was likely either to be expelled by the Russians for anti-Soviet activity or sent home by the British for being compromised by the KGB. As the year went on, the grapevine brought news of various incidents where exchange students had been followed or found themselves targets of entrapment and other forms of KGB attention. Entrapment (*provokatsiya*) meant that the KGB set you up in some compromising situation (sex with a Russian, especially homosexual, which was a criminal offence; black-market dealings; distributing anti-Soviet literature) and then tried to blackmail you: *we won't pursue this if you'll just agree to give us information from time to time in the future.*

I was told in strict confidence by one of our British group that one of the other students had been trapped in this way and—instead of telling the embassy, as we were supposed to do, and being sent home posthaste—had agreed to the KGB offer. The convolutions of possible spying scenarios seemed to be endless. Towards the end of the year, my Soviet friend Sasha, a student who lived in the Moscow University dorm, told me that he thought that this same British student had been tailing him. The whole story seemed wildly improbable, but on the off-chance there was anything in it, the range of possibilities was mind-boggling. Sasha could have been a KGB stooge (though I didn't think he was) trying to stir up trouble within the British group or just elicit some comment from me on the British student concerned. The British student could be spying on Sasha on behalf of British intelligence, though it was difficult to imagine a reason unless it had something to do with the Soviet student's friendship with me. Or, most implausibly, the British student could be spying on Sasha for unknown reasons on behalf of the KGB.

'Are you a spy (*ty shpionka*)?' was the ingenuous question asked me by a schoolgirl in Volgograd. I said no, but in my own mind the answer wasn't absolutely clear-cut. No, I was not a spy: that is, I was not on the payroll or working unpaid for any national or *émigré* intelligence agency. But I knew some spies, broadly construed: my Oxford college, St Antony's, was full of them, admittedly mainly retired; and not long after my arrival in Moscow I was appalled to receive a signed letter through the open post from one of them. How close did a connection have to be to become culpable? We exchange students were often invited to the embassy, where officials (some of whom must have been intelligence officers) showed interest in our experiences and observations of Soviet life; and at the end of the year we all had to write a detailed final report for the British Council, which was probably passed on to the Foreign Office and MI6, on the same topic. There was even the possibility of individual debriefing, as I discovered after my return to Britain, if one was thought to have sufficiently interesting things to report. Where did that come on the continuum between being a spy and being an innocent bystander?

No doubt it was a symptom of our collective paranoid obsession with spying that such thoughts would even come into my mind. In the unlikely event that I had wanted to be absolutely honest in replying to the Volgograd girl's question, I might have said, 'Not intentionally.' But even that might not have been fully accurate, since in my capacity as a historical researcher, I wanted to find out things the Soviet authorities wanted to hide, and they counted that as spying. Given my status as a hunter out of secrets, I never felt totally innocent—but perhaps nobody did in the Soviet Union. The most accurate answer to the Volgograd question might have been: 'I don't think so'. Or even 'I hope not'.

The British group as a whole sailed for Leningrad on 8 September 1966, but I hadn't yet got my documents together and had to miss the boat, along with four other prospective exchange students who were still waiting for visas. I left about ten days later on the SS *Krupskaya*, alone except for Bill Stephenson, a mathematician on the Academy of Sciences exchange, so presumably the other four British Council nominees were refused visas. 'I have British nationality and passport, a Russian visa, and permission to study for ten months at Moscow State University', I wrote to my mother from the boat. 'I have £70 of travellers' cheques from the British Council (who supplement the Russian stipend) and £50 of my own (which is all that we British nationals are allowed to take out of the country because of the Economic Crisis), and two suitcases, one overnight bag and one cabin trunk of luggage.' You can see the effect on my prose of all that last-minute list-making. For some reason I didn't list my violin, but I had that with me too. Our route was via Copenhagen, Stockholm and Helsinki to Leningrad. Someone from the Ministry of Higher Education was to meet me in Leningrad with a train ticket to go on to Moscow.

The *Krupskaya* was rather empty, so I had a two-berth first-class cabin to myself. Remarkably, my memory of that trip, which took about five days with three stops in cities I had never been to before, is of intolerable boredom, an empty life punctuated three times a day by meals. Some drunken Finns got on at Helsinki to continue drinking in Leningrad. There was a bunch of Australian women on board, I told my mother, probably left wing and one of them perhaps Dymphna Cusack, an Australian writer who was a friend of my parents'. I did not make myself known to her, even though she—if it was Dymphna Cusack—had written me a letter of condolence on my father's death only a year earlier. I didn't tell the Australian women that I was Australian, and because I was travelling as Mrs Bruce with a British passport and unplaceable accent, they didn't work it out. I seemed to relish travelling under an alias.

The arrival at Leningrad was a mess. A young woman from Intourist and a man from the Academy of Sciences were there to meet Bill Stephenson, as well as the British Embassy's scientific attaché, but by some bureaucratic confusion nobody had come to meet me. As a result, I didn't have a ticket to go on to Moscow, and we couldn't buy one because foreigners were not allowed to buy tickets for journeys of more than forty kilometres without authorisation. Fortunately, the Soviet bureaucracy had made a second mistake that more or less cancelled out the first one. As I described it laconically to my mother, the Academy of Sciences man meeting Bill

> brought not only his reservation but one for his wife. But he doesn't have a wife. So when the Intourist office closed an hour early, thus preventing Bill from returning his wife's ticket and me from collecting mine for the midnight train, everything, in a sense worked out. I travelled as Bill's wife on a ticket bought by the Academy of Sciences' interpreter, who was paid by the Embassy man who was to apply for repayment by British Council, who would have to get the money back from Intourist.

The negotiations that finally achieved this result went on for hours, but by the end I was feeling quite cheerful. This was partly because of Bill, whom I hadn't had much to do with on the boat but quickly got to know the day of our arrival. He was a friendly and comforting presence who, as I reported, 'ticked me off when I got uppish and patted my head when I got upset'. With Bill around, I felt reasonably confident I wasn't going to be left in Leningrad to rot on the docks.

I arrived in Moscow at 8.15 a.m. the next day, having travelled 'hard' (economy) class with Bill and his Intourist guide, Natasha, overnight. Strictly speaking, it was Mrs Bill Stephenson who arrived, but this time there actually was someone at the station to meet me—or rather, to meet 'Miss Meila Patrick' and escort her to the Moscow University dormitory on Lenin Hills. The rest of the day was taken up by bureaucratic formalities, filling in forms for various officials, some of whom were expecting Sheila Fitzpatrick and others Sheila Bruce. This was not altogether surprising, as the original request from the British Council to admit me as an exchange student preceded my marriage and thus identified me as Sheila Fitzpatrick, whereas my entry visa, issued to me as the holder of my recently acquired British passport, was in the name of Sheila Bruce. I had compounded the possibilities for confusion by writing in my application that I preferred to be known by my second name, Mary. As far as I can remember, this was ostensibly because Maria and its diminutive, Masha, would be easier for Russians than Sheila, but it has the smell of the same kind of identity repudiation as my refusal to make myself known to the Australians on the boat. It didn't matter, in the event, as the Soviet bureaucrats ignored my request. Nobody ever called me Masha and I never used the name. Contrary to my expectations, all educated Russians knew the name of Sheila, pronounced Shayla, because they had read the novels of CP Snow in which Sheila is the narrator's neurotic and suicidal wife. They didn't even have trouble finding a diminutive: Shaylochka.

Wherever they were in the Soviet Union, foreigners had to have their own Foreign Department, shortened to Inotdel. The Moscow Inotdel was headed by the fearsome, red-haired Lilia Pavlovna. Lilia Pavlovna was regarded with suspicion and dislike by many of the exchange students, partly because she had the power to refuse requests and often used it, and partly because of her assumed KGB connections. The Australian writer Robert Dessaix, who in an earlier incarnation as Robert Jones was an exchange student at MGU the same year as I was, recalls her in *A Mother's Disgrace* as a kind of Soviet basilisk who once reduced him to loud sobbing in her office; Katerina Clark, there on the Australian account the year before, had a similar experience. I ended up quite liking her, as she seemed relatively honest and straightforward, within the constraints of her job, and was not ill-disposed to me personally. Still, we started off on an awkward note. The form she had to complete on my behalf included a question about my parents' profession. I said my father had been a historian, at which she wrote down 'teacher'. When I objected that he was a freelance historian but not a teacher, she was momentarily stumped: 'We don't have historians who are not teachers.' It was a relief for her, bureaucratically speaking, to learn that he was dead and that my surviving parent had a more acceptable profession. 'Father, a historian, is dead; mother teaches history at Monash University, Australia', is what she finally wrote. I winced at that: it seemed unkind that my father, a socialist who had had hopes for the Soviet Union, should be so brusquely dismissed.

I distributed a total of ten passport photos for various applications and dossiers that first day, exhausting the supply I had brought with me, so I had to go off to a photography shop on Herzen Street to get some more. It cost me twenty kopeks for six, as I recorded in my diary ('Turn of century atmosphere. Camera with shutters. Negatives pegged on line across room. Subject lit by four or five bare light globes on wall'). With one of these passport photos, I obtained my university pass from Lilia Pavlovna's counterpart at the Inotdel downtown, Viktor Dmitrievich. This was the absolutely essential document, without which I would not be allowed back into the dormitory and would be forced to live on the streets, although that too was forbidden, for foreigners as well as Russians. Viktor Dmitrievich, whom I found a bit smarmier than Lilia Pavlovna, instructed me to sign the document as Sheila Fitzpatrick. I'm not sure why, since the pass itself was made out to Sheila Bruce (in Cyrillic 'Bryus, Shila'), exchange student at the School of Philology from 23 September 1966 to 15 July 1967. All this identity confusion was surely going to make a mess of my Soviet personal file, I thought. But perhaps that was a good thing—harder for the KGB to keep straight who I was.

The students in the exchange group were all British except me, the biggest contingents being in language and literature, with a handful of historians (the others working on Russian history before the Revolution), along with an economist, an economic geographer, an architect, an archaeologist and an anthropologist. In addition to the twenty British Council students, there were two Australians in Moscow (one of them Robert Jones), and a large American group that I tried to avoid, as well as assorted French, Italian, and German in two varieties (capitalists from West

Germany and fraternal foreigners from the East). My diary and letters to my mother in the first months are full of statements about disliking and being irritated by the British group, which I think mainly reflects my depression and consequent antisocial tendencies; by the end of the year, when we all went on a trip around the Soviet Union together, I found I quite liked them. My closest contacts in the group the first autumn were our group leader, Michael Ellman, an economist from Cambridge back for his second year on the exchange, and Caroline Waddington (later Humphrey), a Cambridge social anthropologist, with whom I used to swap bulletins on our latest bureaucratic battles, mine for archives, hers for field trips. Later I also became friendly with a literature student, Ann Barlow. As we had a roster to pick up and deliver English newspapers from the embassy, as well as periodic trips and social functions in the embassy together, I had occasional casual contact with the rest of the group. But I was wary of too much socialising with English-speakers, partly out of concern to improve my Russian and partly because I aspired to live in a Soviet, not expatriate world. That, I felt, was what I had come to Moscow for, and it was a once-in-a-lifetime chance of finite duration. Whether it would be possible to discover a Soviet world to receive me, given the constraints of the situation and my own temperament, remained to be seen.

It was all very well to aspire to live in a Soviet world, but to do that one had to know some Russians. Shyness was the first problem: if I was too shy even to go into the communal kitchen in the dorm, however was I going to meet people? To make it more difficult, I had certain fixed opinions about what kind of Soviet people I wanted to meet. Not alienated young people with a taste for Western consumer goods, like

Vic. Perhaps not even people like Alyosha, since he was so sophisticated and knowledgeable about the West, although in practice I would have been happy if Alyosha had suddenly reappeared. Not dissident intellectuals who knew the Western foreign correspondents in Moscow and were written about by Max Hayward. Particularly not the young celebrity poets who, according to the student grapevine, had a different girlfriend from the British or American group every year. That, of course, eliminated a broad range of the people I could fairly easily meet who might be interested in meeting me. I wanted to get to know the kind of Russians who *didn't* seek out foreigners, and find out what they said when foreigners weren't around. It sounded unachievable by definition, but, in those innocent days before self-reflexivity, anthropologists claimed to have the knack. Although knowing almost nothing about anthropology, I wanted in effect to be an anthropologist with Moscow as my field and find out what made these people tick. Otherwise, I thought, I couldn't write their history properly.

I assumed that the KGB was keeping an eye on me, as on all the other students. In fact, I was reminded of this likelihood soon after my arrival, when Alyosha sent a message to me via his mother saying 'he was glad to have made his contribution to getting me here'. By this he presumably meant that he had given me a good write-up in the report that, as a guide, he had to write on all the people in his tourist group. The report would have gone in the first instance to Sputnik, the youth travel agency he was working for, and thence to the KGB, where it must have become one of the first documents in my file. I was glad to have had a good start.

Shy, uncommunicative exchange students like me must have been an annoyance to the KGB. You can sense this in the Leningrad KGB's report on a Belgian who was later allegedly caught out as an agent of a Belgian intelligence organisation:

> Paul Charl'e, a nice looking young man, a graduate of Louvain Catholic University ... came to Leningrad on the scientific exchange for a ten-month stay ... He soon became known in the postgraduates' dormitory and the university as 'quiet Paul' and 'the oddball exchange student'. His dorm neighbours gave him the first nickname ... He didn't get close to anyone, neither to Soviets nor to foreign postgraduates, and never took part in the discussions and arguments which periodically took place in the dorm. On the contrary, the Belgian exchange student was extremely uncommunicative and even seemed unsociable.

A bad choice for a spy, you might think. I suppose he was in a smaller, more collegial dormitory than mine, as I simply didn't know enough people in my dorm to be nicknamed 'Quiet Sheila' or anything else. But the good thing about the shy ones, from the KGB's point of view, is that if somebody makes a special effort to talk to them, they often respond. In my case, it didn't take much to break through the barrier. Valery, the KGB's first offering to me, was the guide for a British Council student outing to Zagorsk a week after I arrived. I didn't enjoy the excursion much, no doubt feeling an outsider in the British group, who had bonded on the boat, and described the guide in my diary as reserved and sarcastic in manner, with a smooth, beardless face and the unmistakable manner of a member of the intelligentsia. His English was good, though I noted that he seemed to be concealing this, perhaps 'in order to hear more of our uninhibited conversation'. It was not until our next expedition (to

Abramtsevo) that I warmed to him, and that was because he singled me out, recognising, as I felt, my intellectual superiority to the rest. On the Abramtsevo trip, Valery was 'much more talkative. Only to me, though', I noted with satisfaction in my diary. He rattled away about poetry so fast that I couldn't keep up. All the same, I gathered that he was an admirer of the poets Anna Akhmatova and Boris Pasternak but ranked Osip Mandelstam even higher, 'like all the boys (*rebiata*) in the PhilFac'—a nice throwaway line if you came from a place where most boys at the university didn't have passionate opinions about poetry.

Valery was a young man with connections (*sviazi*, one of the ubiquitous words whose vernacular significance they didn't teach you in university language classes). Among his connections were Lilia Pavlovna and Viktor Dmitrievich from the university Inotdel, where his sister also worked. When he disappeared for a couple of weeks in November, the first thing he asked on returning was whether Lilia Pavlovna, who would apparently be annoyed at his unauthorised absence, had asked me about him. 'Why should Lilia Pavlovna ask me?' I wondered in my diary; as far as I knew, she didn't know I knew him. The obvious answer was that he had been sent to report on me, and had been derelict in his duty the past few weeks. I acknowledged this possibility in my diary but still preferred not to think he was from the KGB. For a Soviet student, he seemed strikingly well off: he even, incredibly, had a car, a 1947 Moskvich. His taste in music ran to Joan Baez and Pete Seeger, whose songs he had somehow acquired on tape; and once I accidentally saw him eating lunch at the National, the Intourist hotel, which was not even in the dream world of most Soviet students. Eating out at a restaurant of any kind was a rare occurrence for Soviet citizens, associated only with important celebrations, and the National, which only took foreign currency, was completely unthinkable.

Valery quickly informed me that his father-in-law, a top aviation engineer, worked with the famous Tupolev ('Tupola', I wrote in my diary, not having yet absorbed the fame of Andrey Tupolev, designer of the TU bombers). His own father was also of the elite, being a head of a building trust, although, like Tupolev, he had spent some years in Gulag in the 1940s. Valery and his wife—a student at the aircraft institute of whom he spoke only reluctantly—lived with her parents in what was obviously an elite flat, but I never saw it. All our meetings after the initial ones took place in my room in the dorm, where he showed up with a book to give me the week after our meeting. Being worried about my lack of conversation practice, I asked him how I could find someone interested in exchanging English lessons for Russian. According to my diary, 'he suggested himself. I was surprised because his English is good ... but he may even have come meaning to suggest it—seemed to be hanging around, trying not to be sarcastic and, in general, to be nice. Not sure what he's after ... Left telephone number but not surname' (which I never knew).

I don't remember giving Valery lessons in English. It was all just conversation in Russian, mainly about literature, but he would sometimes say something, usually a bit snaky, about one of the other British Council students. Of the Australian Robert Jones, he once remarked out of the blue: 'He was flirting with me. But then he flirts with everyone.' That surprised me since homosexuality, apart from being a crime in the Soviet Union, was quite outside the normal Russian frame of reference; I wasn't even sure that Valery meant the remark in a directly sexual sense. At least I had enough sense not to take him up on it and ask what he meant, as it was very likely a fishing expedition. Valery didn't flirt with me. What he did was give me a short course on Soviet book publishing and distribution and the importance of *sviazi* in getting the books you actually wanted to read, like coveted small-print-run editions of Akhmatova. 'The books in shops are the leftovers', he told me. 'Do not ask me about them, I do not read such books.' Using his *sviazi*, he brought me lots of rare and specialised books, many published in the 1920s, mostly his choice rather than my specific request, but would never let me pay for them. The price he told me he had paid for one esoteric book on music was a quarter of a Russian student's stipend for a month. Another time it was a valuable 1925 edition of the poet Alexander Blok. I chewed this over in my diary: 'Why won't he take money for them? Because it's discourteous, or because financial transactions are more suspect?'

Valery's idea was that we would swap his Russian books for English- and Russian-language editions published abroad; he particularly wanted an *émigré* edition of Mandelstam. I was willing to give him English-language books, mainly contemporary literature, but balked at *émigré* publications, for fear of being accused of trading in anti-Soviet materials. This was a completely reasonable fear; however, it would have been prudent to worry about English-language books, too. According to the Leningrad KGB book, Ned Keenan got into trouble for giving his Russian friends 'bourgeois literature' like *Life*, the *New York Times* and the memoirs of Lord Keynes, 'which contained brazen slander on the Soviet Union and international communism'. Another student alleged to be a spy had given a Russian friend, who later informed on him, a copy of *Reader's Digest* that, by chance or otherwise, contained an article entitled 'How they treat Jews in the Soviet Union'. I knew it was unwise of me to get involved in this book exchange, even though many other students took similar risks, but found it impossible to refuse outright—after all, it was so nice of Valery to give me all these books that it seemed churlish to question his motives or fail to reciprocate.

The term '*stukach*', the informer or stool pigeon who collects information on people around him and then delivers it to his KGB control, was familiar to me after a few weeks in Moscow, but I did not want to think of Valery in these terms. For one thing, he was of higher social class than I thought a *stukach* would be. The conventional derivation of *stukach* was one who knocked on the door of the KGB office, but I always thought of it in the terms in which it presented itself to me in real life: the person who knocks on your door in the dorm. Naturally I was much quicker to identify other people's Russian contacts as *stukachi* than my own, but this was a universal failing.

My connection with Valery was strictly confined to conversation and book dealings, but my friend Bill, whose wife I had become to get to Moscow from Leningrad, had a more total immersion. Natasha, the girl who first met him at the station on behalf of Intourist, 'has been taking him everywhere and also apparently cross-examining him on his movements in her absence', I recorded in my diary. 'He finds it odd that she is available at all times of day although in theory a student', and her income seemed to be much higher than a student's stipend. 'Having wondered if she was reporting on him, he asked her; she was ... very angry, said "you're crazy" but didn't answer yes or no'

. In return for Bill's thoughts on Natasha and her possible KGB connections, I told him about Valery. It was obvious to him that Valery was sent by the KGB, just as it was obvious to me that Natasha was. But I was aware that I might be applying double standards. Not only Bill but also Michael Ellman and Caroline thought Valery sounded suspicious. 'This depressed me', I recorded in my diary in October. 'I started making classic excuses for him.'

Although Bill had his doubts about Natasha—another diary entry of mine records him as 'rather worried because his spy had stayed the night, claiming inability to get taxi'—he grew used to her and presumably worried less. By early November, when he held a Revolution Day party in his hotel room, they looked like a couple. I disapproved of Natasha, not only because I thought she was an informer but also because she was proprietorial about Bill, whom I liked. 'She has one of those awful Russian accents in English, seems to patronize even if she doesn't mean to, flings her solid body round with horrid animation ... a very overbearing girl', I wrote in my diary. And with no sense of humour, apparently (Valery was not strong in that respect either). When she asked for English books and Bill lent her Muriel Spark's *The Prime of Miss Jean Brodie*, 'she was very cross and asked if it was a joke'.

Valery vanished from the scene after the first few months, and I didn't expect to see him again. It was a surprise when, three years later, he suddenly showed up close to midnight at my door at MGU (a different door, of course, from the one I'd had in 1966–67), claiming to be a friend of my neighbour (a different one from 1966). He was full of the fact that he had been in Egypt 'and become a man'. The Arab–Israeli conflict was a big thing by this time, with the Soviets more or less secretly involved, so this information was obviously dangled in front of me to encourage me to ask in what circumstances a Soviet civilian would find himself becoming a man there, an obvious spy question. Having lost my earlier illusions about Valery, I didn't bite. He had looked everywhere for me at New Year, he said, not explaining why it had suddenly become so urgent to see me after a three-year hiatus. But that wasn't hard to work out: he had presumably been assigned to investigate my new English boyfriend who had come over to see me at Christmas–New Year—a natural object of interest because he was a well-placed journalist in London who knew Russian—and showed up too late. 'Slipshod work', I commented to the journalist.

As for Natasha, I don't know the end of that story, but she was still around as Bill's girlfriend at the end of the 1966–67 year. It was evident that despite her presumed initial assignment from the KGB, she had developed her own agenda, which was to marry Bill and go to England with him. The KGB warned her off him as a marriage prospect by telling her he had a girlfriend back in England (presumably information obtained by reading his letters home), but she ignored this attempt at discouragement. I don't know if she got Bill in the end or not. My impression was that having its informers developing a personal agenda, at least where foreigners were concerned, was a perennial problem for the KGB. True, it was hard to get permission to leave via marriage, but the potential pay-off, as seen by many young Soviet women, was enormous. Conversely, if you were a Russian who had met and fallen for a foreign student *without* authorisation, the personal entanglement inevitably led to a degree of entanglement with the KGB, or at least unwelcome interest.

That first year, my neighbour (*sosedka*) in the block was Galya, an unsophisticated Russian girl from Uzbekistan, who had no foreign languages and very little concept of life outside the Soviet Union. She talked a lot about her Mama, a midwife in Samarkand who regularly sent her grapes and jam, but not at all about Papa, so I assumed for a long time that he was dead, and was surprised when a passing mention indicated the contrary. Some foreign students became lifelong friends with their neighbours, despite the fact that the neighbours obviously had to report on them: it was a big privilege to have such a nice room all to yourself in MGU, and that had to be paid for. In fact, the reporting obligation was so clear that it had bled into the meaning of the word 'neighbour' in colloquial Russian. I didn't become close friends with Galya, and indeed ended up rather hostile to her for setting me up for a KGB entrapment, as will be explained later. But at first I liked her reasonably well. We even had an early heart-to-heart conversation when she asked me about my Mama and Papa and I said that my Papa was dead and started to cry, which of course created an immediate bond, and kept us talking until 2 a.m. Galya had no visible boyfriend but lots of women friends who flocked to her privileged single room and made a lot of noise—their harsh greeting cries of '*Gal'! Svet! Tan'!*' sounded like a flock of unappealing birds. Still, with her orthodox views and lack of sophistication, I found Galya an interesting object of study: Soviet Student Exhibit A, as it were. 'Healthy-minded', I called her in my first diary entry. I was inclined to attribute her orthodoxy not so much to caution as to lack of imagination and intelligence. 'Life itself dictates', explaining why something was the way it was, was a typical Galya tautology. She told me—and I think she really believed it—that all the books in the Lenin Library's collection were in its public catalogue, a statement that would have been unthinkable from a Valery or Alyosha, as would her assertion that the shortage of all interesting editions in Soviet bookshops was 'due solely to the insatiable love of literature of the broad public'. Admitting that *Novy mir*'s print run was set well below public demand (a fact generally known by the intelligentsia, and also at St Antony's), she ascribed it to 'technical reasons outside our understanding'.

Even among the Svetlanas and Tanyas of her circle, Galya was something of an innocent about the outside world. She once asked me if I were an Australian Aborigine in the presence of some of her raucous friends, who laughed immoderately. Like other Soviet students of this period, Galya had had to work for a couple of years at a factory to earn 'proletarian' credentials to get into university, one of Khrushchev's 'back to our revolutionary roots' projects that was, understandably, intensely unpopular with the intelligentsia. In the course of this work, which she found uncongenial, she had lost the tips of several fingers, which had got caught in the machine. She was very self-conscious about the damaged fingers and habitually kept a handkerchief wrapped around them. At school, she and the other pupils had been called up every year for a couple of weeks to help on the collective farms; in Russia, they usually worked on the potato patches, but in Samarkand it was the cotton fields.

The Leningrad KGB materials included the example of a foreign student with an innocent lad from Yakutia as a neighbour who intentionally sowed ideological doubts and then complimented him for the 'boldness of his thought' and 'capacity to think for himself'. It never crossed my mind to try to develop critical thinking in Galya; I wanted her to stay just the way she was, so that I could take notes. Just as I had learnt to mimic the Oxford style, so I was developing the capacity of talking like Galya—though only when I was talking to her, in a kind of echo effect. In that first conversation about our families, 'I found my family as described to her to be almost a mirror image of hers, just as when she talked about the Soviet literary world I started to think exactly as she spoke and had difficulty working out what discordant point of view I would normally have held'. 'There is something terribly solid about Galya's view of things', I wrote to my mother. Listening to her, I could see how, if you were a Soviet intellectual living among Galyas, intellectual sophistication might start feeling really phoney, a matter of disarranging evident truths out of irresponsibility or malice. 'I can see this even when I know quite well that she is out of her depth or simply misinformed.'

It was from Galya that I first got a sense, as opposed to an academic knowledge, of how terrible World War II had been in the Soviet Union. About two-thirds of her class at school lost their fathers, she said, and that was in comparatively sheltered Uzbekistan. Her father was on the Japanese front and survived, but apparently in a kind of half-life that explained his invisibility in her stories of her family. 'I asked if he was wounded; she said no, but his teeth started to fall out from malnutrition', and there were 'nervous disturbances' and fears. An uncle, too, came back a nervous wreck after fighting all the way to Berlin. No-one returned from the war undamaged, she said matter-of-factly. And then conditions at home when they returned were so bad that it was hard for them to get back on their feet. When I asked Valery about the war, he told a similar story. His father, twice wounded, nevertheless remained in a tank company for the duration, but ended up with partial paralysis of the face, 'a sick man'. The West, Valery editorialised, didn't understand how Russia had suffered during the war. In my diary, I

> suddenly imagined a whole generation of crippled neurotics. No wonder people refer to their mothers instead of fathers as head of the house. Had never thought before how incredibly bad the war was for Russia. *Vechernyaya Moskva* [Moscow's evening paper] is publishing a diary of 1941. Imagine those thin, bitter, legless-armless-parasitical old men who sit hunched up, slightly drunk, in buses, in 1941 going to the front through Moscow suburbs. Probably they're not old—45–55. Younger than my father.

I was a 1941 baby; my mother always said she had been in the maternity hospital giving birth to me when Hitler invaded the Soviet Union. (Later I worked out that, with a 4 June birthday, this was unlikely to be literally true, unless they kept you in hospital for two and a half weeks back then, but in my twenties I took it to be gospel.) My father hadn't been called up because of short sight or, in my mother's version, because they were afraid he would stir up trouble in his unit; the two uncles of mine who served had come through intact; and in my class at school, only one girl had a father killed in the war. The scale of Russian suffering, and the contrast with Australia's comparatively easy ride, left me awed and a little guilty.

My world was broadening a little, and my mood improving. In November, around the time that Valery's visits were tailing off, the KGB sent me someone new: Misha the acrobat. I really liked Misha, though given the circumstances of our first meeting it was hard to convince myself that he was anything other than a plant. One evening there was a knock on the door and an unknown young man appeared, asking to borrow a screwdriver. Screwdrivers were hard to find in Moscow, like all tools, but I had brought one with me from England and probably shown it to Galya. I was surprised by the request and the unexpected visit, but lent the screwdriver to the young man, who said his name was Misha (no surname, of course), even though he was totally unknown to me and didn't live in our Zone—in fact, his presence there as a non-student and non-resident, in a building where only pass-holders were admitted, was never explained. He brought the screwdriver back a bit later that evening, at the same time presenting me with a small volume of reproductions of the artist Petrov-Vodkin (which presumably he just happened to have with him) and inviting me to an exhibition of paintings by Robert Falk, one of the modernists of the 1920s who had worked in obscurity through the Stalin period. Pushing away the obvious conclusion that he had knocked on my door because he knew that an English student lived there, I comforted myself with the fact that because of my non-English accent in Russian, he had taken me for Romanian or Hungarian, or so he said. Misha had only rudimentary English, which could be taken as KGB recognition—assuming they were really paying attention—that my linguistic skills were improving. Although I had already seen the Falk exhibition, I liked the look of Misha and accepted his invitation.

The visit to the Falk exhibition was a great success. Misha further identified himself as aged thirty-one, recently returned from five years in Siberia (not stated in what capacity), now working in radio journalism with construction as his speciality; father an architect. Up to the age of sixteen, he said, he had been trained in a circus school to be an acrobat, which seemed plausible in terms of his short, compact build, if not in his extremely poor sight (minus seven in both eyes, he told me, whereas I, also pretty short-sighted, was only minus three on the Soviet scale). The Siberian experience showed itself in a touch of frontier spirit: he wore an anorak instead of an overcoat, and no hat, gloves or scarf. Misha was a lively, gregarious type, talking to everybody at the exhibition and borrowing their glasses on my behalf (I had recently broken mine), since his were too strong. When we went on to the Artistic Cafe after the exhibition, he socialised with everyone there, too. His acquaintance with Australian culture was quite striking: not only did he know Frank Hardy and Alan Marshall, both of whom had work translated into Russian, but he had even heard Sir Bernard Heinze, a noted figure in Australian music, conduct a concert at Voronezh when he was at the university there. If I hadn't wanted to think otherwise, I would have had to conclude he had been briefed.

Like all Russian intellectuals I had met, Misha looked at paintings not as visual objects but for their message, which often meant their subject matter. Thus, among Falk's paintings, he particularly liked 1950's *View from Studio Window*, featuring a Revolution Day parade in the square below where the Red flags suggested bloodstains on a drab grey background. By the end of the afternoon, Misha was using the familiar form of address to me, the first Russian to do so, though I stuck gamely to the polite form. It felt to me that he was 'more interested in me as a girl than as foreigner. But he is quite presentable. So why pick me up?' I asked the diary. Why indeed? He became nervous and excited towards the end of the outing, seemingly torn by some kind of conflict, and saying 'I don't know, I don't know' rather comically in English.

Misha soon disappeared from my life; a week after we met, he went off on a business trip to the Ukraine to write a piece on a new industrial town and didn't show up again, with the exception of one brief unexpected appearance at my door at 11.30 p.m. a month or so later, leaving me feeling rather bereft. 'I knew he was too good to be true', I wrote in my diary. I made up a romantic story to explain his disappearance, based on 'I don't know, I don't know', in which Misha, though sent by the KGB, found he really liked me and so felt it dishonourable to continue the acquaintance. This was more of a fantasy than something I really believed, although years later I was interested to read Andrey Sinyavsky's account of how, when instructed by the KGB to make friends with a foreign student he liked, he tried to communicate his dilemma to her in similarly enigmatic phrases.

By this time, I had acquired some Russian acquaintances without the KGB's help. I looked up Alyosha's mother, Zoya Vladimirovna, a motherly woman who invited me over several times for tea and cakes, her husband, Mikhail Mikhalyov, the *Oktyabr'* editor, being always absent or offstage in the study, typing. Having been told that guests should take flowers to the hostess, and finding that, unlike most purchases, this was comparatively easy as they were sold at the entrance to Metro stations, I always arrived with my sheaf of blooms until the day Zoya Vladimirovna said, 'My cavalier!', which made me feel I was doing something wrong and I stopped going. Anyway, it was a long trip—a Metro ride plus two buses.

I'd taken on a job by this time, working two hours a week at the Institute of Foreign Languages. The pay was minimal, a rouble an hour, but I enjoyed the work, which consisted mainly of recording texts and advising staff members on current colloquial usage. I made friends there, particularly with the Professor of English, Elena Borisovna Cherkasskaya. She seemed old to me, although she couldn't really have been, with a sixteen-year-old son, Borya, a maths Wunderkind, as well as a Yiddish-speaking mother, both of whom I met in my visits to her home. 'Very pleasant and homely', I wrote in the diary after my first meeting with Elena Borisovna, with 'rather wild orange/white hair'. In fact, as I discovered, the hair colour fluctuated wildly: just before every public holiday, Elena (whom I always called by name and patronymic, out of deference to the age difference) had it dyed orange, and then in the following months it gradually faded to white, until the next holiday came around. Elena's English was fairly fluent but non-idiomatic. I became Shaylochka to her outside the institute, but at work she sometimes called me 'Mrs Sheila', which her juniors in the English Department, a married couple called Victor Aronovich and Viktoria Leonidovna, knew wasn't right. They called me Sheila, 'he with great archness', as I recorded in my diary, because the lack of patronymic seemed so intimate. Victor Aronovich spoke an elaborate formal English which made him sound almost Indian. After one contretemps, a scheduling mistake, I think, he explained to his wife on the telephone in my hearing that 'the charming Mrs Bruce had graciously disregarded the awfully awkward incident'.

After the New Year, the centre of my Moscow life shifted elsewhere, and I stopped working at the institute. But I still dropped in from time to time to see Elena Borisovna, and reported sad developments to my mother in May:

> My friend Elena Borisovna has been defeated by the plots against her in the Institute and not re-elected to the chair. Her English had gone off considerably, with everybody attacking it, and she kept using odd formal phrases not quite appropriately. But she was very pleased to see me, and embarrassed me considerably by telling me the whole story for forty-five minutes in the common room in a conspiratorial whisper. Her explanations are all mixed up, and it is obviously a terrible blow; in fact she is in that awful state of persecution where everything she says about it sounds slightly mad. She wants me to go and tell the Dean how good her English is, but I can't do that, and it wouldn't help anyway. Fortunately she didn't make a direct request, but said the Dean was offended by my not visiting him …

I asked my mother to send photos of herself and my brother so that I could give them to Elena. 'It is so hard to make affectionate gestures, which she obviously needs. They told her among other things that all her staff disliked her. It isn't even true.'

During this time of distress Elena told me a remarkable story. We were walking along one of the institute's many corridors—it was an eighteenth-century building, three storeys high and built around a courtyard—and she suddenly said, 'It was here that he jumped out.' 'Who did?' I asked in confusion. 'The spy', she said. It was on 16 October 1941, the day of the great panic about evacuation in Moscow, with the Germans already in the northern Moscow suburb of Khimki and looking set to capture the capital. Elena's husband was away at the war; a young son (not Borya, but an older son, who died) and her mother constituted her household in Moscow. All day she had been phoning back and forth to her mother, trying to get her to agree to come to the institute with her things to be evacuated with Elena; a truck was coming in the late afternoon to take staff members, families and luggage to the train for transit east to an unknown destination. Her mother remained adamant that she would stay in Moscow, throwing Elena into a state of terrible indecision. The spy who jumped out so unexpectedly was a German, quite an ordinary nice-looking young man, fair haired, good Russian, who asked her to remain and work with the Germans when they took over and told her that she would be well treated. Elena was appalled, at a loss for words. They turned a corner in the corridor and, when she looked around, he was gone as mysteriously as he had come. Elena, terror-stricken at this brush with a spy who had asked her to collaborate, and not even received a straightforward refusal, decided on the spur of the moment that the only safe thing was to leave Moscow, and in fact got on the truck and then took the train to Siberia that same evening. She didn't see her mother again for the duration of the war.

Friends from an older generation were easier for me at this point: I was much happier chatting to Elena Borisovna or playing piano duets with Caroline's supervisor, the gentle ethnographer Professor Tokarev, than with my own contemporaries. But, as I see from the diary, I was beginning to make some contact with people of my own age. In November, when I'd gone to the House of Composers to check their concerts for the coming month, I got talking to some girls outside, Lena and Nina, and they urged me to come in to hear the evening's program, unexcitingly advertised as a discussion of amateur music-making (*samodeyatel'nost'*). It turned out to be part bard concert, part lively debate on various forms of popular music, conducted in the spirit of the Thaw ('We need to be more open!'). The bards were guitar poets who sang their own poetry, usually on topical or wryly romantic themes; they were enormously popular with young people and tolerated, rather than encouraged, by the authorities. This audience was young, keen and well informed, with Bulat Okudzhava among their favourites, and contemporary French chansonniers within their frame of reference. (The notes on the discussion in my diary are so detailed that one has to conclude that my Russian comprehension had taken an upward leap.)

The evening lasted from 6.30 p.m. to 11.45 p.m., and I sat in rapt attention the whole time, being particularly taken with some delightful settings of Samuil Marshak's translations of AA Milne, much funnier than the English originals. I even enjoyed an intervention from the floor by a crazy young man who wouldn't stop singing his own composition, warbling the same passionate phrase—'golden autumn (*zolotaya osen'*)'—over and over again. The one performance I strongly disliked was a song called *Baby Yar'* (on the Yevtushenko text? In any case, about the Nazi killing of Jews in the occupied Ukraine during the war), rendered with 'bared teeth', as I noted in the diary, and a kind of growling delivery. In retrospect, this sounds like a knock-off of the style popularised by Vladimir Vysotsky of the Taganka Theatre in the 1970s, in which angry songs about Gulag were a staple. But I hadn't yet heard of Vysotsky, who didn't seem to be part of the world of my new friends, though they later took me to the Taganka Theatre to see Brecht's *Good Woman of Szechuan*. Lena invited me to dinner at home, too, and I met and liked her family, but then we dropped out of contact. It was probably my fault: I liked Lena, just as I had liked Alyosha, but she was the kind of person you would expect me to make friends with, and I was looking for something different.

Tomiko qualified as different because she was Japanese, a junior member of the faculty at Waseda, the women's university in Tokyo, whose field was Soviet literature. A person of gentle manners and steely determination, she dressed almost entirely in shades of grey, perhaps because she felt that her decision to become a scholar excluded the possibility of marriage. We met on an overnight British Council excursion in the autumn in which the small Japanese group was included; Tomiko was the only woman in her group, as well as the only young person, and when we had to pair off to share rooms, I invited her to join me. No doubt this was partly preparation for my future life as wife of a Japanologist, but I also had a fellow feeling for her as another outsider. For the rest of my year in Moscow, she was the foreigner with whom I spent most time.

As Russian was our only common language, we would chatter away in our variously accented versions on the bus, earning curious looks from other passengers. Despite decades of instruction in multiculturalism (called 'friendship of nations'), Russians were not so keen on 'orientals', even their own from the non-Slavic republics; and they normally took Tomiko for Chinese, against whom prejudice was encouraged because of the Sino–Soviet rift. At the same time, we encountered at least one example of a notable *absence* of racial discrimination. One day when I showed up at the Lenin Library without Tomiko, the cloakroom attendant for the First Hall asked where my friend was—'you are so much alike, I can't tell you apart'. Indeed, we were much of a height and age, and both had short dark hair cut in a thick fringe, so if you discounted skin colour and features (Russians usually took me for Jewish because of my big nose), it was a reasonable comment and gave us a lot of pleasure.

Another thing we had in common was our topics. Tomiko was a specialist on the writer Maxim Gorky, I on Lunacharsky. It didn't exactly give us a shared world view, since Tomiko was much more respectful of her man than I was of mine, but there was enough overlap that we knew quite a lot about the other's field of study and shared a supervisor, Alexander Ovcharenko of MGU's School of Philology. Gorky studies and Lunacharsky studies were such basic subfields of Soviet literature that they had their own names: *gor'kovedenie* and *lunacharskovedenie*. From an orthodox Soviet standpoint, the two belonged together as famous cultural arbiters and patrons of the 1920s and 1930s. This translated at St Antony's into the view that they were pretty much of a piece as deluded intellectuals who had sold out and ended up manipulated by the political bosses. Both were admired in the Japanese circles Tomiko moved in as exemplars of socialist culture. Among the younger Soviet generation, Lunacharsky was being reconfigured as a species of liberal, whereas Gorky remained trapped in a quasi-Stalinist persona, force-fed to schoolchildren and consequently boring. Our joint supervisor, Ovcharenko, was primarily a Gorky specialist, though Lunacharsky had recently become a second string to his bow. It was to be assumed, therefore, that he was not in the progressive camp as far as Lunacharsky studies were concerned.

I first met Ovcharenko a few weeks after my arrival when, a draft of my Scholarly Plan in hand, I met him by appointment at 7.30 p.m. on one of the two days a week he held office hours in the downtown PhilFac—they were called 'showing-up (*yavochnye*) days', meaning that professors were rarely to be found at work on any other day. The Plan was the first hurdle for foreign exchange students. You had to give your project a title (Lilia Pavlovna and I had settled on the umbrella formulation of 'AV Lunacharsky: Life and Works') and list all the library and archival materials you would need to consult, as well as any necessary research trips outside Moscow. Both title and Plan needed to be approved by your supervisor before acquiring formal validity; after that happened, they were set in stone for the duration of your stay. I had put in all the archives I could think of—State, Party and Literary—although I was not at all sure that my unknown supervisor would let me keep them in the Plan, particularly as he didn't have the reputation of a liberal. Still, it seemed worth trying.

Ovcharenko turned out to be in his mid forties, good-looking, very thin (there were rumours of tuberculosis), with black-framed glasses and a rather un-Soviet touch of elegance of dress and carriage. Contrary to expectations, our first meeting was a great success. It was the rapprochement with Valery on the Abramtsevo trip all over again: *He likes me! He thinks I am intelligent!* He was remarkably helpful about my Plan, accepting my entire archives list as well as adding a couple of extra provincial archives, and telling me I should write in research trips to consult them. 'Then next year', he said, 'off you go to New York and Stanford'. I couldn't believe my luck in getting this cosmopolitan response, and, according to my diary, was 'grinning like a fool all the time, even flirting with him (and, of course, vice versa), as if I had turned into some other person ... Looked in mirror on way out—pink cheeks, black circles under eyes, face rather round and Russian and appealing; a second-class Natasha ...' (this was a *War and Peace* reference). In other words, it wasn't just Valery all over again, but *better* than Valery, given that I thought Ovcharenko thought I was attractive.

The positive impression continued at the next meeting, despite the 'incredible confusion and, one would think, strain on nerves' from meeting students in a room where three other professors were doing the same thing. Ovcharenko wrote out my Plan for me, presumably correcting the mistakes in Russian along the way, though he was kind enough not to point them out. He used the form for Soviet graduate students, since there was none available for foreigners, and earned my admiration by instantly recognising my name on his list, even though it appeared as Fits Patrick Sheilin. With the urgent business of the Plan to deal with, there wasn't much time for me to say what I was after with my dissertation, but, as I noted in the diary, 'he started off very well informed'. This was probably meant as a back-handed tribute to KGB briefings of Soviet supervisors, as well as an indirect dig at Hayward, for not knowing much about Lunacharsky. The Plan was submitted expeditiously, thanks to Ovcharenko's businesslike approach. The next stage was approval by the PhilFac, which was more or less automatic, and the granting of permission to work by the various archives on my Plan, which wasn't automatic at all—any one of them might reject my application, even if my supervisor and the PhilFac had signed off on it.

Ovcharenko gave my project a new title, 'Lunacharsky as People's Commissar', and added dates, 1917–29. An uncharitable explanation of this contraction of scope would be that he wanted to push me away from the controversial territory of Lunacharsky's engagement in philosophical argument and cultural politics towards safer ground. Whatever his motives, I think in fact that I owe him a debt of gratitude. Without those dates, which were relatively broad in a Soviet context, no archive would have given me anything. With 'People's Commissar' in my title, the State Archives were much more likely to accept me (although I'm not sure that I understood this at the time) because, being the repository of the archives of People's Commissariats, they could scarcely claim not to have materials on my topic.

The People's Commissariat of Enlightenment (Narkompros) had jurisdiction over education and the arts, which meant that, with my new formulation of project, educational policy suddenly became as relevant to me as cultural policy. I didn't know much about education, and Ovcharenko didn't either—the Lunacharsky *Works* he had edited were culture-focused, just as my research in Oxford had been—but nevertheless he was firm about the need for me to educate myself in the field in preparation for work in the State Archives. When he set me a reading list, mainly on education, I protested that culture was my main interest, but he ignored my protests—'quite rightly, as I found reading the books later', as I recorded in the diary. I was starting to see how, using the Narkompros education materials as a base, I might be able to get a wholly new angle on the workings of Soviet government and politics.

From the reports of our early conversations in my diary, it really seems as if Ovcharenko was excited by the topic he had given me: that he thought an institutional study of Narkompros, Lunacharsky's Commissariat, would be new and interesting, and possibly also that only a foreigner could do it, given the constraints on Soviet historical publication. This may be extrapolating too far—the man was an anti-liberal, after all—but it is at least a possible interpretation of his repeated statement that, with this topic, I would be going into territory unfamiliar even to Soviet scholars. 'He kept telling me that my work on Lunacharsky was covering new ground, both from the Soviet and the Western point of view', is one diary entry (I noted on this occasion that he was in 'great good humour' and that Tomiko said he 'smelt of wine'). On another occasion, his answer when I asked him to recommend a good Soviet study of some particular topic was that unfortunately no such work existed; I would just have to write it myself. That wasn't the kind of thing Soviet supervisors normally said to their foreign students, judging by the student grapevine. The norm was to emphasise the wealth of Soviet scholarship to be mastered, with special reference to the relevant wisdom of Marx and Lenin, before the foreigner could dare to think of making a contribution of her own. I can't remember Ovcharenko ever mentioning Marx to me, and Lenin figured in our conversations only as a historical actor, not as a source of ideological authority.

Re-reading my diary, I'm tempted to think that Ovcharenko was entertaining himself by a bit of brinkmanship in our early conversations, flirting not only with me but with the kind of discussion of political history that simply wasn't acceptable in Soviet publications, though it was standard fare in the West. On one occasion, according to my diary, he took me out of the crowded common room where all the professors were meeting their students into an empty lecture room (empty, that is to say, except for three or four women sitting around and one woman typing), where conversation was much easier. He had already told me that Lunacharsky was not doing the real work in Narkompros, so I asked him who *was* doing the work. This was bold because several of Lunacharsky's deputies, who were the probable workhorses, had fallen into political disgrace, seriously enough in at least one case to have become unmentionable in print. Ovcharenko rose to this challenge without batting an eyelid, making an impromptu speech on the power structure in the institution and its internal politics, topics that were essentially taboo in Soviet public discussion. Then, even more daringly, he introduced the forbidden name of Nikolay Bukharin, a still unrehabilitated rival of Stalin's who had been killed in the Great Purges of the 1930s as a spy and traitor. This would have been really difficult to explain away if someone had decided to report him on it, since Bukharin's connection with Narkompros (the topic on which Ovcharenko was supposed to be supervising me) was very tenuous; clearly, Ovcharenko had strayed into the realm of high Party politics, which he had no business discussing with a foreigner. He pronounced Bukharin's name 'not at all furtively, indeed quite loudly', I noted in my diary—adding that 'it may have been at that point that all the women [in the room] stopped pretending to work and just sat and listened'.

I was surprised by Ovcharenko's frankness, particularly when I went off and read some of his scholarly work. For one of his research monographs, he had chosen the ultra-orthodox and apparently totally boring topic of *Gorky as Publicist*. In a letter to my mother, I described its style as 'sound, cautious and flat', completely lacking the liveliness, intelligence and sometimes malicious wit of his conversation: 'I think he must have spent his youth acquiring the art of writing in a way that looks stupid but isn't'. It still seemed to me that any Soviet scholar who was intelligent was bound to be liberal, so Ovcharenko was a puzzle. The most I could say for *Gorky as Publicist* was that the archival research was thorough, which made it 'admirable in an odd way'.

There were charismatic lecturers in the PhilFac who worked on great but controversial literary figures like Pasternak and Mandelstam and were worshipped by their students. Obviously the author of *Gorky as Publicist* was not one of them, although in his own (unfashionable) subfield of socialist realism he was certainly the best thing going. Ovcharenko's boss, Aleksey Ivanovich Metchenko, was a union-boss physical type of about sixty whom I instinctively cast as a thug, and I noticed that when Metchenko was around, Ovcharenko became very official and unhelpful in manner. Professor Petrov taught a very dull seminar on socialist realism that I found good for my Russian when, at Ovcharenko's suggestion, I attended it. I described him in a letter to my mother as 'a charming old baby, petted by all the faculty secretaries (who do little else). He has small feet and wears black shoes, very clean and smart, with rather pointed toes, and a very neat black suit'. These small feet obviously caught my attention, as in another letter, reporting the latest meeting with Ovcharenko, I said that 'little Professor Petrov' was in the room the whole time, 'swinging his feet and listening' because he had nothing else to do.

I fell into the habit of turning up for appointments with Tomiko (I used to call and make the appointments for both of us, a result of Tomiko's gentle insistence that Russians could understand me better), and this seemed to amuse Ovcharenko who, as I told my mother, 'regards us as a rather exotic phenomenon'. Tomiko, along with assorted professors, supplicants and secretaries, was usually an auditor of my conversations with Ovcharenko after the first meetings, and I appreciated her presence. Demure and diffident herself, being constrained by Japanese conventions about female behaviour in public, she marvelled—though with a hint of teasing—at my boldness and determination in dealing with the Soviet world. It was a great help to me to have to live up to Tomiko's professed belief that I knew neither fear nor embarrassment.

By mid November, my Plan had been officially accepted by the PhilFac, and Lilia Pavlovna was sending in my applications to all the archives listed in it. More confiding outside the office, Lilia Pavlovna had told me in a chance meeting on the bus that my Plan was so unusual that 'she would not have liked to accept it if not written personally by Ovcharenko'. By this time, I was so well disposed to Ovcharenko that I was wondering if I couldn't have him as official supervisor for my D.Phil. in Oxford, as one of my friends on the British exchange had apparently managed to organise something similar in Cambridge. 'I'd like to be independent of St Antony's and Hayward if possible', I told my mother, noting that Ovcharenko understood my questions in bad Russian much better than Hayward understood me when I spoke English. It's true that Ovcharenko, like Hayward, was a literary scholar, not a historian, but he had much more of a feel for archives and sources. When I told him about a particularly useful set of bureaucratic documents I had found in the Lenin Library, 'his eyes lit up: he is certainly a historian by temperament, even if a literature man by profession'.

Another side of Ovcharenko emerged unexpectedly in November: the rising Party man, or perhaps *Ovcharenko as Publicist*. Ovcharenko disappeared for a couple of weeks from his usual office hours, and it turned out that he had been sent to China as a member of a Friendship Delegation. Since the Sino–Soviet split at the end of the 1950s, however, friendship between the two nations had been in short supply; moreover, the Chinese Cultural Revolution, with its xenophobic and anti-Soviet aspect and Red Guards partially out of control, was in full swing. Not surprisingly (indeed, this may have been the whole point of the visit), the Soviet delegation was 'insulted' by Chinese 'hooligans' and returned early in a much-publicised huff on 20 November. Along with the rest of the Soviet public, I read all about this in *Pravda*, which said that the decision to return had been made suddenly on 18 November. To my great satisfaction, I knew this to be wrong: I had rung Ovcharenko's home on 15 or 16 November to find out what had happened to him, and his wife had told me then that he was in China and would be back on the 20th. So the huff was at least partly stage-managed.

Regardless of any element of state theatricals, it was a traumatic experience for Ovcharenko. He had fallen ill in China, and when I saw him at his regular seminar ten days after his return, he was still looking very tired and a bit battered, the thinness more pronounced. Instead of giving a seminar, he talked about China, which was the topic on everyone's mind. As I recorded in my diary, he seemed angry and impatient at what was going on. This so-called Cultural Revolution was anti-cultural hooliganism, in his view (and *Pravda*'s, but he didn't sound like someone parroting the official line), not deserving of the name of revolution. It was hard to find out who was giving the orders, but the people the Soviet delegation had met at the Cultural Revolution headquarters in Peking were mainly postgraduate students and undergraduate seniors from one of the Peking universities. He was insulted by placards reading 'USSR—Enemy No. 1' and overwhelmed by the crowds, which closed in on the Soviet cars, threatening to overturn them, and the noise: gongs and drums were beaten and slogans chanted outside their hotel in Peking all night. The Chinese who were supposed to be hosting the Soviet delegation wouldn't conduct normal conversations but banged on the table and shouted abuse.

The odd thing was that Ovcharenko and I had been talking about cultural revolution a few weeks before he left for China. It wasn't the Chinese Cultural Revolution that was the subject of the conversation but a short-lived Soviet Cultural Revolution (the same Russian term was used) of the early Stalin period, long forgotten in the Soviet Union and unnoticed in Western scholarship. I found out about it in the course of my research on Lunacharsky, who ran into a lot of trouble in the late 1920s from young Communist militants, briefly enjoying support from the Stalinist leadership, who went on the rampage against 'liberal' administrators like Lunacharsky and the 'bourgeois' intelligentsia he protected. Since this episode was unknown in the West, I was naturally intrigued, and asked Ovcharenko about it, carefully avoiding any suggestion of a parallel between the Soviet and Chinese manifestations, given the passion with which Soviet media had been denouncing the Chinese Red Guards ever since I arrived in the Soviet Union. For all my caution, the parallel was on the face of it pretty obvious, and Ovcharenko didn't deny that; he just said, I thought for form's sake, that the phenomena were different. At the same time, he was clearly intrigued and a bit excited by the issue; and, as I recorded in my diary, the parallel somehow 'hovered in the air' throughout the conversation. This seemed to be not only because it was on my mind but because of Ovcharenko's 'own, it seems almost whimsical, thoughts'. I suppose what I meant by that was that he seemed to be flirting with the idea of a parallel, as he did when a conversation was becoming politically risqué. I don't know if that discussion stayed in Ovcharenko's mind when he encountered the real-life Chinese Cultural Revolution a few weeks later. For me, it was the beginning of a train of thought that in New York in the 1970s led me to produce the first Western study, *Cultural Revolution in Russia, 1928–31*.

I had one more important piece of business with Ovcharenko. Ever since writing my article for *Soviet Studies*, I had wanted to make contact with IA Sats, the Lunacharsky scholar whose work I particularly liked. My friends Zoya Vladimirovna and Elena Borisovna had both confirmed that this was the same Igor Alexandrovich Sats who was Lunacharsky's brother-in-law and former assistant and now worked at *Novy mir*. They also confirmed that the IA Lunacharskaya who sometimes published on Lunacharsky was indeed his daughter, Irina Anatolevna, but neither of them knew her or Sats personally or had any way of finding out their telephone numbers. So I asked Ovcharenko if he would contact them and introduce me. He said Sats lived outside Moscow and was not on the telephone (not true, as I would soon find out) but agreed to ring Irina Lunacharskaya and ask if she would see me. I noted in the diary that at this meeting I 'didn't like [Ovcharenko] as much as usual, but couldn't decide why. He seemed to leer a bit …' This slightly unfavourable impression persisted at the next meeting, when I asked him a lot of questions about the Lunacharsky family, and he answered 'slyly', according to my diary. Still, he had called Irina Lunacharskaya, as promised, and she was willing to see me; he gave me her telephone number to call and make an appointment. I didn't yet know it, but this was the end of good relations with my Moscow supervisor and the prelude to a whole new chapter in my life.

4

Irina and Igor

I owe Irina to Ovcharenko, and indirectly Igor too. That doesn't mean they liked each other. As soon as I mentioned Irina and Igor to Ovcharenko, the atmosphere changed and conversation became awkward. It sounded as if he didn't like Sats at all—that, if I remember rightly, was how he referred to him, not the usual polite form of first name and patronymic (Igor Alexandrovich). His references to Irina Anatolevna were more polite, and at least he was evidently on speaking terms with her, as he had her home telephone number. All the same, it seemed gratuitous on his part to mention that, for all her devotion to her father's memory and proprietorial airs about him, she was not Lunacharsky's natural daughter but an adopted one. Her natural father, Lev Rosenel, had been killed during the Civil War in unknown circumstances, Ovcharenko said; I took that to imply that Rosenel might have been on the White side, or at any rate not an active supporter of the Reds.

I gathered that Ovcharenko's closest contacts were not with Lunacharsky's second family, now headed by Irina, but his first. A few years after the Revolution, Lunacharsky had left his Old Bolshevik wife, Anna Alexandrovna, sister of the Marxist philosopher Alexander Bogdanov, and their son, Anatoly, for the woman who was to become his second wife, Natalia Alexandrovna Rosenel-Sats, Irina's mother and Igor's sister. Many of the Old Bolsheviks were survived by more than one family, and there was often bad blood between them. All the same, the Lunacharsky case was egregious, with much criticism of the break-up in Old Bolshevik circles at the time, and an endless stream of malicious gossip about the new wife, an attractive young actress with a taste for fashion and luxury and no visible interest in politics. When Lunacharsky died in 1933, the two families inserted competing death notices in the newspapers, one in *Pravda*, the other in *Izvestiia*.

Irina Anatolevna and Igor Alexandrovich fully reciprocated Ovcharenko's dislike, as I quickly discovered. Even on my first meeting with Irina early in January, she was pretty bitchy about him, making it clear that she didn't think he should have been put in charge of the Lunacharsky *Works*: he was an interloper, didn't care about Lunacharsky, and was really a Gorky specialist, not a *lunacharskoved* at all. Used to thinking of Gorky and Lunacharsky as birds of a feather, I was surprised by the sharpness of her references to Gorky. Ovcharenko was about to edit a new collection of Gorky's works, about which Irina commented 'God knows who needs it. But I suppose it's easy work'. During that first meeting, she rang up one of the Lunacharsky scholars she approved of and told him 'I have here a very nice, very good girl from Oxford who has fallen into Ovcharenko's hands', the last said with a wealth of meaning. When I met Igor Sats a week or so later, he made his feelings about Ovcharenko even clearer, being 'very scathing about my poor supervisor, for whom I still have friendly feelings', as I wrote to my mother. According to him, Ovcharenko, a Ukrainian born in Kazakhstan, had first made his reputation as a young literary scholar in Moscow in the 'anti-cosmopolitan campaign' of the early 1950s, 'unmasking' Jewish literary critics who were writing under Russian noms-de-plume. In Igor's eyes, he was an anti-Semite and probably a Stalinist.

My friendly feelings for Ovcharenko didn't survive a conversation with him in early February which, unfortunately, I considered too politically sensitive to write about at any length either in my diary or in my letters to my mother. Untypically, this was a conversation without witnesses (Ovcharenko must have located an empty office), and I found it extremely spooky. He said Igor Sats was a sinister man who had very likely murdered Lunacharsky, as he was the only person with him in his last illness in the south of France. (I later heard this story from Russian *émigrés* in Los Angeles, who emphasised, as did Ovcharenko, Igor's Jewishness.) Confirmation of the story, according to Ovcharenko, was to be found in the diary of Lunacharsky's son, Anatoly, who had gone out to Lunacharsky's deathbed. The diary remained in the hands of the first family after the son died in the war, and Ovcharenko had access to it. He was prepared to give me access too, but under certain conditions. Lunacharsky (the father) had also kept a diary in his later years, and it remained in possession of the second family. Unfortunately, Irina kept a tight hold on it and wouldn't let Ovcharenko or other good Lunacharsky scholars read it. If I understood him correctly, Ovcharenko was offering me a deal: you persuade Irina Anatolevna to let you see Lunacharsky's diary, and I'll get you the diary of the son with the sensational stuff about the murder.

This conversation shocked me, partly because I was a stiff-necked honourable young person and partly because I saw myself being dragged into deep waters. I thought of it as a bit of private enterprise on Ovcharenko's part, but in retrospect it looks rather like the dirty tricks the KGB used to get up to, giving foreigners sensational materials on Soviet 'liberals' that would discredit them (and, in Igor's case, the journal he worked for, *Novy mir*) abroad. Of course, it might have made more sense to give me the sensational materials directly, but perhaps that's where Ovcharenko's private enterprise came in—or perhaps they were afraid I would just take the materials to Irina and Igor and spoil the plot.

In any case, that was more or less the last of Ovcharenko as someone I liked and trusted. And I suppose vice versa, as I was probably not so poker-faced during this conversation as I intended to be. I said it was all very interesting and surprising (by which I meant totally implausible—not for a second did I think the murder allegation might be true) and that it would be very nice if Irina Anatolevna showed me the diaries. Nothing about passing them on. I meant it as a polite deflection of Ovcharenko's proposal, though I was too cautious (or frightened?) to give an outright refusal. Ovcharenko surely understood this, and also understood that I had gone over to the enemy; that is, the camp of Irina and Igor. He treated me accordingly thereafter. Granted, this was an extreme situation, because of the degree of hostility between Ovcharenko and the second Lunacharsky family, but it was also a general condition of Soviet life, or at least Soviet intelligentsia life: if you were in one 'circle', you couldn't be in another. I had almost involuntarily stepped from Ovcharenko's orbit into Irina and Igor's. It was one of the lucky breaks of my life.

Irina was my friend for thirty-five years, until her death in a car accident in the early 1990s. It seemed tragic that she should have died just then, and yet I wonder how she would have made the transition: her survival skills were outstanding but extremely Soviet. Irina was a science journalist by profession, quite successful, but her real mission in life was to tend the flame of Lunacharsky's memory, somewhat tarnished by his loss of reputation in the Stalin years. That meant keeping a tight rein on Lunacharsky scholars to make sure they portrayed her man appropriately as both impeccably orthodox (disagreements with Lenin had to be forgotten) and tolerant. A great and eclectic patron of the arts, he should be shown to have supported writers in good repute with the contemporary intelligentsia but not those now seen as Stalinists. 'Loyal' (*loyalen*), meaning hewing to her line, was a big word with Irina: Ovcharenko was not loyal, but I should be. She was a kind of entrepreneur of Lunacharsky studies who was at the same time its censor: I only wiggled out of her clutches and saved our friendship by dropping any idea of writing a Lunacharsky biography, which in my hands would certainly not have lived up to her standards of hagiography. Irina was a fluent, persuasive conversationalist and a virtuoso of the telephone, with a well-honed instinct for the limits of the possible in any given situation. You could never win an argument with Irina; she simply veered off in another direction. I once watched her run out of space when writing a letter and, without a second's pause, make a left turn and continue up the side of the page. That was Irina, and I couldn't help but admire her self-confidence and immunity from self-criticism.

Irina was beautiful, elegant, worldly and an irresistible force. She lived in one of the most desirable buildings in Moscow (8 Gorky Street, apartment 53), where she was a neighbour of her friend Alexey Adzhubei, former editor of *Izvestiia*, who was married to Khrushchev's daughter Rada, a science journalist like Irina. Irina's apartment was palatial by Soviet standards: eight rooms for a family of four—Irina and her husband and two sons, or six if you counted the old family servant and the *babushka*, her mother-in-law, whom Irina treated much as she did the servants, that is, as a family member of a lesser sort. The apartment, exuding an atmosphere of aristocracy, contained a lot of fine eighteenth-century furniture and china, presumably goods confiscated from the rich in the name of the Revolution and acquired by Lunacharsky in the first Soviet years. Particularly impressive was the remarkable hexagonal study off the front hall, with shelves full of objets d'art, where Irina would interview people visiting for the first time (later, you moved to the impressive dining room, and finally to the small and quite ordinary kitchen). It was startling in a Soviet, or indeed any other, context; I had never been in a place like it. For that matter, Irina was the first person I knew with a live-in servant, though this was not uncommon among elite families in Moscow: generally, as in Irina's case, the servant had been brought as a young girl from the village in the 1930s and stayed on as a quasi–family member.

The younger son, Andrey, was a precocious and consciously charming eleven-year-old when I first met them, physically resembling Irina and much indulged. The older son, Sergey, more like his father, was in his twenties, completing his scientific studies and planning to marry. This led to a lot of criticism from Irina, who probably thought the fiancée was not his social or intellectual equal (not real intelligentsia is how she would have expressed this thought). Sergey's marriage meant that Irina would have to buy him a cooperative apartment in the suburbs, an innovation of the Khrushchev years that was a striking departure from the norm of renting from the state with more or less guaranteed tenure. Irina's apartment (rented, as all but the new co-op apartments were) was in the very centre of the city, and she couldn't see why anyone would want to live anywhere else.

In later years, Irina added a dog to the household, Nessie (named for the Loch Ness monster), to which she was passionately attached; when Nessie was knocked down on Gorky Street, Irina told me that she lay down in the gutter with her arms around her as she died. Of course, there was often a dose of dramatic exaggeration in Irina's stories. Her husband, Rafail Naumovich Sterlin, was a gruff chemist in the military with the rank of colonel, notably lacking Irina's charm and aristocratic bearing. I was frightened of him because of his brusqueness, and thought he disliked my presence in their home, though Irina took not the slightest notice of any absence of welcome in his manner. He used to disconcert me by firing unanswerable questions like how much a set of spanners cost in England (I had no idea) or what I thought of the great socialist-realist writer Boris Lavrenev (I hadn't read and had barely heard of him). Rafail Naumovich was Jewish, as was Irina (from her mother and natural father, though not from Lunacharsky), but this didn't seem to be an issue—except perhaps to people like Ovcharenko—and was not discussed. They were an odd couple. As it was later explained to me, back in 1937 captivating young Irina, a spoiled child of privilege whose high-placed family friends had suddenly been declared 'enemies of the people' in the Great Purges, found herself shunned by all her fellow university students except for one humble admirer, Rafail Naumovich, whom she married. Although I appreciated this story, I privately thought that, even after being kissed by the princess, the frog had remained a frog.

On that first meeting, Irina turned on her best steamroller act, completely overwhelming me, talking non-stop (sometimes simultaneously to me and someone on the telephone), peppering me with questions but scarcely giving me time to reply. *Why had I chosen this thesis topic? Was it chosen for me? Who was my English supervisor? Write his name in Russian ... How old was I, was I married, when would I get my doctorate?* She told me right off that as Lunacharsky was little known in England, we needed to publicise him—evidently I was already enrolled in her enterprise. I had just received a letter from the British publisher Frederic Warburg, of Secker & Warburg, asking me if I were interested in writing a Lunacharsky biography, and told Irina about it. She said, 'Wonderful!', though she might not have thought so if she knew about Warburg's Congress for Cultural Freedom connections (I probably didn't know about them at the time myself). But even at this early stage of our acquaintance, I probably got the message that a biography would be wonderful as long as I wrote it under her close supervision.

I came to Irina's in the early afternoon and had an appointment with Ovcharenko at 5.30 p.m., which seemed reasonable as the PhilFac was only a couple of blocks away.

But Irina hadn't finished with me. When the time came, she absolutely wouldn't let me go, teasing me so relentlessly with her questions (*Why do you have to go? Do you have an appointment? With whom?*) that it seemed she must have divined that I was meeting the enemy, even though I had only just been informed that that was what he was. I didn't admit to having an appointment, since I didn't want either to lie or to say it was with Ovcharenko, and Irina totally defeated my intention to leave, so I missed the appointment. At 6.30 p.m. I tried to leave again, this time telling her that I had a ticket to a concert at the Conservatorium at 7 p.m., which was true. Irina insisted—insistence was typical of her—that I had to eat supper before I left, and took me off into the kitchen to prepare it (that meant heating up some soup and giving me some bread and sausage; cooking was not one of Irina's skills). I choked it down, Irina all the while urging me to eat more, and managed to leave at about ten to seven. The atmosphere, I noted in my diary, was 'very friendly by this time'. At the door, Irina 'disapproved of my coat and my way of putting on hat and scarf, straightened them, kissed me goodbye and told me to ring in a week', and I staggered out shell-shocked into the night.

From this time on, regular ringing of Irina became part of my life, and quite a tormenting part, too, as I hated the telephone at the best of times, and hated it particularly in Moscow. Irina probably had no notion of how difficult it was for me to call her at the appointed hour—from the archives, the Lenin Library, the street, the dorm or wherever I happened to be—after finding a public phone that was neither occupied nor out of order and standing in line with my two-kopek pieces at the ready—but if she had done, it would have made no difference. It was harder speaking

Russian over the phone than face to face, and when I did reach Irina, usually after several unsuccessful attempts, her opening gambit was often to reproach me for not having rung earlier. She would never make a firm appointment more than a day or two in advance, a Soviet habit I never came to terms with, so half the time the upshot of one telephone call was an arrangement to make another call two days later. My sense of burden is conveyed by my comment to my mother at the end of January, when I was working long hours in the State Archives, that 'I am usually pretty tired in the evenings, with barely enough energy to ring up Irina Anatolevna, which I am always having to do'. We met several times in January, Irina assuming an ever more proprietorial attitude towards me. When I think about it, the whole story of Rafail Naumovich as last remaining suitor is implausible: if Irina had wanted to marry someone else, the man wouldn't have had a chance.

About two weeks after our first meeting, I had a cold, and used this as an excuse for not having rung her. According to my diary entry, she made a great point of telling me that, if I ever got sick, I was without fail to ring her. I noted that that was 'very kind', but also that I had better be careful in the future not to mention ever having been ill, to avoid reproaches about not having got up from my bed of sickness to tell her about it. On medical matters, as about everything else, she was full of categorical advice which could not be argued with. This could be slightly ludicrous, as when she would hold forth on something like the price and availability of sausage, about which she obviously had no first-hand knowledge, there being other people in the household to do the shopping. Her sons would, on occasion, protest—'Mama, you know nothing about it!'—which she took in good part; she was not easily offended, although she could turn on a good show of indignation if she wanted to make a point. While Irina had no expertise in shopping of the everyday kind, she had a great array of connections (much broader-reaching than Valery's) and was unbeatable in her knowledge of whom to call to access various luxury goods and services. Once, later in our friendship, I found myself with roubles left over at the end of my stay, and Irina marched me off with great efficiency to buy a gold necklace, selecting 'red gold' because of its superior quality. She was the only person I knew in Moscow who owned any jewellery other than a wedding ring.

As Irina talked, I began to realise how she operated as a manager both of the community of Lunacharsky scholars (not all being amenable, as in the case of Ovcharenko as editor of the *Works*) and of her father's reputation. She really loved her father, who was the focal point of her emotional life, but in addition she was a very talented PR woman for the Lunacharsky cause. Her references to her mother, who had died a few years earlier, were few and noticeably less warm. Irina would tell me all sorts of off-beat things about Lunacharsky, little vignettes of his relationship with Stalin and other leaders, jokes he had told, *bons mots*. Her general stance on Stalin, about whom she had no real personal memories, was that of a moderate de-Staliniser, in other words, standard Moscow intelligentsia in those years; and she would freely criticise Khrushchev (out of power since 1964), whom she knew quite well and for whom she had some affection. On Brezhnev, still fairly new in the top office, she had little to say in the first years of our acquaintance, though later, like everyone else, she told jokes about him.

But on Lenin or other questions involving the basics of Party history she was completely inflexible: Lenin and Lunacharsky were as one, Lunacharsky never deviated from the Party line, or if he did, he later acknowledged the error of his ways. All this, of course, I took with a pinch of salt, having done my own research on these matters, but there was no gainsaying Irina—Ovcharenko the cynic was a lot easier to talk to on such matters. Neither Irina nor her husband sounded like 'liberals', though Irina was very respectful of Igor, who obviously was one; Rafail Naumovich sometimes struck me as an unreconstructed Stalinist. Both Irina and her husband could be quite aggressive in their assertion of Soviet orthodoxies, pushing you into a corner and trying to make you agree, but he did it without humour, whereas Irina's ideological challenges always carried a hint of flirtation. Once I got over my surprise at Irina's formidable fluency in right-thinking, her orthodoxy struck me more as a good-humoured performance than a matter of deep belief. Her words were orthodox (although, like everyone else, she enjoyed telling political jokes), but her practice was far too enterprising and assertive to fit that mould; she was like a good lawyer, who can always find the appropriate legal argument for the case he is making.

About the capitalist West, Irina had the right Soviet sentiments of superiority and suspicion, but she was also proud of her fluent French—a high point of our relationship in later years was when I brought along a French historian friend of mine, American but with a Parisian gloss, whom she interviewed in the hexagonal study and bowled over, to her great satisfaction. She was a pillar of the Swiss-Soviet

Friendship Society, through which she could occasionally get trips to French-speaking Switzerland. She spoke some English, too: well enough to be an occasional guest at functions at the American and British Embassies in Moscow as well as the French, although with me she always spoke Russian. It was a rare privilege, of course, for Soviet citizens to be on the guest list of Western embassies, but Irina took it for granted; she was used to mixing with the top people. (I was at first a source of disappointment to her, knowing so few important people in England and looking blank when she dropped references to ambassadors names; later she was truly pleased, on my behalf as well as hers, when my range of acquaintances in the US began to include a few recognisable names.) In the St Antony's perspective—which was getting more and more distant from me in Moscow, but I could still remember the basics—the Novosti press agency, where she worked, was regarded as a propaganda agency with strong KGB connections. But it was clear that Irina had contacts everywhere that mattered. It would have been strange if this had not included the KGB.

As a science journalist, Irina had a few scoops in the time I knew her, but the job always seemed secondary in her life. She certainly didn't work anything like 9 a.m. to 5 p.m., Monday to Friday, but then it was hard to find a Soviet elite member, or perhaps any Soviet citizen, who did. The central activity and purpose of Irina's life seemed to be protecting Lunacharsky's posthumous reputation and gaining official and popular recognition of his achievements. It puzzled her a little that I didn't have the same instinct in regard to my own father, whom she knew (from her extensive cross-examining of me, and perhaps from other sources as well) to have been a staunch fighter for civil liberties and a socialist critic of capitalist government back in Australia. Why was I, or at least my mother, not more active in arranging republication of my father's work and encouraging scholars to write articles extolling his legacy? 'If you were only Russian', I wrote jokingly to my mother,

> you would have had a better time [I meant in the aftermath of my father's death, eighteen months earlier], trying to get the flat turned into a Fitzpatrick Memorial Museum. When Irina fixes me with her eye and says 'This is my duty to Papa' … I find myself almost envying her: some day I am sure to tell her that my father was also a good, cultured man (*kul'turnyi chelovek*) and a fighter for peace against the oppressors.

'Almost' was the kind of reflexive qualifier with which my mother and I filled our letters; I envied Irina, no question about it, and marvelled that a father could be remembered with such unambiguous affection and respect.

Irina wasn't the only keeper of the flame I met in Moscow; it seemed an almost inevitable life choice for Soviet children of the famous, especially those who died under a cloud and needed a bit of rehabilitating. There was the Gorky granddaughter whom I met with Tomiko; and the appealingly unorthodox Ivy and Tanya Litvinova, widow and daughter of Maxim Litvinov, Soviet foreign minister in the 1930s, whom I encountered later in the year. I had noticed with Irina that building up her own great man involved a certain pulling down of competitors like Gorky, and it was the same with the others. When I told Ivy Litvinova my dissertation topic, as I wrote to my mother, 'she did a great pantomime of astonishment that anyone should want to write about the dear well-intentioned man' (that is, Lunacharsky), and followed up with a series of disrespectful anecdotes about him. Tanya and Irina had been great friends in childhood but then had not seen each other for twenty years, meeting again, as it happened, shortly before my encounter with the Litvinovs. 'Irina thought Tanya had let herself go, and her husband is an old Jew with a beard (unquote)', my report to my mother continued. 'Tanya said Irina dyed her hair; lucky she didn't meet her husband the colonel or she would have said worse.' There was in Irina's attitude a reserve about someone who was not only personally eccentric but also probably had unorthodox views (this was obvious even before Pavel Litvinov, Ivy's grandson and Tanya's nephew, became notorious as a dissident); and in Tanya, a reserve that implied a suspicion of KGB connections.

Irina had grown up in a tight-knit group of children of the high Soviet political elite, who saw each other constantly at school and as weekend neighbours at the *dacha* (country house). I wish I had taken better notes of her stories about this milieu in my diary, which concentrates heavily on Igor and my conversations with him: perhaps I thought they were just gossip, like the tales that circulated at St Antony's, and didn't allow her the status of a primary source I accorded to Igor. The parents of Irina's childhood friends also made cameo appearances in her stories, as did various eligible Soviet bachelors who had made passes at the teenage Irina or been admirers of her mother's after Lunacharsky's death. Maya Kaganovich, daughter of Lazar, was most frequently mentioned, though Irina never offered to introduce me: it was strange to hear in passing of the ailing elderly father, once Stalin's much-feared right-hand man, who was the object of Maya's protective concern.

One of Irina's best stories, polished by frequent retelling, was about how, on applying for entrance to Moscow University in 1937, she had to fill out a form requiring her to name any enemies of the people personally known to her. ('Enemy of the people' was the term applied to high officials who had been or were about to be purged on fantastic allegations of spying and terrorism; they were either shot or disappeared into Gulag for twenty years.) As a good Young Communist, Irina dutifully started her list: 'Trotsky, Zinoviev, Kamenev, Rykov, Bukharin, Radek ...'—in other words, a litany of the most notorious Party oppositionists, who were currently being obsessively vilified in the media and in show trials. Irina's answer had already gone onto a second page when some highly placed protector—it could even have been Kaganovich—intervened and instructed her to throw the list away and write 'None'. It was hard to imagine that Irina had ever been that naïve, but easy to believe that, even in those terrible times, she and her mother still had a few good contacts.

I often felt wrong-footed by Irina, as I wrote to my mother, because of my temperamental inability to see things in black and white; 'I keep trying to straighten out my naturally oblique and conditional way of expressing myself into absolute enthusiasm or absolute rejection'. My gift of mimicry, which worked in a variety of Soviet situations, didn't help with Irina, whose way of articulating clichés was so flamboyant that I could never have reproduced it without sounding absurd. Not surprisingly, Irina sometimes worried about my lack of 'guiding ideas', though after I got to know Igor, she deferred to his judgement on such matters. I never had any sense that she worried about my being a spy, despite (or because of?) what I had told her about St Antony's. She thought of me, perhaps a little patronisingly, as a true scholar, hence rather lacking in worldliness and survival instincts. This meant that I—unlike some American diplomats Irina could name, and Australians too—belonged to the intelligentsia, a Soviet concept that almost defies translation, since it implies not only higher education and superior social status but a moral commitment to high culture. Being a member of the intelligentsia was an important self-identifier to Irina: 'after all, I am an *intelligentka'*, she would say, explaining her inability to tolerate some instance of vulgarity, rudeness or poor taste.

Early in February, Irina took me to a concert, a recital given by her friend Nina Beilina, a violinist who was a pupil of Oistrakh and winner of the Tchaikovsky competition; she played Stravinsky, which was slightly daring in Moscow in the 1960s. I met Nina only on this one occasion, although later, when her husband fell ill, Irina mobilised me to bring in medicine for him from England. Interested though I was in the music, it was the social aspect of this occasion that riveted me. Irina, flanked by her husband wearing all his military medals, knew everyone, greeting them all effusively and introducing me as a wonderful young English scholar of Lunacharsky. The only one whose name seemed familiar, though I couldn't immediately place it, was Alexey Adzhubei, and I almost asked him if he was a composer—lucky I didn't, as Irina would have been chagrined by the mistake. I must have run into Adzhubei again with Irina, but without her husband, because I remember him asking in a rather sarcastic way, 'How's the colonel?' (Rafail Naumovich's insistence on military rank, although he had not been at the front in World War II, provoked quite a lot of comments of this sort.)

Irina more or less observed the conventions of silence during the musical performance, but as soon as it was over she was 'hissing in my ear in between clapping with hands over her head and greeting all the other important people in the hall'. Part of the hissing was a run-down on who they were, much of which was lost on me. The thing I took in was that she had just arranged a meeting for me with the fabled Igor Alexandrovich Sats. I must realise, she impressed on me (and I reported to my mother), that he is 'a Very Important Person, and I must ask intelligent, important questions, and take notes of his answers'.

Igor Alexandrovich Sats was in his mid sixties, bright white hair flopping over his forehead, a big nose (one could see why he was cast as First Jewish Murderer), and an expression that was at once wily, charming and benign. He was to be a central part of my life for fifteen years, until his death in 1979: not just a friend like Irina, exasperating sometimes but valued and, above all, familiar, but more like an adoptive father. In fact, it now occurs to me that my attitude to him was much the same as Irina's to *her* adoptive father, Lunacharsky. Perhaps I learned it from her, as I didn't seem to have the knack with my real father. Irina was very fond of her uncle Igor, and as time went on, this became one of the bonds between us.

I have no memories of our first meeting, which took place at the beginning of February, but it is described in detail in a letter to my mother.

> This was a most nerve-wracking day which I spent entirely preparing my speech to Igor Sats and ringing Irina Anatolevna to find out if he could see me. Finally at 4.30 she managed to get hold of him and told me to come at once, have supper, and go to meet him before he went somewhere else at 7. So I flung on thick socks, boots, hat, scarf, anorak, coat and two pairs of gloves, threw myself on the bus, then into the metro, fought my way up Gorky St and arrived at 5.15... We had to get a taxi because, if I understand Irina Anatolevna rightly, the chauffeur had toothache (at any rate they do have, or have access to, a car). So we arrived at Uncle Igor's. Irina Anatolevna said I would like him, and I did. But I did not perform very well ... I was at a disadvantage talking to him with Irina Anatolevna there because one cannot argue with her, although obviously one can with him ... However it is established that I will come and see him, and he will direct my work ... and I am fairly confident that everything will go very well. At least I don't think I can go any further in search for the Real Authority on Lunacharsky; obviously this is the man.

It's the second visit, free of Irina's inhibiting presence and the sense of being rushed, that I remember vividly, almost cinematically. Igor Alexandrovich (as I always called him, using the polite form of 'you', as he did with me) lived on Smolensk Square, in an apartment on the sixth floor above Moscow's grocery shop No. 1. It was an early 1930s building, built when communalism reigned, a single-family apartment consisting of small kitchen just inside the front door, Igor's bedroom-cum-study on the right, a living room with grand piano (for his son Sasha, a pianist) and further on another bedroom, his wife Raisa Isaevna's, who was more or less an invalid in these years, often in hospital or a sanatorium. It was a spacious apartment in Moscow terms, and very well located on the Arbat, but with the great disadvantage that it had no bathroom—for lavatory and shower, you had to go down to the end of the corridor, known as 'taking the key' (you also took toilet paper with you). My knowledge of its layout is all of a later vintage: in the first months, all I knew of the apartment was the kitchen, the key, and Igor's study.

I see myself standing on Igor's doorstep (no nonsense about buzzers to let you in in those days), nervous and cold in my unsuitable coat: dark-green wool with gold buttons, made to suit a British winter rather than a Russian. Igor opened the door. 'An English girl wearing the uniform of the Tsarist Ministry of Railroads! What a pleasure!' he exclaimed as he ushered me in. 'But why are you wearing an autumn coat instead of a proper winter one? We should find you one.' We never found the coat: Igor was an old socialist who was indifferent to material possessions, a point of difference between him and Irina. If he had ever seriously tried to get someone a winter coat, it would probably have been by asking Irina to arrange it, but his dislike of such networks of contacts meant that the need would have had to be extreme—a penniless wife with tuberculosis trying to join her convict husband in Siberia, for example. His immediate concern about my welfare touched me: it wasn't the norm for academic supervisors, in my experience, and after all, it was in the capacity of student consulting informal supervisor that I had come. Igor, however, had already dropped the 'supervisor' mode of our first conversation and almost never returned to it (the sole example I can recall is when I brought my book manuscript to him a couple of years later and he gave me a formal oral critique in the presence of a Soviet Lunacharsky scholar). Unlike other people in Moscow, Igor did not appear to see me primarily as a student or a foreigner. He saw me, evidently, as a waif who needed to be adopted, so he adopted me.

Igor was a great collector of waifs and strays. People in trouble—and there were many of them in the Soviet Union—found a natural ally in him. The trouble could be arrest, political disgrace, family problems (many single mothers and children orphaned by divorce), loneliness, psychosis (Igor's acquaintance included a broad spectrum of psychotics and depressives, as well as alcoholics), or physical illness (made particularly burdensome because of the deficiencies of the Soviet pharmaceutical industry: doctors would prescribe drugs that could only be got on the black market or, through 'informal channels' like me and other foreign students, from abroad). The literary critic Vladimir Lakshin, a younger colleague of Igor's at *Novy mir*, who wrote an affectionate memoir of him, recalled that Igor would look after the sick in the most basic ways: getting their medicines (a task requiring ingenuity and perseverance in the Soviet Union), sitting by their bedsides, feeding them, changing sheets, bringing bedpans. He kept vigil over the dying, visited the widows and looked after the orphans. When his wife, Raisa Isaevna, fell ill and had to have a colostomy operation, which happened not long before I met him, it was a matter of pain to him that, out of squeamishness, she wouldn't let him help her with the awful chore of bandaging and cleaning the wound. They did colostomy operations in the Soviet Union but didn't make the plastic bags for waste disposal that made life after the operation bearable.

Outside of the family, the only criteria for deserving Igor's help were need and being considered by others to be of no importance in the world. At some point in his life, evidently long ago, Igor had decided to reverse the common habit of deference to 'people who mattered' and dismissive indifference to those who didn't. Nor did he practise contempt for the great, famous and well-connected in a passive Tolstoyan manner; he could be so rude, sullen and aggressive to such people—Lakshin says even to the point of fisticuffs, but I never saw this myself—that his friends tried to keep him out of their way. Confronted with a Soviet elite member or officeholder whom he considered a worthless person, or virtually anyone trying to exercise authority or pull rank over him, Igor would stick out his bottom lip and start radiating a hostility which might or might not remain silent. Bastards (*svolochi*) was his preferred term of abuse for such people; son of a bitch (*sukin syn*) was also a favourite. Cattle (*skoty*) was his collective epithet for Moscow University professors in the humanities and social sciences like Metchenko, while Ovcharenko individually was an unambiguous *svoloch'* in Igor's book. Igor was also, I was told, a virtuoso of *mat*, Russian cursing, but he didn't show off this talent in the presence of women.

Privilege aroused the same responses in him as authority, and he did his best not to use any of the privileges to which he was entitled, for example as a member of the Writers' Union. He had to make compromises on this, particularly with regard to medical treatment for Raisa Isaevna, but he didn't like doing it. He paid no attention to clothes, and in my memory always wore the same shabby jacket, overcoat on top if it was really cold, plus a scarf and a worker's cap (he didn't own a fur hat). He rarely took a taxi, and when, in the early 1960s, he had to have all his teeth out in four mammoth sittings (they had rotted in the marshes of the Smolensk Front during the war, he told me), he reportedly returned home on the Metro, a bloody handkerchief over his mouth, and kept the taxi money Raisa gave him for vodka. (I am not sure about this story, which comes from Igor's friend and drinking companion, the satirist Vladimir Voinovich; in my day, Raisa Isaevna didn't exercise this kind of infantilising control.) Even the privileges of age were unacceptable to Igor. In the Metro, in Voinovich's accurate description, he would always stand 'sticking out his chest, his whole bearing demonstrating that it would be pointless to offer him a seat'.

The aversion to using privilege and connections was an irritant in his relationship with Irina (and, before her, her mother and his sister Natalia), who lived their lives according to different rules. Out of loyalty, he kept his criticisms of their lifestyle more or less silent in my presence, but there was often a satiric edge in his voice when he spoke of the Lunacharskaya-Sterlin household. Irina was a good woman, he would often remind me and himself, energetic and generous. Irina's attitude to him was much warmer and more admiring, though she could never quite reconcile herself to his anti-careerism; he must have been a glamorous figure to her as a child—dark, handsome, brooding, wounded in battle, and fifteen years older. Irina was very fond of Raisa, who returned her affection, though remaining basically on Igor's side as far as luxury and privilege were concerned. With her great capacity for overlooking anything she didn't want to see, Irina serenely ignored Igor's disapproval of luxury and fashion, though it pained her that he was so hostile to the idea of her pulling strings to get him a better apartment, when this was so clearly called for in light of Raisa's health. (In the end, Irina prevailed, over tremendous grumbling and complaint from Igor.) Privately, Irina would say to me that, if Igor had a fault (apart from womanising, drinking and neglecting to make a career), it was his absurd refusal to do the things necessary in Soviet life to maintain a decent standard of living, like cultivating connections.

But that, perhaps was the nub of it: Igor had started out in Soviet life with connections that were unbeatable, back when he was Lunacharsky's secretary and brother-in-law in the 1920s; and on top of that, he was a child of the prosperous pre-revolutionary bourgeoisie, which was something to be ashamed of after the Revolution. He lived in Lunacharsky's luxurious apartment in the Arbat, art nouveau in design, complete with minstrel's gallery, built for a flamboyant and successful lawyer before the Revolution; he mixed with the famous and powerful; and it could be argued that when this phase of his life ended with Lunacharsky's death in 1933, he spent a lifetime atoning for his well-connected and privileged youth. Even when he was young, it was notable how unwilling he was to 'make a career' in any normal sense. Early on, he had a succession of mentors—his piano teacher Boleslav Yavorsky first; then Lunacharsky; then the philosopher Georg Lukaćs, with whom he worked in the 1930s—whose efforts to push him forward he resisted, but to whom he was devoted and remained loyal. He also had his own objects of protection, such as the writer Andrey Platonov, in deep disgrace from the end of the 1920s and consequently ostracised by many. Alexander Tvardovsky, under whom Igor worked at *Novy mir*, was both Igor's patron and the object of his protective care. The 'nanny' of Soviet literature was what

Igor sometimes called himself; that self-denigrating phrase, which others then repeated, was meant to underscore the idea, dear to his heart, that he was not and would always refuse to be a contender.

Igor's father, Alexander Mironovich Sats, was a successful Jewish lawyer in Chernigov and later Kiev. His politics were liberal, and he was a friend of Cadet (Constitutional Democratic Party) leader Paul Miliukov, an amateur violinist whom the young Igor sometimes accompanied on the piano. It was a musical family. Of the six children of Alexander Mironovich's first wife, one was the composer Ilya Sats, who had a brief, brilliant career before dying young in 1911, and another was an opera singer. Igor, born in 1903, was the second child of the second marriage. His older sister, Natalia Alexandrovna, was to become Lunacharsky's second wife. To complicate the story, there was another Natalia in the family, almost exactly Igor's age but his niece. This was Ilya's daughter Natalia Ilinichna, who was to have her own meteoric career under Lunacharsky's patronage as founding director (as a teenager!) of the Moscow Children's Theatre.

Igor seemed destined for a musical career, enrolling in the Kiev Conservatorium at fourteen as a student of composition and piano under Professor Boleslav Yavorsky. That meant that he never graduated from gymnasium (academic high school); in later life it gave him great pleasure to identify himself on official forms as having 'unfinished secondary education' as his highest academic level. In the meritocratic Soviet Union, where formal qualifications counted, this served to reinforce his lifelong claim to non-elite status. Igor didn't finish his musical studies because the Revolution intervened: at the age of fifteen, he ran away to fight with the Reds, saying goodbye to Professor

Yavorsky but not to his family. The Bolsheviks sent him into White territory as a scout and saboteur—looking like a bourgeois schoolboy was an advantage—and he claimed to have blown up two railway stations. He joined a Red Army regiment commanded by the legendary commander Nikolay Shchors and fought with it until severe head and back wounds ended his Civil War combatant career.

He was in hospital for almost a year, his condition exacerbated by typhus, and barely survived. He emerged, physically and psychologically shattered, into a Ukraine which, like the rest of the new Soviet Republic, was a place of hunger, chaos and misery. As far as I could tell from his story, he did not or could not contact his parents—his father was working as a lawyer for the Kiev Soviet but died in 1922—either during his stay in hospital or after his release in April 1922. Still weak, with diminished concentration and injuries that had ended his hopes of a musical career, he got a job as an armed guard in state provisions warehouses in Kiev and spent his free time alone, reading French and German books. It was in this miserable state that he was accidentally discovered and rescued by Professor Yavorsky.

Yavorsky had relocated from Kiev to Moscow during the Civil War, and so had the two Natalias, Igor's sister and niece, where both were doing well—Natalia Alexandrovna as an actress at the Maly Theatre and Natalia Ilinichna as director of her Children's Theatre. All of them, including Yavorsky, owed much to the patronage of Lunacharsky, who, in addition to being Natalia Alexandrovna's suitor, was also an old acquaintance of the Sats family, having been a classmate of one of Igor's and Natalia's elder half-brothers in the Kiev gymnasium. Yavorsky got Igor a job as music reviewer for a new journal he was editing for

Lunacharsky; and Igor also worked for a while in the proletarian culture association Proletkult, which he later remembered as full of half-crazy intellectuals—no actual workers in sight—putting out competitive avant-garde manifestos and fighting with each other. Igor was still in bad shape, and Lunacharsky and Natalia took him into their household, which included the toddler Irina and, I think, Igor's and Natalia's mother. They were living in a grand apartment in the Arbat district—in the 1960s, Irina managed to have this turned into a Lunacharsky Museum—and Igor had a little room in the attic. In recalling these years, Igor always described Lunacharsky as the one who was concerned for his welfare, not his sister Natalia. Almost thirty years older, Lunacharsky called him Gorya or Gorenka (the only person ever to use a diminutive for Igor in his adult life, as far as I know) and it was probably a quasi-filial relationship. After a few months, Lunacharsky invited Igor to become his personal assistant.

Igor remained as Lunacharsky's assistant for ten years, until Lunacharsky's death in 1933, which gave him an extraordinary vantage point for observing the top Bolshevik milieu, as well as a lifelong disinclination for joining it or any other elite group. Undoubtedly, given the constant scandals in the press and the Party about Natalia, and the fact that Igor's appointment could be viewed as nepotism, his position in some respects was an awkward one. But he must have been extremely useful to Lunacharsky, not just because of his unshakable loyalty but because of his literary and editing abilities. According to Vyacheslav Polonsky, one of the foremost literary critics of the time and a close associate of Lunacharsky's, Lunacharsky was far too busy as People's Commissar to write all the articles on literary and cultural themes that were required of him, so he would dictate impromptu reflections to a stenographer and Igor would turn them into articles. Igor never made any such claim to me, but then he wouldn't have. It adds a nice twist to his activity as Lunacharsky editor in the 1960s if the texts he was editing were in fact his own.

As well as working for Lunacharsky, Igor was a student at the Institute of Red Professors in the late 1920s, a kind of social-science and humanities graduate school for young Communists on their way into top jobs. He enrolled unwillingly, as far as I could gather, and never graduated, but it was another opportunity to observe one of the liveliest intellectual milieux in Moscow at close range. He got to know Nadya Alliluyeva, Stalin's young wife, there, as well as the young Communist militants of the Cultural Revolution, whom he liked less than Nadya. The institute was an ultra-politicised place in Igor's day, reproducing all the Party's factional struggles (Trotskyists, Zinovievists, Stalinists, Bukharinists) in spades, and Igor could have got Lunacharsky into a lot of trouble had he joined them. He didn't, and apparently was never tempted, having a sceptical attitude to all the leading oppositionists, including Nikolay Bukharin, the one he knew best, for whom he had some liking but little respect.

Lunacharsky was in quasi-disgrace in the last years of his life, having resigned from Narkompros in 1929, after more than a year of attacks from the Cultural Revolutionaries and clashes with Molotov and the industrial authorities on education policy. He was finally appointed Soviet ambassador to Spain to get him out of the way. The plan, so Igor told me, was that Igor should commute back and forth between Moscow and Madrid, keeping Lunacharsky's shop open in Moscow so to speak, while Raisa Isaevna Lindner

(Sats's future wife, probably already his girlfriend) would be with Lunacharsky fulltime, acting as translator since she knew Spanish. But Lunacharsky, who was already in bad health, died in Menton, in the south of France, on the way to Spain.

After Lunacharsky's death, refusing Bukharin's invitation to work with him, Igor drifted into the Institute of Philosophy, where he encountered two people who were to be of great importance in his life: Georg Lukaćs, a Hungarian Marxist already famous in international Communist circles for his work on history and class consciousness, and Mikhail Lifshits, a near contemporary of Igor's specialising in aesthetics who became a passionate opponent of modernism in art. They coalesced as a group around the journal *Literaturnyi kritik*, which played a provocative and surprisingly independent role in the Stalinist 1930s, as *Novy mir* was to do in the post-Stalin period. *Literaturnyi kritik* was a vehicle for Lukaćs's provocative philosophical and literary work on Hegel, the Russian novel, and other topics, mainly written in German and translated into Russian by Igor (perhaps one day we'll find out that Igor wrote these articles, too, though in Lukaćs's case, I doubt it). Among the journal's many provocations was its publication of original prose work by Igor's close friend Andrey Platonov. As a result of Stalin's intense dislike of his satirical novella about collectivisation, Platonov was generally considered too hot to handle, but *Literaturnyi kritik* managed to get his stories into print despite being a journal of literary criticism with no mandate to publish literature. It must have been somewhere around this time that Igor was accepted into the Writers' Union as a literary critic, a prudent career move that he was probably ashamed of (he hated and despised the union when I knew him, though he remained a member, and never told me the circumstances of his joining it).

The Great Purges of 1936–38 hit the Soviet Communist and artistic elites with devastating force, sweeping away much of the upper echelons of the Party, government and military, as well as most of the Cultural Revolution militants Igor had known at the institute and famous avant-garde figures like the poet Osip Mandelstam and theatre director Vsevolod Meyerhold. The Lunacharsky-Sats family came through relatively unscathed, with the exception of Natalia Ilinichna, who was arrested along with her husband, the minister for trade; the husband of Igor's younger sister, Tanya, was also arrested. Lukaćs and the *Literaturnyi kritik* group also survived, although in general foreign Communists like Lukaćs were at even greater risk than homegrown ones.

The Purges were a topic that was on everyone's mind in the 1960s, though it was still considered controversial and publications were often censored. Igor talked to me a lot about the Purges. He told many stories about people of his acquaintance who had fallen victim and also tried to analyse the process (much of his analysis is reflected in Chapter 8 of my book *Everyday Stalinism*). I asked him very early on why he thought he had survived, with so many obvious risk factors like high elite connections and acquaintance with victims. It was a question I would not have dreamt of putting to anyone else, but I wanted to know and assumed he would give me a truthful answer. The only survival strategy worth anything, according to Igor, was simply to disappear, like the friend of his who went down south, stole a chicken, and sat safely in prison

Sheila and Igor Sats, in his study, 1969.

Igor and Lunacharsky playing chess, in the summer of 1924. The back of the original photograph is inscribed by Igor: 'To dear Sheila, in memory of our conversations and friendship, 7 July 1967.'

Irina and Lunacharsky in his study, circa 1928-9.

Irina Lunacharskaya; with me in her eighteenth-century study, and with her husband Rafail Naumovich Sterlin and their dog Nessie, both circa 1980-90.

Lunacharsky and his wife, Natalia Alexandrovna Luncharskaya—Rozenel, 1926.

Alexander Ovcharenko (right)—my supervisor in Moscow—encountered in 1981 at the Woodrow Wilson International Center for Scholars, Washington DC, with an unidentified Soviet colleague.

The St Antony's College annual photo, 1964. I'm seated third from the left, the Warden FW Deakin ninth from the left, and Max Hayward third from the right, all in the front row.

Moscow University, photograph by author, 2013.

State Archives of the Russian Federation, photograph by author, 2013.

Sovetskaya Rossiya *article:* 'He who is obliged to hide the truth', *16 June 1968.*

КТО ВЫНУЖДЕН ПРАВДУ СКРЫВАТЬ...

Томас Манн никогда не был коммунистом, но он был большим писателем-гуманистом. Именно это и позволило ему назвать антикоммунизм самой большой глупостью нашего времени. Среди буржуазных пропагандистов нет больших писателей, но зато более чем достаточно антикоммунистов. При этом, что весьма примечательно, многие из них выдают себя за любителей и ревнителей изящной словесности, в особенности советской литературы.

Чем же объясняется такое пристрастие?

Ответы на этот вопрос в какой-то степени содержатся в высказываниях самих «ревнителей» и «любителей». Так, сравнительно недавно некто Людмила Келер в американском журнале «Рашен ревью» писала: «Есть такая публика (особенно в вузовской компании), которая хвалит все, что приходит из России».

Хотя автор статьи дама и профессор Питтсбургского университета, хотелось бы обратить внимание на тот «изящный стиль», коим она объясняется, когда дело касается оценки произведений советских писателей общественностью США. Впрочем, даже сквозь полицейский жаргон мисс Келер легко разглядеть ее боязнь растущего влияния советской литературы.

Еще более четко эта боязнь прослеживается в высказываниях Юргена Рюле. Вот что писал он на страницах западногерманского журнала «Остойропа» («Восточная Европа»): «Целый ряд крупных писателей — как в советской сфере влияния, так и за ее пределами выступал в пользу коммунистической партии, а в творчестве их хорошо известно читающей публике за рубежом, чтобы можно было выступить против него с открытым забралом. Именно поэтому Хэллетт с тщанием, достойным лучшего применения, собрал и опубликовал на английском языке всю ту брань, которой осыпали некогда «Тихий Дон» рапповские критики и другие «леваки» и демагоги. При этом выясняется любопытная деталь: симпатии автора-антикоммуниста всецело на стороне РАППа, деятели которого, казалось бы, только и грезили, что о мировой революции. По уверениям Хэллетта, «независимые взгляды (РАППа) на марксизм в литературе стали источником затруднений для советского строя» (?!), ликвидация же РАППа означала не что иное, как «полное исчезновение» ограниченной творческой свободы, существовавшей ранее».

Поистине цирковые трюки проделывает мистер Хэллетт. Ведь даже из его собственной статьи видно, что произошло, если бы партия не избавила советскую литературу от рапповской «опеки»: в этом случае «Тихий Дон» попросту не увидел бы света.

Поскольку, однако, этого не произошло и «Тихий Дон» существует, Хэллетт делает еще один трюк. Он пытается противопоставить социалистическому реализму... самого М. А. Шолохова. Для этого английский «литературовед» соотносит «Тихий Дон» не с подлинным социалистическим реализмом, а с площадной карикатурой на него, сфабрикованной им самим же.

Оказывается, по уверениям мистера Хэллетта, советские писатели «должны при выборе темы основываться на достижениях советского правительства», а вот-де Шолохов не пошел на это и создал героя, «образ которого может считаться трагическим». Тем самым, заверяет Хэллетт, М. А. Шолохов «не осудил безоговорочно общественный строй, существовавший до большевистской революции». Иначе говоря, в «Тихом Доне» якобы наличествуют какие-то элементы одобрения буржуазно-помещичьего строя, свергнутого народом под руководством партии большевиков. Вот аж куда занесло мистера Хэллетта!

Нужно сказать, что автор статьи в лондонском журнале отнюдь не отличается оригинальностью мышления. Попытки «отлучить» М. А. Шолохова от советской литературы предпринимались реакционными буржуазными учеными и до этого. К тем же приемам, что и Р. Хэллетт, прибегает другой английский «советолог» — С. Фицпатрик, выступивший в прошлом году в журнале «Совьет стадиз» со статьей «Новейшие советские переиздания и толкования». Правда, в отличие от своего коллеги Хэллетта, Фицпатрик пытается оторвать от советской литературы уже не М. А. Шолохова, а А. В. Луначарского. Начинает Фицпатрик с беспардонной клеветы в адрес А. В. Луначарского и основоположника советской литературы А. М. Горького — инициатора выпуска серии «Жизнь замечательных людей». «Первоначальным назначением (серии) было не писать историю, а создавать мифы и образы героев, достойных подражания... Если он (Луначарский) заслуживает место в «Жизни замечательных людей», то не как ученый, администратор, политический деятель или герой, достойный подражания. Он антигерой, который не признавал «монолитности»,— витийствует Фицпатрик.

Попробуем разобраться в этих более чем сомнительных упражнениях Фицпатрика. «Монолитность», которую, по его уверениям, не признавал А. Луначарский — друг и соратник Ленина,— это ленинское единство партии и народа, без которого не было бы ни Советской державы, ни советской литературы. Что думал об этом сам А. В. Луначарский, нетрудно установить. «Она,— писал Луначарский о коммунистической партии в своем очерке «Ленин»,— для того чтобы руководить и не допустить ошибок».

Более хитро, нежели Келер и Фицпатрик, действует антисоветский поэт Георгий Анненский, эмигрировавший в свое время из Советской страны и ныне подвизающийся в США. В молодости Анненский был знаком с А. Блоком, С. Есениным, В. Маяковским и вот теперь развязно выступает от имени всех названных поэтов, пользуясь тем, что они давно умерли и не могут поймать его за руку. Анненский ссылается, разумеется, не на творчество поэтов, а на слова, якобы сказанные ему великими писателями с глазу на глаз. В результате оказывается, что великий советский поэт В. Маяковский, по уверениям Анненского, плакался ему в жилетку, когда приезжал во Францию...

Жаль, что нет в живых Владимира Владимировича, а то бы с помощью его гневных строк господин Анненский мог войти в литературу со всей своей геростратовой славой. Впрочем, живы и борются, дают достойную отповедь фальсификаторам нетленные произведения Маяковского.

Нам же остается лишь сказать, что приемы идеологических диверсантов не очень-то отличаются от приемов буржуазных разведчиков. Это не дискуссия и не полемика, а просто провокация, бесчестная игра. Она свидетельствует не о силе кривды, а о страхе буржуазной пропаганды перед истиной. Как писал Роберт Бернс:

Правдивой страницы
Лишь тот и боится,
Кто вынужден правду
скрывать.

В. ГОЛАНТ,
кандидат исторических наук.

Wearing my 'Ministry of Railways' coat, by the Moskva River in the winter of 1969. Smolensk Square is visible in the background.

Igor Sats, portrait sent to me in Oxford and inscribed 'to Sheila, with love, 12 October 1970'. *This remarkably gloomy portrait was no doubt intended to convey his state of mind after being fired—alongside Tvardovsky—from the editorial board of* Novy mir.

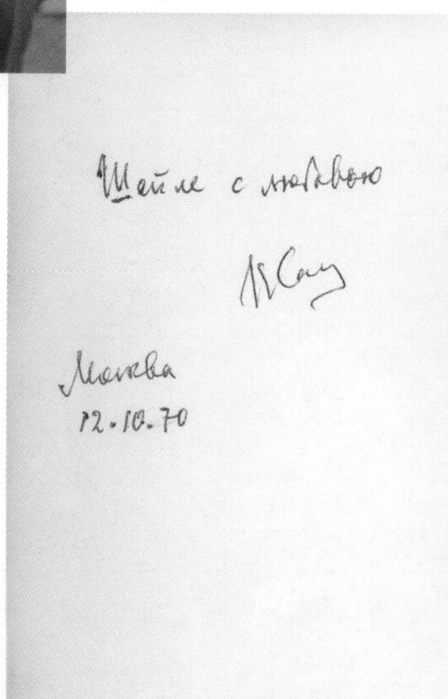

as a petty thief while the storm raged outside. But that one knew only with hindsight. For his personal survival, Igor said there was no reason but blind luck, though it may have helped to be low-profile and not hold high office. It would have been nice to have known in advance that one was going to be lucky, he added, which was as close as Igor came to describing what the experience had been like for him.

Ironically, Igor's most dangerous moment came in 1939–40, as the Purges were winding down. The danger came from two directions. The first was Igor's friendship with Platonov. Stalin's belief that he was an important writer, if not one whom he personally liked, may have saved Platonov from arrest, but he was under close surveillance. As agents of the NKVD (the KGB's precursor) reported, Igor was a close friend of Platonov's, one of only two people entrusted with his manuscripts. When Platonov's teenage son was arrested on a charge of terrorism, Igor went to the Lubyanka with Platonov to try to find out about the boy's fate. Though Igor never mentioned it when telling the story, this was a much more dangerous action for him than for Platonov: by Soviet convention, immediate family had the informal right to petition about a relative's arrest and could even assert the victim's innocence with relative impunity, but if an outsider joined in, that constituted anti-Soviet activity and possible conspiracy in the eyes of the secret police. The son was not released, but he was not shot either, and returned from Gulag after what was by Soviet standards a relatively short term.

The second danger to Igor were the attacks on *Literaturnyi kritik* that started in the literary community and ended up provoking Politburo intervention. In the spring of 1939,

Igor and others from the journal were harshly criticised at the Writers' Union. One highly placed apparatchik suggested that the security police ought to look into their activities, which provoked Igor—who had clearly already developed his aggressive and unconciliatory manner to such people—to respond rudely (the rudeness is evident even in the edited minutes) that the police had no place in literary squabbles. The literary militants of the Cultural Revolution—including Alexander Fadeev, a survivor who had risen to a dominant position in the Writers' Union—had never liked Lukács and his group. They denounced the journal editors, including Igor, as an 'anti-Party' faction that was trying to monopolise Soviet literary criticism, and in November 1940 the journal was closed down.

The war came as a relief to Igor; he immediately volunteered for the Red Army, glad to see the last of the corrupt Soviet literary world. He probably hoped, as well as expected, not to come back. He and Raisa Isaevna were back together by the outbreak of the war, having drifted apart in the mid 1930s (she had a son, who turned out to be schizophrenic, by a poet who, if I remember rightly, fell into disgrace and committed suicide). Igor adopted the poet's son, and at the beginning of 1941 Raisa gave birth to their own child, Sasha. Before Igor went off to fight, they married—having previously regarded marriage as a pointless bourgeois convention—to protect Raisa and Sasha's legal rights and give them the status of family of a soldier on active service.

Igor was in the army from the autumn of 1941 to 1946, serving first in field intelligence in the Thirty-Ninth Army and later being seconded (probably because of his knowledge of Polish) to the First Polish Army, recruited from

Polish refugees and deportees on Soviet soil in the middle of the war on the initiative of a Polish writer much admired by Stalin, Wanda Wasilewska. The Great Patriotic War, as it was known in the Soviet Union, turned out much better for Igor than the Civil War had done. He relished the male companionship of the army, free of the ambiguities and betrayals of civilian life, and admired his generals, especially Ivan Konev and Konstantin Rokossovsky, whose strategy and tactics he was willing to talk about for hours. He was proud of his field-intelligence skills and told me many stories about his exploits crawling close to enemy lines to listen in on their conversations; once he even took me out to a forest reserve on the outskirts of Moscow to demonstrate his expertise in tracking. He was even prouder of the field spies (*razvedchiki*) who had served under his command, and never failed to attend the unit's reunions, nostalgic drinking sessions that took place on public holidays. At one point, Raisa Isaevna was notified that Igor had been killed at the front, but one of his *razvedchiki*, who happened to be in Moscow at the time, rejected the idea out of hand: Igor Alexandrovich wouldn't have been so silly as not to come back from his forays into enemy territory. That comment greatly pleased Igor when he did finally reappear.

Igor telling me the story of his life was hard to separate from Igor teaching me Soviet history. I'm not sure that he strongly differentiated between the two himself, which was not unusual at that period, when the individual lives of everyone over forty had been so buffeted by public events of the recent past like the Purges and the war. From the start, he made it clear that I had to learn to understand contemporary Russian history, 'because for me Lunacharsky is only the beginning', as I reported to my mother. That 'for me' is puzzling: I doubt that he discerned a great future historian in the impressionable English girl who had shown up on his doorstep. What he probably did see was someone from the West, where nobody understood Soviet history, who might with luck absorb a bit of understanding and spread it around when she got back. In other words, he had an implicit agenda for me, like Irina, but a less personal one. It worked better than Irina's. I had ambitions in Soviet history, and for me, too, Lunacharsky was just the beginning. If it was disinformation about Soviet history that Igor was spreading (as Ovcharenko and the KGB might well have thought), he had found the right agent.

Soviet history as Igor understood it was a kind of black comedy. That's not wholly unlike seeing it as a tragedy, which is a standard Western view, but there are significant differences. In Igor's version, there were no deep-laid conspiratorial plans to enslave the people and use the Party dictatorship to create a totalitarian state. Igor's Bolsheviks were not at all averse to violence—they were revolutionaries, after all—but once they had taken power, they found that violence, almost their only tool, was a blunt instrument. It made people react but not necessarily do what you wanted them to do. It was constantly generating unintended consequences, which hapless bureaucrats tried in vain to keep in check. The worse things got in practice, the more high-flown the rhetoric about glorious successes. The Soviet Union was a theatre of the absurd, in Igor's telling—the world of the great Soviet satirists, from Mikhail Zoshchenko and Andrey Platonov to Vladimir Voinovich, who not coincidentally were all friends of Igor's.

The literary satirists, though enormously popular in the Soviet Union, often got into political trouble because they were thought to be mocking the society and its leaders, and obviously the same objections could be made to Igor's version of Soviet history. To this, his answer was simple: it was *his* history. Born in territory that became the Soviet Union, he had chosen his political allegiance once and for all when he joined the Bolsheviks at fifteen. One Party and one country was the hand he'd been dealt and there weren't any second choices, he told me once when I asked him why he was still a Party member. That didn't mean he had to admire the people who ran the Communist Party and the Soviet Union or like everything they did. On the other hand, if he could have used the phrase 'Soviet patriot' without a satirical glint in his eye, he would have said he was one. I think he was.

Few of the Party leaders came out well in Igor's stories. Trotsky had dealt ruthlessly with his troops in the Civil War, Zinoviev was a fool, Alexey Rykov a nice man but a drunk, Bukharin a lightweight. As far as the leading Stalinists were concerned, Vyacheslav Molotov and Georgy Malenkov were unspeakable, and Lazar Kaganovich energetic and good-humoured but a bully (Igor did a fine imitation of Kaganovich backing a subordinate up against the wall and shouting in his face like a sergeant-major). On Stalin himself, the picture was less clear, perhaps because Igor had had fewer opportunities for personal observation. Igor knew him at second hand through Nadya Alliluyeva, his fellow student at the Institute, for whom Igor felt considerable sympathy (she committed suicide in 1932). He also knew him through Lunacharsky, who—rather surprisingly—had a certain respect for Stalin, for all Stalin's crudeness. Always a contrarian, Igor was no more inclined to join the anti-Stalin bandwagon set in motion by Khrushchev than he had been earlier to sign on to the Stalin cult, about which he had many acid jokes to tell; he was more interested in working out what made Stalin tick than compiling an indictment against him. But basically he didn't think that understanding Stalin was the key to understanding Soviet history—he was too much of a Marxist for that. From his viewpoint, societies and political parties tend to get the leaders they deserve.

The two people from the world of high politics of whom Igor always spoke highly and never criticised were Lunacharsky and Lenin. In the case of Lunacharsky, this was a natural product of loyalty and affection, and the fact that I was a scholar writing a study of him. I had a definite sense that Igor could have shown me more of Lunacharsky's fallibilities and weaknesses if he had had a mind to, and this is confirmed by a couple of irreverent Lunacharsky anecdotes Voinovich remembers being told by Igor that I never heard. In the first months of my acquaintance with Igor and Irina, I wrote to the *Journal of Contemporary History* in London withdrawing my Lunacharsky article (written in my St Antony's belittling mode) from publication in the April 1967 issue. It was done out of respect for Igor's and Irina's feelings; but, while I thought Irina would be hurt as well as annoyed to have her father belittled, I guessed that Igor would have wryly recognised my portrait, even if he saw it as something of a caricature.

Igor's Lenin worship was another thing entirely. Lenin could do no wrong in his book; even the most dubious of his actions and pronouncements were given ingenious and elaborate justifications. He enjoyed Lenin's polemical prose, his cunning and his aggressive embrace of contradictions ('Dialectics!' [*dialektika*], Igor would exclaim). Lenin was one of only three or four topics at which my eyes would sometimes glaze over at Igor's, along with Franz Liszt (whose piano music Igor liked more than I did) and Lukaćs's totalist Marxist-Hegelian philosophy. Still, I preferred Lenin to the other two, and professionally it was useful to be given a crash course in Lenin's works. I wasn't the only beneficiary of Lenin instruction among Igor's younger friends: Lakshin was another, though he was too polite or prudent in his (Soviet-published) memoirs to object; and so was Voinovich, who (according to his post-Soviet reminiscences of Igor) thought Lenin was a terrible person who had done great harm to Russia, and said so. Igor's response was that he didn't know what he was talking about: couldn't he, as a satirist, see that Lenin was also a satirist on the level of Russia's greatest, Mikhail Saltykov-Shchedrin from the nineteenth century and Zoshchenko from the twentieth?

Since the 1990s, we've had a plethora of inside stories, memoirs and sensational archival disclosure about the seamy side of Soviet politics. But this was the 1960s, before *Let History Judge,* Zhores Medvedev's insider essay in de-Stalinisation, had made it into print, or Khrushchev's memoirs appeared. Nobody knew inside stories like Igor's then; his accounts of Soviet high politics astonished me. I sat with popping eyes as Igor talked about a chance meeting at the height of the Great Purges with Yevgenia Yezhova, whose husband Nikolay Yezhov—'sword of the Revolution', as the catchphrase went—was head of the NKVD and chief purger, though before too long he and his wife would both fall victim themselves. 'A nice woman', Igor said; 'we all knew her [i.e. in the literary world], but now she was distraught because of what was happening and she had a terrible rash all over her face'. (I wrote the name down in my diary as 'Yershova', which shows how much I knew about Soviet history at that point).

One of my heroes, Nikolay Sukhanov, author of *Memoirs of the Russian Revolution*, was a favourite subject, though not particularly a hero, of Igor's. Sukhanov, a former Menshevik, met his end in the Menshevik show trial of the early 1930s. According to Igor, there actually was a Menshevik plot, or at least conspiratorial contacts involving some of the other defendants and an *émigré* journal, but Sukhanov probably wasn't a part of it; he was in dock with the others because of his visibility. 'Nobody tried to defend him; Lunacharsky took no interest', I wrote in my diary, summarising Igor's account. 'I asked whether that wasn't a pity. He shrugged—"Of course it was a pity" (*konechno, zhalko*).' Soviet history was full of things that were a pity, or worse, I understood him to be telling me; people like Lunacharsky had to pick their battles. It was up to Sukhanov's son-in-law to agitate on his behalf (which he did, though to no avail).

The story I liked best, and recorded almost word for word in my diary, was about a spy, the Chekist Yakov Blyumkin, who happened to live in the next flat to the Lunacharskys. I could see that Igor had enjoyed Blyumkin, a lively Jewish lad from Odessa only five years older than him; and the glimpses he gave of the milieu of the GPU (secret police, successor to the Cheka and precursor of the NKVD) in the 1920s had a tinge of nostalgia, like somebody remembering Chicago in the days of Al Capone. Blyumkin was an adventurer, Igor said, prone when bored to lie on his bed firing his pistol at the ceiling. While working for the secret police in Istanbul in 1929, he met the exiled Trotsky, and—in a reckless move—carried back letters from him to former oppositionist leaders back home. Karl Radek, one of the addressees, refused to accept the letter for fear of entrapment, telling Blyumkin he was going to inform on him. Blyumkin, according to my notes of Igor's story, 'would have killed him, but there were people in the flat, or close by'. He tried to make a getaway but found there were people waiting for him at all the railway stations. So he came home and told the Lunacharskys that the game was up. About a week later, he rang from prison asking them to get the cleaning woman to send a change of linen—he was being given a week to write his memoirs, then he would be shot. A GPU acquaintance whom Igor ran into on the street shortly afterwards confirmed that 'Yakov is no longer among the living' (*Yakova uzhe net*).

In those early months, I was always wondering why Igor was willing to spend so much time talking to me, and why he wasn't afraid that I was a spy. I asked him the last question and he simply laughed: as if he, of all people, couldn't recognise a spy! I explained about St Antony's and the 'not unknown' Max Hayward (as the Soviet press liked to refer to him—strangely, as he was quite unknown to the Soviet public, though not to the KGB), and he listened with interest but became no more cautious. It bothered me that I could have gone and published his stories abroad and got him into great trouble; I thought he should at least ask me not to do this, but he never did. 'I kept telling him reasons not to trust me, I was so startled that he did', I wrote to my mother once I was safely back in Oxford. But he had decided to trust me; who knows why. Probably it wasn't as remarkable as I thought at the time: Igor was quite reckless in speech around those he liked. He could suddenly clam up when someone he didn't trust was around, but in general, he couldn't be bothered being too cautious. What had he got to lose? It wasn't 1937. This attitude to life used to worry Irina, and I'm sure Raisa Isaevna too.

One of the reasons I was puzzled by Igor's spending time with me was that I thought that in Russian I was very boring. I was mainly silent in our early conversations, just interjecting a few factual questions and nodding when I understood or agreed with a point. My linguistic command wasn't up to humour or irony at this moment, though I could recognise it in others, and I felt that without these attributes I was not myself. I explained this to Igor, in my pedestrian Russian, and he waved it away. I didn't have to talk; he could read my face. Perhaps this was true, though at the time I doubted it.

I started off going to see Igor every Sunday (when archives were closed and libraries were on reduced hours), but by mid April he was suggesting I come round during the week as well. By May, our conversations were becoming 'longer and longer', as I wrote to my mother. By June, having run out of archives, I was going round to Igor's every second day and staying most of the day—eight hours, I recorded, on 24 June. Raisa Isaevna was away much of the time, in hospital or convalescing at the sanatorium. Igor had started to feed me (omelettes) and provide me with reading matter (selected articles from *Novy mir*, unpublished manuscripts, closed-circulation documents) when he had business to attend to. I would sit on the wooden chair in his room, and he would sit on the bed, a hard-divan type that rose alarmingly in the middle and looked extremely uncomfortable.

The telephone would ring often, and, as at Irina's, there was never any question of my leaving the room for him to talk in private. 'Private' was not an operative concept in the Soviet Union, given the crowded housing conditions. If you wanted to say something out of the hearing of others (including the KGB), you went for a walk.

In my diary and letters to my mother, I continued to pick over the question of why Igor wanted to talk to me; it seemed such extraordinary good fortune. After all, as I wrote to my mother in April, it wasn't as if he was 'a lonely old man in retirement but a very occupied man in the centre of all sorts of things and fighting all sorts of battles', as well as looking after a very sick wife. Was there an ulterior motive, I wondered. Spying was what I meant (it was the Soviet Union, after all), not sex. But 'I cannot think of Igor Alexandrovich except as an honest man, if a shrewd one', I wrote in my diary. Indeed, had any of the Lunacharskys been regularly reporting on me, it would surely have been Irina, who was inclined to cross-examine me about my life, attitudes and contacts in a way Igor never did. Little by little, I came to accept my good fortune and explain it in the simplest possible manner: as I wrote solemnly to my mother, 'I have come to the conclusion that Igor Alexandrovich likes me coming round'.

I'm not sure when it occurred to me that sex might also be a factor. I have a memory of Irina warning me about Igor's womanising tendencies, noting particularly the recent family scandal about his affair with his widowed daughter-in-law (the affair was over, but I knew her, as she still brought the grand-daughter to see him), reminding me of Raisa Isaevna's ill health, and warning me not to have an affair with him. I don't know exactly when that happened, but it was probably in the early summer, when Raisa Isaevna was in hospital, Sasha was off somewhere, and I was spending my eight-hour days at Igor's. That was the time that Igor made the nicest possible pass at me: that is, he kissed me and said, 'Of course, I am too old for you'. I agreed that this was so, expressing regret, which I felt. This is one of the few sensible decisions I made in my personal life in these years, and it was purely instinctive, not thought out in advance. It would have been disastrous to have had an affair with Igor, not least that it would have felt like incest. So I was able to tell Irina with a clear conscience that I wasn't about to have an affair with Igor, and I suppose she believed me, otherwise she wouldn't have let the topic drop. After that, she just took my closeness to Igor as a fact of life. For such a proprietorial person, it's odd that she was so ready to hand me over without resentment, but that's my memory of it. We remained good friends, but as long as Igor was alive, he was the one I called first when I arrived in Moscow, and Irina only second.

The sexual aspect of Igor's interest in me can't have come as a complete surprise, as he always talked as freely about sex and the women in his life as he did about politics. He was completely straightforward talking about sex, never prurient, and often very funny. In Igor's book, where close relations existed between a man and a woman, they were assumed to be sexual unless the contrary was explicitly stated—in which case, Igor often felt it necessary to offer a sympathetic explanation (*He was impotent, poor fellow; it was a neurosis he brought back from the war …*). Sex came into many of his stories about the great and famous, since he considered it an important part of life without which his thumbnail characterisations would have been incomplete.

He even talked quite a lot about Lenin and his lover, Inessa Armand, partly because he (Igor) was friends with her children. Only Lunacharsky was exempt, presumably out of respect. I remember Igor's comment on his own father, remembered without affection, that the reason he had nine children was not that he was so keen on children, or that he was particularly fond of his wives, 'it was the activity itself [that is, sexual intercourse] he liked'. This, I thought, was probably something they had in common. But Igor loved the women in his life, remaining fond of them and concerned about their welfare long after the affairs were over.

There were some waifs and strays among Igor's past affairs, but the lovers from the past he spoke about most were strong, independent women, whom he admired for their intellect and force of character. Elena Felixovna Usievich, daughter of the famous revolutionary Felix Kon, a feisty but well-connected literary critic, who worked with Lukaćs and Igor on *Literaturnyi kritik,* was one of them. Another was Wanda Wasilewska, the Polish writer whose 'socialist realist' novels were so admired by Stalin that he put her in charge of forming the First Polish Army, which is probably where Igor got to know her. While there is an extensive Polish and Russian literature on Wasilewska, a great celebrity in the war years, married to another celebrity, the Ukrainian writer Alexander Korneichuk, none of it tells much about her private life; and even Stalin's personal archive confirms only that they met in his office from time to time during the war. If I correctly understood Igor, however, Wasilewska was having an affair with Stalin in the 1940s at approximately the same time she was having an affair with Igor. (I didn't write this down in my diary, and I can't swear that Igor was explicit about the nature of the relationship in either case.) Of course, this made a considerable impression on me. Only two degrees of separation from Stalin for Igor! And for me, consequently, only three.

Perhaps I was slow to notice sex as a factor in Igor's attitude to me because I was preoccupied with something else: love. The word appeared quite early in my diary, though qualified ('a kind of love') and referring to something reciprocal. It may be a bold claim, but I think in the course of our thirteen-year friendship I made it onto the list of women Igor loved. Probably the last of them—at least that's what I gathered from Raisa Isaevna when we became friendly after his death—and from the family standpoint comparatively harmless. Certainly I loved him. For that decade and a half, from our meeting at the beginning of 1967 to his death at the end of 1979, Igor was the person who mattered most to me in the world, on a par with my father earlier and my husband Michael Danos later. I'm not talking here about his help to me as a budding historian, though that was enormous: I learned so thoroughly to see the Soviet world through his eyes that he could almost be called a co-author of all my books (like Lunacharsky's!), particularly those on everyday and social behaviour. It was on the personal level that he mattered so much, and the role—as his framing between my father and Misha suggests—was something between father and lover, with me pushing towards the first and Igor towards the second. I knew, or thought I did, why Igor was so important to me. It was because he was a living contradiction of my fear, when my father died, that now all love would have to be earned and conditional, for who else but a father would love you *no matter what*? I thought of Igor's love as unearned, gratuitous, and it seemed to me a miracle.

5

In the Archives

Two extraordinary things happened to me in the first months of 1967: Igor and the archives. It seems contradictory to say that all my attention was on both of them, but that's what it felt like. It was a time for doing the impossible, like paying 100 per cent attention to two different things at the same time. As far as time allocation went, the archives had slight priority, in that I wouldn't go to Igor's during opening hours, but it was a near thing. Everything else, including Irina and the Lenin Library, came a distant second.

Although Igor and the archives were separate spheres, there was an overlap. I was reading the archives of Lunacharsky's Commissariat of Enlightenment (Narkompros) from the 1920s, when Igor had been working with Lunacharsky. As literary secretary, he didn't have any direct connection with Narkompros, but he heard all about the important policy issues from Lunacharsky, and could generally remember what the stakes were and who was on which side. If he didn't remember, he would sometimes ring up one of the old Narkompros staffers who had been closer to the action and ask them; sometimes he invited them round to talk to me. I knew how lucky I was having Igor, but I don't know that I realised what an extraordinary advantage it was to have Igor and the archives at the same time. It's a wonderful thing to have archives, especially if nobody else has used them. But untapped archives plus a primary informant willing to give you a running commentary on what you read in the archives the day before is something that only happens once in a lifetime.

Soviet history was in its infancy in the West, and it was almost unknown for Western scholars to get permission to work in Soviet archives for the period after 1917. This lack of access to archives was one of the reasons given by Russian historians in the West for considering the Soviet period not a legitimate object of study for historians. The boundaries of what history is are always debatable. Up to the 1960s, British archives still followed a fifty-year rule, implying that World War I was history, but not the 1920s. But the new-fangled discipline of contemporary history was gaining ground, not without resistance from the old guard. Contemporary history had no fixed boundaries, but historians often assumed its furthest limit was about a generation back, or thirty years. A similar readjustment of boundaries was in process in many Western archives: 1967 was the year when the British Public Record Office switched from a fifty-year rule to a thirty-year one, bringing my topic (as far as British archives were concerned) firmly into the purview of history.

But Russian historians in the West, many of them *émigrés*, were unusually conservative: it was still generally assumed that Russian history stopped with the Revolution, and that everything that followed was the domain of political scientists. I considered this to be pure prejudice, like the refusal of major research libraries to have a catalogue entry for

'Soviet Union' (rescinded by the Library of Congress in the 1980s, only a few years before the Soviet Union itself ceased to exist). One of the underlying causes of my excitement in that first year in the Soviet Union was that I thought (correctly, as it turned out) that I was in at the birth of a new field of scholarship, Soviet history.

Unlike British archives, Soviet archives had no formal fifty- or thirty-year rule restricting access, though their assumption that 1917 was a breakpoint brought them in practice close to something like a fifty-year rule. The good side of this was that if a rule has not been codified in law, you don't have to stick to it; the bad side was the automatic Soviet habit of restricting access to information in every possible context, especially with respect to foreigners. It's strange that, coming from Britain, which at the time of my departure for the Soviet Union still had a fifty-year rule, I should have had such a sense of righteousness in demanding Soviet archives that would barely have come within a thirty-year rule—and even stranger, in retrospect, to think that the period I was working on, now so distant, was then only a generation away and still vivid in the memory of Igor and his contemporaries.

Getting into the archives was a key aspiration of mine from the beginning of my stay in the Soviet Union. This was in part the result of my strict training in the History Department of the University of Melbourne, where archival research was considered a *sine qua non*, but no doubt intensified by my frustration with the St Antony's people for not understanding the importance of primary sources for historians. But, in addition, I knew from my Oxford reading of recent Lunacharsky publications that at least some Soviet scholars were now getting access to archival material going up to the early 1930s; that meant that conceivably I could get access too.

Later in my life as a scholar, when my archival successes became known and commented upon in the field, I used to say that, coming from Britain with a literary scholar as a supervisor, I was too naïve to know that I would never get Soviet archives on the post-1917 period, and that's why I brought it off. This was a useful defence against the implied suggestion that I got into the archives through some kind of sinister pull ('Communist father' was the rumour in the US). Re-reading my letters and diaries, however, I have my doubts about this version: I don't come across as naïve, just very determined and with big ideas about what I was going to achieve as a Soviet historian. My stubborn, almost aggressive, insistence on archives contrasted oddly with my general shyness in Moscow. I was obsessed with them, according to my friend Tomiko (who, as a literary scholar, was more interested in texts), and behaved 'as if life without archives is impossible'—which, as I told my mother, was actually how I felt. Elaborating her favourite theme of my freedom from fear and embarrassment, Tomiko would construct great fantasies in which archivists were overcome by my 'impetuous demands'. Of course, those were my fantasies too.

The process started when Ovcharenko signed my Plan—with State, Party and Literary Archives all included in it—and Lilia Pavlovna from Inotdel sent off applications on my behalf to each of the archives. That was in late November, at which point I was still mentally focused primarily on the Central Party Archives, where Lunacharsky's personal papers were. As I wrote to my mother, 'they don't like having foreigners work in the Party archives and they may easily refuse. But then my Plan *has* been accepted'. While Lilia Pavlovna was always doubtful that the Party Archives would let me in, Ovcharenko was much more upbeat: there was a precedent, he said, for a British exchange student to get into the Party archives, so there was hope for me. That student, who had also had Ovcharenko as a supervisor, was a literary scholar working on Lunacharsky's plays, some of the manuscripts of which were in the Party Archives, so in a sense his case was stronger than mine.

After relations with Ovcharenko soured, I questioned whether he had ever genuinely supported me as far as the Party Archives were concerned. There's something a little fishy about his gratuitous comment (recorded in my diary early in December) that he wasn't sure about Lilia Pavlovna's commitment to getting me in, as if he were preparing to make her the villain if permission were refused; and, for what it's worth, this warning note was sounded in the conversation that turned chilly when I asked about meeting Igor. Looking back, after decades of experience with graduate students and Soviet archives, it strikes me that if Ovcharenko really wanted to maximise my archival chances, he might have formulated my topic differently, something like 'Lunacharsky as People's Commissar and Party Figure', so that the Party Archive people couldn't say that all the relevant material was in the State Archives. On the other hand, Ovcharenko had presumably supported his earlier British student's access, and he spoke of his success with satisfaction. I found it strange, back then, that a non-liberal like Ovcharenko should want to broaden access to information, but now I think that was a fundamental misconception, based on taking ideology too seriously. Liberal or not, it was a coup to get your foreign student into Party Archives, a feather in your cap as far as colleagues were concerned (*See how important and well-connected I am, bet you couldn't have brought it off ...*)

Getting permission to do anything was a big problem in the Soviet Union, involving endless visits to bureaucrats who demanded ever more documents and didn't care how much time you both had to waste. Petty officials were prone to make you wait for hours outside their little windows and then, when you finally got to the front of the queue, slam them down triumphantly in your face (*Closed for lunch! Closed for the day! Closed for repairs! Closed forever!*). More senior personnel simply instructed their secretaries to stonewall and disappeared. Archival permissions were the worst of all, except perhaps for permission to marry (which, being married already, I never attempted). Archives were under the jurisdiction of the Central State Archive Administration, until recently part of the state security apparatus; in the 1960s, the archival directors and senior archivists still had the security mindset by which the contents of archives were state secrets, and foreigners who wanted to see them were probably out to discredit the Soviet Union. The Party Archives had never been under the security police, but they were in the jurisdiction of the Central Committee of the Soviet Communist Party, which was no better. In fact for non-Communist foreigners it was worse, because the Party Archives people could always say that only Communists could work in Communist archives—an infuriating position, given that in the Soviet context the Party was not some kind of special-interest body like a church or private foundation that might reasonably want to keep non-members out of its files, but the country's ruling institution. That's not to say that there couldn't be exceptions about the Communists-only rule: there were exceptions everywhere in Soviet life, since it ran on such personalistic lines, with patrons like Ovcharenko always trying to get the rules bent for their clients. As with literary censorship, the degree of restriction changed almost with the weather, and the trick was to grab the right moment—the proper conjunction of forces (*kon"iunktura*), in SovietSpeak—to enable the string you were pulling to work.

My permission from the State Archives came through just before the New Year break, as I remember, although I was so focused on the Party Archives that this is glossed over in my diary and letters. Ovcharenko was still optimistic about the Party Archives when I spoke to him on the telephone shortly after the New Year break. But then something went wrong. On 23 January, Lilia Pavlovna told me that the Party Archives had refused permission for me to work there. She said she had had the sense of a 'change in attitude from positive to negative' in the stratosphere above occurring sometime earlier in the month, but I'm not sure that I believe that, as she had never mentioned this positive attitude before, always expressing doubt that I would get in. Lilia Pavlovna showed me the letter, signed by the deputy head of the Institute of Marxism-Leninism where the Party Archives were housed. It said that the archival base for my topic was the State Archives—in a way, unarguable, given my project title, 'Lunacharsky as People's Commissar'—and that I didn't need material from the Party Archives. The refusal was so definite, Lilia Pavlovna said, that she had no possible grounds for appealing the decision, though Ovcharenko might do so, if he were so inclined, when the archive director returned from a trip to Czechoslovakia (a nice touch of legitimacy-conferring specificity, though very likely untrue, as such touches often were).

I didn't fight Lilia Pavlovna about the refusal. Nor, I think, did I go immediately to Ovcharenko. Instead, I decided to go round to the Party Archives in person and argue my case. This might sound straightforward, but in the Soviet context it was a bold move: foreigners were not supposed to know the address of the Central Party Archives, unless they had been given specific permission to work there, and there were of course no telephone books to look it up in. I knew the address because of my intensive study of guide-books to Moscow and its architectural monuments, one of which identified a historic building on Soviet Square as 'now the seat of the Institute of Marxism-Leninism' where the Central Party Archives resided, and because it was just around the corner from Irina's apartment. In any case, I turned up on the doorstep and brazenly asked to speak to the director about my application to do research in the archives. Being caught off balance, they fetched him, or at least a deputy, which was already a success. My memory is that I spoke to him in terms of my rights and the contractual obligations of the Soviet Union to Britain under the exchange agreement. In the story of the incident I often told later, this was further sign of my naïvety and lack of understanding of how the Soviet system worked, which was certainly not by strict observance of law. I think, however, I already understood that; it was a question of finding some sort of justification, however weak, for my request. What I probably hadn't yet fully grasped was the importance of personal connections, otherwise I might have tried to get Irina to look in her address book to find someone who knew someone who was a friend of the director, who could call him on my behalf and prepare the ground. Still, my strategy could have worked—earnest young women can be disarming, and occasional breaking of rules is one of the pleasurable exercises of bureaucratic power—but, as it happened, it didn't. He told me politely that what he had in his archive were Party documents, and unfortunately I was not a member of the Party. I thanked him for his time and departed unchastened by the refusal, which I evidently expected, and in fact rather pleased with my adventure. Probably I had some analogy with the British Council at the back of my mind: I had pestered them for more than a year to get on the Soviet exchange, and then, when the right conjuncture appeared, they let me in, and were even glad to do it.

I could afford to take the longer view about the Party Archives—which, after all, did let me in twenty years later, though it took the imminent collapse of the Soviet Union to do it—because the State Archives were panning out so well. I started work there in the middle of January, and by the end of the month I was writing to my mother that these archives had turned out to be 'the best of all' because I had a window into the workings of government—and on top of that, I was seeing documents I couldn't get in Britain because of the fifty-year rule. The State Archives were not as centrally located as the Party ones, requiring a longish walk from the Metro coming from the university or going on to the Lenin Library, though in compensation there was a good bus for getting to Igor's. The archives building was a big, grey Stalinist elephant squatting on the road to the Novodevichy cemetery. Actually it was a whole complex of buildings of varying ages and architectural styles, but I didn't find that out until much later because we weren't allowed to roam around. There was a special reading room for foreigners, most of them from fraternal (socialist bloc) countries, not capitalists like me. The entrance was round the corner from the main entrance, used by Soviet citizens and giving access to the general reading room and main cloakroom, so we were effectively cut off from them. The only Soviet citizens we saw were archivists and the attendants at our special foreigners' coatroom, fragile elderly men and women scarcely capable of lifting our briefcases and heavy coats over the counter. They were said by the fraternal foreigners who shared our reading room to be returnees from Gulag.

We weren't allowed to go to the archives snack bar or cafeteria because that would have meant wandering unsupervised around the building; in consequence, the generally kind-hearted women who sat guard over our reading room had to make tea for us and allowed us to eat sandwiches at our desks, dropping crumbs on the state secrets. Some of the Americans (all working on the Imperial period, so not in my state of pioneering excitement) left at lunchtime to get a bus to the embassy for lunch, but even had I been an American with an embassy snack bar at hand I would never have considered this. Getting into the archives was such a momentous thing that I couldn't miss a moment of it: I was there from the opening to the closing every day, barely interrupting my labours for one trip per day (at first with escort, later without) to the downstairs women's lavatory. The archivists, despite working for an institution not long out of direct subordination to state security, were trained historians, mainly women, some of them young and quite well disposed, within the limits of the permissible, to foreigners. The women on duty in our reading room were just watchdogs, I think, without special historical training. It was a boring job, all the more in that, unlike the Soviet citizens you saw on the Metro, they didn't seem to read. The one I remember best used to spend hours rubbing cream into her hands from a little tin, probably not a Soviet product. If I had been a bit more savvy about Soviet life, I would have gone and bought her some more from the foreign-currency stores—which was probably just what some of our fraternal foreigners in the reading room had done.

The young professional archivist assigned to us—mine was Natalia Dmitrievna—were meant to bring us material relevant to our themes, sticking strictly to the exact formulation of topic and dates we had given in our applications. The trouble was, we didn't know what kinds of materials the archives held, as we were forbidden to see archival inventories (*opisi*) or catalogues. We couldn't order files by number, either, if we happened to have found a citation in the footnote of some scholarly monograph or dissertation; that would have raised the possibility of collusion with Soviet researchers, stuck well out of our reach in their own reading room, with entrance from a different street. The convention in the foreigners' reading room was that no Soviet scholars, with the possible exception of our supervisors, existed or were known to us.

If you didn't have inventories or catalogues, you really had to know something about the structure of your chosen archive to make an intelligent request. The State Archive contained the files of the central government institutions, so what you needed to know before starting work was how the Soviet central state bureaucracy was structured and what kind of paper it generated. Child of a freelance historian and teacher, I knew absolutely nothing about bureaucracy; I had never worked for one, and the only ones I had ever dealt with were the Commonwealth Scholarships and the British Council (with a brief foray into the Commonwealth and Foreign Offices when I was trying to get on the British exchange in 1965). I had no conception of ministries (called People's Commissariats in the Soviet Union before the war, to sound revolutionary), what they did, or how they did it. Ovcharenko had given me no clues, perhaps because as a literary scholar he didn't know much about Narkompros's bureaucratic structure and functioning either; he had talked to me about its high politics, but anything about high politics was on the banned list in Soviet archival terms. No Western historian had worked on any Soviet People's Commissariat, still less on its archives, and as Ovcharenko had remarked, there weren't many Soviet studies of this kind either.

When Natalia Dmitrievna came down and asked what materials I wanted, I had a sinking feeling; my mind was empty of inspiration about what to ask for. I think I mumbled something about minutes, but I didn't know minutes of what. Perhaps the Narkompros executive council (collegium), headed by the People's Commissar? This suggestion must have come from Natalia Dmitrievna, as I had never heard of the collegium (though had I been better educated in Russian history, I would have recognised it as a venerable Russian institution dating back to Peter the Great's time). But there were no minutes preserved from the collegium. The word 'protocols' surfaced, again surely from Natalia Dmitrievna. Yes, protocols were definitely what I was after. Protocols of the collegium, I said firmly. They brought me the protocols for 1918, and I saw that the stars had aligned themselves on my side. Protocols were '*exactly* what I want', I wrote to my mother on 18 January.

After a while, I learned a few more tricks. You got a richer haul if you asked not just for 'protocols' (agendas, with rapporteurs on the various items and resolutions and lists of those present) but 'protocols with materials', the materials usually being draft resolutions sent up from subsections of the Commissariat with supporting data. I mastered my Commissariat's organisational structure, with the help of some extraordinarily dry Soviet monographs on the subject, which were freely available in the Lenin Library. Ordering in the archives was always a guessing game. Everything connected with the Communist Party, the security organs and the military was off-limits, so you weren't going to get a file headed 'Correspondence of Narkompros and the Party Central Committee'. However, if you asked for 'Correspondence of Narkompros with other institutions', you just might get lucky. I learned where you might find real statistical data, and I also learned to avoid the vast array of pseudo-statistics that came under the heading of 'socialist competition'. I became a diligent hunter out of special-purpose meetings because minutes were often taken of them instead of just protocols, and the minutes included discussion, where speakers were likely to go off message and start pursuing their own agendas. All my strategies were designed to enable me to find out what conflicts and disagreements had preceded the final decisions and what lay behind the bland generalisations of formal resolutions. In other words, any suspicious archives director who thought I was trying to find out the secrets of Narkompros was dead right.

The requirement that you were only allowed archival files on the topic formally registered, interpreted in the narrowest and most literal way, was particularly vexatious. What happens when you do research is that you keep finding new avenues to explore and your understanding of what your topic is keeps changing. In the Soviet Union, your topic was unchangeable, and new avenues, if they meant searching in different institutions from the one you were pledged to, were ruled out. If Narkompros started fighting the People's Commissariat of Health over school lunches—the kind of thing that happened all the time—you could read Narkompros's version of the story but not that of the people over in Health. If Lunacharsky, as People's Commissar, had a run-in with Narkompros's political education department, I couldn't get files from the political education department because Lunacharsky wasn't a member of it; still less could I follow the archival trail when the political education people ran off to the Party Central Committee for support. If Lunacharsky went to a plenary meeting of the Party Central Committee, I couldn't read the text of his speech or the discussion of it. The same was true if he reported to the highest government body, the Council of People's Commissars—that wasn't 'on my topic'.

But I learned to work within these restrictions. I became very good at picking up clues to disagreements on policy and reading the silences when someone was falling into disgrace. I had Igor and the former Narkompros staffers to fill in some of the gaps. I discovered that Narkompros and various of its departments had published regular bulletins and newsletters of the kind that would normally be preserved only in archives, but were in fact held by the Lenin Library and even included in its public catalogue. There was, of course, a mass of classified material in the State Archives—even larger than I supposed—that by definition was withheld from me in Soviet times, though it became accessible after the collapse of the Soviet Union. As it turned out, I had found out most of Narkompros's secrets without them.

All this talk of difficulties, in any case, should not obscure the fact that the Narkompros archive was a goldmine. I was lucky, in hindsight, that the Party Archives didn't let me in. They would have kept me in a Party-centred world, thus encouraging me to see the Soviet political process the same way everyone else did, Western and Soviet. The conventional wisdom was that everything was decided in the Party Politburo (the executive body of the Central Committee) and nothing happened anywhere else. It was true, of course, that the Politburo's word was law—when a matter came before it, and to the degree that the executive branch subsequently did what the Politburo's law instructed. But all sorts of things happened in other places, particularly in the 1920s, before the question of Party–state balance was definitively decided in the Party's favour. You couldn't find out much about that in the Politburo archives because it was done out of sight of the Politburo. Where you found out about it was in the archives of the government bureaucracy. Any part of the bureaucracy would have served the purpose, but for me, it was Narkompros.

Western Sovietologists believed that the Soviet system of government was monolithic, which put them right in line with Soviet orthodoxy, except that the Soviets thought being monolithic was good and the Sovietologists thought it was bad. But one of the first things that struck me, down in the trenches of Narkompros, was that things weren't monolithic at all. Every policy decision was preceded by fights, with the demarcation lines sometimes being political–ideological grounds but more often institutional. For example, the industrial authorities might support a change in technical education policy which Narkompros opposed; the Central Committee of the Young Communists might throw its vocal and militant support to industry while the Council of People's Commissars weakly backed up Narkompros. (This was, in fact, the issue on which Lunacharsky finally resigned as People's Commissar in 1929, and the details were visible in the Narkompros archives as well as etched in Igor's memory.) Some days, I felt completely carried away by the sense that I now understood how the Soviet system worked AND NOBODY ELSE DID because they had never seen a Soviet state archive.

The nice thing about working on the very first years of the Soviet government was that my surprise about the existence of all these bureaucratic conflicts was matched by the surprise of the protagonists—innocents in office, at first, radical intellectuals who knew as little about the workings of bureaucracy as I did, whose study of Marx had given them some understanding of economic interest but none of institutional. It was a shock to members of the first Soviet government when they found that being socialists, bound by Party discipline, did not automatically produce consensus once they were put in charge of a particular sector—industry, education, the army—and started to see the world through its eyes. Most of the leaders adapted in practice without changing their theoretical view of government, but Lunacharsky had an enquiring mind and was bothered by the fact that Narkompros, under his leadership, seemed so often to disagree with the Party Central Committee. He wrote an article, hidden away in a very obscure publication, about how conflict based on institutional interest, though not recognised in the classic Marxist analysis, was probably inevitable and not necessarily a bad thing.

Apart from this maverick essay of Lunacharsky's (which seems to have passed unnoticed at the time and by later scholars), orthodox Soviet analyses ignored institutional interest as having no place in the monolithic Soviet system of government. The only word available to describe it (*vedomstvennost'*, the tendency of a state institution to see only its only interest and not the larger good) carried a strong negative loading. American social scientists had a concept of institutional interest in democratic contexts, but rejected its applicability in the Soviet context because they too defined the Soviet system as monolithic. I was very pleased by my discovery that, whatever was happening at the very top, the second level of Soviet politics was driven by conflicts based on bureaucratic interest.

Over time, I developed a further hypothesis: that scholars tend to absorb the bureaucratic perspective of the institutions they work on. This was borne when, a few years later, I ran into an English scholar (Bob Davies from Birmingham), whose Moscow archival topic was industrial development in the late 1920s. Bob had researched the conflict over technical education that led to Lunacharsky's resignation from the industrial archives; I had researched it from those of Narkompros (I did ask for the industrial files, but they were refused, as being not on my topic). The interesting thing was that to Bob it seemed obvious that industry had the stronger case, whereas I had been taking it for granted that Narkompros was in the right.

This led me to fantasise about how the Soviets, who were generally quite inept at influencing Western scholarly opinion, could improve their performance. What they should do was give Western historians access to the most taboo of all Soviet archives, those of the security organs, but to no others, so that the scholars would automatically absorb the perspective of the institution and incorporate it in their work. Institutional archives are full of self-justification and tend to show the institution in the best possible light. Thus the archives of the Stalinist NKVD would surely show the security police as battling for the general good against the laziness and stupidity of other institutions: Narkompros, for example, which kept trying to put adolescent delinquents in its own inferior reform schools instead of those of the NKVD; industrial enterprises, which brazenly failed to pay proper wages to the NKVD's convict labourers; provincial and republican authorities, which omitted to provide food and housing for deportees the NKVD had settled in their regions; district soviets, which failed to set up kindergartens in the native language for children of ethnic deportees (Narkompros would be blamed for this, too); the cadres department of the Party Central Committee, which persisted in reassigning any Gulag officers who showed signs of competence and sending the Gulag administration nothing but duds ... (My theory about the gullibility of scholars working from one archive was never tested, but when the Gulag archive finally opened to Western scholars in the 1990s, this was exactly the kind of thing that was in it.)

I was working extraordinarily hard the first two months of 1967, dividing my day in a complicated manner between archives and libraries, which were open in the evening when the archives were closed. My routines were mainly determined by intellectual need, but I have to admit that considerations about eating also played a part. There was no food in the archives, except what you brought with you, and the food in the Lenin Library stand-up cafeteria was unspeakable. But if you picked the right route between the two, you might be able to buy a bun or some chocolates to keep you going. (Soviet chocolate was my staple in the first year in the Soviet Union; later I used to smuggle Western muesli bars into the library.) The Lenin Library was a deeply hierarchical institution in which the First Hall, reserved for academicians, full professors, and exchange students from capitalist countries, had its own cloakroom and was much less crowded than the others. It had a wooden floor, almost free of polish because of repeated mopping, on which were arranged, like clumsy ships at berth, two-sided desks—quite spacious if there was only one person sitting on either side, but often occupied by two, an elderly professor and his younger female research assistant, who would keep up a soft but constant and annoying stream of conversation. It was warm, except for the couple of times a day when, regardless of the outside temperature, all the windows were thrown open for fifteen minutes' ventilation and everyone froze.

The First Hall was two floors up from the basement lavatories, but the stink wafted up the staircase, along with smoke from the cigarettes in the smoking room outside the lavatories. The story of the Soviet absence of toilet paper has been told so often that it need not be repeated. The usual library substitute was order slips, but being on good-quality, almost glossy, paper with dimensions of about two inches by three inches, they were not ideal for the purpose.

There was cold water in the bathroom to wash your hands in, but almost invariably no soap. In the halls, readers sat and worked in their fur-lined boots but without overcoats, which were compulsorily left in the downstairs cloakroom. You also had to leave briefcases and bags downstairs—but if the bags were too heavy (full of books, for example), they were likely to be rejected. The lines for the regular cloakrooms were very long, which made the First Hall privilege of a separate line very useful. But even for First Hall clients, the attendants could be stroppy, coming back with the familiar 'I too am a human being' response if asked to do anything beyond the bare minimum.

The Lenin Library card catalogue had many defects. You would not find anything in it if you looked under Trotsky, Lev Davidovich, or Bukharin, Nikolay Ivanovich, though both were prodigious publishers in their day. Lunacharsky, Anatoly Vasilevich, was much better: you could find all sorts of interesting minor publications from the 1920s there, although some of his heretical pre-revolutionary works were probably absent in the 'special collection' (off-limits for foreigners and most ordinary readers). But there were wonderful things in the Lenin Library catalogue, and you could often find them by looking not under author or title but under institution. I used to spend a lot of time in the library simply going through the catalogue under the big entries like 'Communist Party of the Soviet Union' and 'State Statistical Administration', with their dozens of subheadings. The Lenin Library was a deposit library, so all the many journals of the 1920s were there, enabling me to track down small articles by Lunacharsky (or Igor!) that didn't make it into the collected works.

It wasn't all plain sailing. You weren't always given the books and periodicals you ordered, though they usually came if you tried again. Books from the 1920s containing forbidden names such as Trotsky or Bukharin were likely to have had the names inked out (the Lenin Library did it in purple) or, in some cases, inked out and then painstakingly restored in a librarian's hand. Presumably the restoration was a product of the Thaw. Generally you could still read the names anyway, but it gave a nice frisson of the forbidden. Finally, though this didn't really bother me until I moved into social history, there was the infuriating matter of local newspapers. The Lenin Library had a fine collection of regional and republican newspapers, but they kept them up in the northern suburb of Khimki, notable for being the furthest point of advance for the German Army in October 1941, hence presumably the place Elena Borisovna's spy had come from. Lenin Library readers had to go up to Khimki to read the newspapers, but the problem was that Khimki, though only a short bus ride from the last Metro stop, was closed to foreigners. The Soviet Union was even more skilled at generating these catch-22 situations than Joseph Heller's US Army. Some years the library would bring down small numbers of regional newspapers if a foreigner ordered them, some years not; the tug of war went on inconclusively for decades.

The advantage of a Soviet-type system where access to information is routinely made difficult is the ecstatic moments of discovery. One of my familiar routes took me from the State Archives to the Fundamental Library of the Social Sciences, a modern building with an upscale clientele and a good snack bar. You might almost have thought you were in the West there but for the usual smelly lavatories, located centrally, by some extraordinary architectural misjudgement, at the top of the handsome stairs leading to the reading room. This library had inherited the collection of the old Communist Academy of the 1920s, an elite institution set up to compete with the (non-Communist) Academy of Sciences, of which a number of Party leaders were members. Trawling through the catalogue under the heading 'Communist Party of the Soviet Union, Congresses', I came across something called 'Material' relating to a Party Congress in 1930. When I ordered it, it turned out to be a numbered copy of a document marked 'Top Secret. For Congress delegates only' containing a transcript of police interrogations of engineers and industrial administrators conducted in preparation for a show trial. If this document had been in an archive, as it should have been, I would never have got it because it was classified. I copied out the whole thing word for word by hand.

Telephone directories were an interest of mine because they were so hard to get in the Soviet Union. Before the war, Moscow telephone directories had existed and been available to the population in the normal way, although even then they had been on the prohibited list for export, so are not to be found in Western libraries. I tracked them down in the Lenin Library catalogue through the institutional entry (I think it was 'Moscow. Moscow Telephone Network') and, sometime in the 1970s, ordered a run of them for the prewar period. I had various minor research aims like checking addresses for my biographical files, but my main purpose was exactly the kind of purpose that foreign historian-spies were supposed to have: I wanted to find out a state secret, namely to calculate the impact of the Great Purges on two subsets of the Soviet population: Moscow telephone subscribers and top industrial managers.

The dimensions and comparative impact of the Great Purges were matters of great interest and controversy in the West, but little hard data was available, since statistics relating in any way to the Great Purges were strictly guarded. The idea of using telephone directories had come to me when I made another serendipitous find in the Lenin Library catalogue, an in-house telephone directory of officials at the People's Commissariat of Heavy Industry for 1937. That was another document that I had painstakingly copied out by hand—before ordering the telephone books, as I did not want to order them all together for fear of arousing the librarians' suspicions. Having received the telephone books for 1937 and 1939, I set about tracing the retention rate for my top officials and comparing it with a random sample of subscribers. But '1937' always rang alarm bells in the Soviet Union, and I noticed one of the librarians drifting past behind me as I worked, evidently trying to see what I was doing with my telephone books. They left me to it that year, but when I came back the next year and ordered the telephone directories again, the order was refused. That went on for a decade or so, since I didn't give up and kept ordering every time I was in Moscow, only to be told by the librarians that the telephone directories for the 1930s were lost, in use with another reader, too fragile to read, or had simply never existed. But I wore them down, or perhaps it was just the system collapsing. Finally, in the late 1980s, I got the telephone directories back.

The Literary Archives at first refused my application to work there, probably on the same ground as the Party Archives—that the source material for 'Lunacharsky as People's Commissar' was in the State Archives. The Literary Archive had two separate Lunacharsky collections. One had been deposited by Lunacharsky's first wife, Anna Alexandrovna, and was closed to scholars without permission from that family. If I had remained in Ovcharenko's good graces and made the deal with him, perhaps I could have had access to this. The second Lunacharsky collection had been deposited by Irina, who had similar rights to give or deny access. When my refusal came from the Literary Archives, a friendly woman from the State Archives rang up to appeal on my behalf, but Irina was the real key to reversing the decision. Once she told them I had her permission to work on the materials she had given them, they let me in.

The Literary Archives were miles away, 'in the mud near the reservoir' as I described it to my mother, not just a long Metro ride but also a long hike from Metro station to archive. They let me read a few microfilms (not from Irina's materials, so they had evidently forgotten or decided to overlook the basis for admitting me). After finishing off the microfilms, I went off to negotiate for more in a spirit of duty rather than enthusiasm: microfilming was a new technique in the Soviet Union, and they were so mean with the film that the first and last pages of text, being about half an inch from ends of the reel, were impossible to read without taking them off the machine and holding them up to the light. The files that had been deposited by Irina were not microfilmed, thank God, but they were still in the process of being catalogued. I managed to find the woman who was working on them, someone I had met at Irina's, and she agreed to let me read them. 'In these archives', I wrote to my mother, 'Irina Anatolevna's name carries weight, and they treat me kindly because I am associated with her'.

It's odd to think of this kind of privatisation of access in the supposedly totalitarian Soviet Union, but actually it was extremely characteristic of the system in practice—the Russian system, no doubt, rather than specifically the Soviet, as remnants of it remain to this day: just a few years ago the family of Stalinist henchman Anastas Mikoyan was still restricting access to the unedited manuscript of his memoirs in the former Party Archives (now the Russian State Archive of Socio-Political History). As I later discovered when archival access broadened in the late 1980s, privatisation of a kind extended even to scholarly users. When I asked the State Archives for the files of a peasant newspaper from the 1930s, I was told that they had been moved to a distant room in the archives to be worked on by the team of Professor Viktor Danilov, and would not be available to others for the foreseeable future without his permission (fortunately, I knew him, and he gave me permission). As far as I could work out, the archives were all honeycombed with complicated 'special privilege' arrangements like these—but of course, in the old days, we knew nothing of this. If Professor Danilov or whoever had commandeered a particular set of files you needed, you might be told that they were 'being used by another researcher' (an answer we tended to disbelieve), but the standard answers of 'lost' or 'non-existent' were equally likely.

Irina had contacts with the Party Archives as well as the Literary ones, and from Irina's standpoint, the Party Archives were the sexiest source for Lunacharsky studies: this was where various Soviet *lunacharskovedy* were finding documentation of high-political secrets (like Lunacharsky's clashes with Molotov in his last years at Narkompros) and doing their best to publish them. It wasn't always easy, because in addition to the regular pre-publication censorship mechanisms, the archives themselves might refuse permission to cite their materials—which sometimes led to the absurd situation that a scholarly article would make a disclosure, which was actually based on archival research but appeared without any citation of source. Irina was generally in favour of publication of secrets, as long as they didn't reflect badly on Lunacharsky. If anyone had published the Party's Central Control Commission's file on Lunacharsky (which I read in the Party Archives in the 1990s) containing an array of denunciations of Lunacharsky and his wife, for various peccadillos, she would surely have considered it an unfriendly act and called it pure 'sensationalism'.

Irina had had business dealings with both the Party and the Literary Archives. This startled me when she first mentioned it, as the atmosphere of high mystery surrounding the archives didn't seem to go with mundane issues of acquisition, still less with transactions involving money. Irina's story of the papers started with Lunacharsky's death in December 1933, when the NKVD swooped into the apartment—the one Irina and her mother were still living in—and took all the papers they could find. This was evidently standard practice of the period as far as important Party figures were concerned rather than a reflection of the fact that, at the time of his death, Lunacharsky was in political disfavour. The material seems to have ended up with other personal papers of Lunacharsky's in the Party Archives, though I'm not sure when the security organs handed it over. But some papers were saved because they were in a secret drawer that Irina knew about from sitting reading in her father's study as a child (I think her mother, Natalia Alexandrovna, played a role in saving the papers in the version Irina originally told me, but by the time she came to write about it twenty years later, it was all Irina). In any case, Irina became the custodian of the papers after her mother died in 1965. She made it known to the Party and Literary Archives that the family was willing to part with some of the Lunacharsky papers it had retained, and a bidding war ensued, at the end of which part of the collection went to the Party Archives and part to the Literary Archives, and the family was richer by an amount unknown to me.

Even then, Irina didn't give up all the Lunacharsky papers in her possession. In the last years of his life, Lunacharsky had kept a diary, the one coveted by Ovcharenko, which remained in Irina's flat and was never let out of her hands. She also kept letters from Lunacharsky to his wife, sent when he was travelling in Europe. Irina said these materials were not suitable for the archives because of some deeply personal material (mainly sexual, I gathered), but there was also political stuff, including some surprising reflections on Stalin as, in the late 1920s, an acceptable leader who was not necessarily a foe of high culture (despite his short-lived sponsorship of the Cultural Revolution) and, it generally seemed to Lunacharsky, an improvement on his competitors for Party leadership. Irina told me about these entries, and even waved what may have been the relevant pages around a few feet from my face, but would never let me read them or take notes; and she must have followed the same pattern with other *lunacharskovedy*, as this story never got into print. Evidently she judged the time not ripe for these revelations—or perhaps she worried about the possible impact of a relatively positive assessment of Stalin on Lunacharsky's 'liberal' reputation in the Soviet Union.

There is a postscript to this story, rather painful to remember. As the Soviet Union collapsed at the beginning of the 1990s, Irina started thinking about the future, and how she could use her (diminished) assets in the new post-Soviet situation. The Lunacharsky diaries and letters to his wife were among these assets. It was essential, she decided, to publish the 'real story' of Lunacharsky's last years in the West, and I was to be the conduit. I tried to explain tactfully that the subject had less resonance in the West than in the old Soviet Union, that Western commercial publishers were ruled by the market and might not think they could sell books on Lunacharsky to a broad audience, that the end of the Cold War had made Soviet topics less attractive, and so on, but to no avail. Irina just didn't want to hear or accept that people in the West were not clamouring to hear the truth about Lunacharsky.

Academic publishers for Irina's work were a possibility, but there was the problem of style of presentation: in the first post-Soviet years, scarcely any of the professional Soviet historians could write articles that were publishable in the West, let alone a non-professional like Irina, used to writing in the now defunct genre of Soviet popular journalism. Irina had never been inclined to listen to objections, and in this period she was almost hysterical in her desire to take immediate purposeful action to establish a beachhead for herself and Lunacharsky in the new post-Soviet world. This was scarcely surprising, given that the whole structure that made his life's work meaningful, and by extension hers, had crumbled, but it was hard to handle.

I agreed to take one of Irina's articles and look for an outlet, though my heart sank at the prospect of peer review, a completely alien concept to Irina, whose Soviet experience led her to think that if a senior scholar with clout wanted something published, that's what would happen unless the censor intervened. The article was about Lunacharsky's resignation as People's Commissar, and it argued both that Lunacharsky and Stalin were not enemies and that Lunacharsky's resignation showed him to have been the sole honourable man in the Soviet leadership. I took it to the editors of the American Slavic journal *Russian Review*, which, to my great relief, somehow worked it into shape and got it through peer review. But the piece took ages to translate and edit, and by the time it came out in 1992, Irina was dead. It remains the only scholarly article drawing on Lunacharsky's diaries and letters to Natalia Alexandrovna, because Irina was the only person with access to those sources. They are now in the hands of her son, Andrey, still inaccessible to scholars.

My sense of myself as a historian-spy who had hit pay dirt may have somehow communicated itself to the KGB by the spring of 1967. Or else they got more suspicious of me because of the connection with Igor or an unfavourable report from Ovcharenko; or possibly, since individual exchange students seemed to come under KGB attention for short bursts at different times, it was simply my turn to be spied on. Up to that time, Valery and Misha had been the only signs of KGB interest in me. But something odd happened early in March. I was buying a snack at the basement cafeteria at the university when the saleswoman stepped back and said, with an uncharacteristically friendly smile, 'Let your boyfriend take your picture', indicating a man, unknown to me, who was indeed taking a photograph from the shadows and looking very annoyed at being made visible. Why such a photo should be useful is hard to imagine, as I was alone, innocently getting myself something to eat, and had moreover supplied ten passport-size photos on my first day in the Soviet Union, and probably another dozen to various institutions since.

One Sunday not long after that, I went for lunch to a restaurant with Andrzej, one of the fraternal foreigners from the State Archives reading room. Andrzej was a sophisticated Pole, a specialist on the seventeenth century, who never ceased to be amazed that anyone would be so perverse as to try and do honest historical work on the Soviet period. Once married to a Russian, he had an excellent sense of Soviet society and a varied set of contacts, helped, he told me, by his skill at training dogs (dog ownership was a recent Moscow fashion, but the new Russian owners didn't know how to look after their dogs or make them obey). Our restaurant excursion was outside my normal repertoire, though possibly not Andrzej's. In the Soviet context, restaurants were just for special occasions, and involved a lot of drinking as well as eating. The Leningrad KGB's cases of foreign-student misbehaviour often included frequenting restaurants and getting drunk instead of working. Andrzej and I did the proper restaurant thing and drank a lot. Emerging together into the street at about 4 p.m., we were heading for the Metro when Andrzej said we were being followed. I had to take his word for it, being unused to noticing 'tails', as well as short-sighted and rather tipsy. It must be you that brought this on us, I said, to which Andrzej sharply replied that of course it was not him, a harmless fraternal foreigner they were following, but me, a capitalist. I went back to the dorm, lay down to rest for a few minutes, and went to sleep.

I was abruptly woken up about 5.30 p.m. by my neighbour Galya knocking on the door, speaking with uncharacteristic excitement. There was a scholar from East Germany who wanted to see me, she said; he had rung up earlier in the afternoon (using the number of the collective telephone on the floor, on which I rarely got calls) and she had taken the message (if true, something she had never done before). It was very urgent that he make contact with me immediately, as he had rare Lunacharsky material. You must ring him back, ring him back now, she urged. I was still muzzy—who was this man? I had never heard the name (Horst Bott) and didn't want to ring him, but it seemed to be the only way to shut her up. I found a two-kopek coin and went and rang the number. The man answered and, with an insistence equal to Galya's, said he lived quite close by, I must come over immediately to see his wonderful Lunacharsky documents. I think he said Ovcharenko had put him in touch with me. Going out again was the last thing I felt like on that cold evening, but with my strong sense of obligation to follow up each and every lead on Lunacharsky, I unwillingly agreed.

Horst Bott was a personable man in his twenties, living apparently alone in a two-room apartment. I noticed, as I took off coat, hat, scarf and boots (the standard way of entering a Soviet apartment in winter) and was ushered into his main room, that the door to the other room was closed. I had scarcely sat down on the couch and formulated my first question about the Lunacharsky material when Horst sat down next to me, too close, and said he had a lovely bathroom with an actual bath (MGU had only showers); wouldn't I like to have a bath while I was here, to relax? No, I said, thanks all the same, but tell me about your Lunacharsky material and what your research topic is. I never did find out what his alleged research topic was, though he finally did produce a small card index with a few bibliographical entries on Lunacharsky in it, and suggested we should collaborate and share our research. I think, though at this point I cannot swear to it (and I didn't write about it to my mother, for security reasons), that he asked me about Igor and Irina. But his main objective, as became clear very quickly, was to get my clothes off and seduce me. Fighting down a feeling of panic, I calculated my chances of getting off the sofa (not easy, with him essentially holding me down under the guise of amorous advances), putting on hat, gloves, boots, scarf and overcoat, and getting myself out the door if he tried to restrain me, and decided they were about zero. I also developed a spooky conviction that there was someone else in the apartment behind that closed door, but not someone who would help me; my conviction, in fact, was that he was there to take photographs once Horst had got my clothes off.

Whether this was at all plausible, I can't say; it could just have been an elaboration of the stories I had heard about staged entrapments, where a foreign student had gone to bed with a Russian, only to have a photographer burst in, sometimes with a second person posing as an aggrieved spouse. Entrapments were most effective when the sexual encounter was homosexual, since that was a crime both in Britain and the Soviet Union at the time. But I had heard of them succeeding—or at least resulting in the embassy sending the student home—even with a heterosexual encounter, when the threat was to tell one's own spouse (I was, after all, married) or academic supervisor.

I did not try to fight off Horst because I thought it would be hopeless; instead, I resorted to cunning. Allowing him to kiss me, but resisting (in a maidenly rather than violent way) his efforts to go further, I said I liked him very much; it would be nice to get together with him, but not today; it just wasn't the right time ... I am a little appalled as I relate this, but it worked. Disentangling himself, he produced some chocolates and wine (I accepted the first but not the second), and after not too long allowed me to excuse myself on the pretext that I was tired. I said I would look forward to seeing him, perhaps next week, and departed in relatively good order but extremely rattled. He didn't escort me to the bus stop, which in Soviet terms was unusual, but said he would ring me in a few days. When I got home, Galya was hanging around waiting for me, her face one big question mark. I was so angry with her I couldn't bring myself to speak; she had set me up, an act of betrayal, and I didn't want anything more to do with her.

But what to do about Horst? I was really scared that he would pursue me and try again, and felt that with Galya as his accomplice I wasn't safe even in my room. After all, I hadn't confronted him and said I thought he was a spy; I had behaved as if I took him at face value. I wanted to make sure the KGB called him off, which I assumed would happen if they knew I had rumbled him, but I wasn't sure how to send the message. In retrospect, it occurs to me that Lilia Pavlovna might have been the person to go to, both because of her assumed KGB connections and her likely sympathy with a young woman subjected to sexual harassment. But at the time the only way I could think of to send a message was via the British Embassy, whose offices were all presumed to be bugged, even though that had the disadvantage that sometimes, when the embassy found out that a student had been compromised, they sent them home forthwith, and I wanted at all costs to avoid that. The trick was to tell the KGB bug that their agent had been detected while at the same time assuring the embassy that their student had not been compromised. So I went off to see the British cultural attaché, a sensible man well versed in Soviet lore, who also happened to be related by marriage to James Bond's creator, Ian Fleming. Speaking clearly and slowly, I told him that an East German spy had tried to entrap me but had been unsuccessful; there would, I trusted, be no follow-up, but I just wanted to put the embassy in the picture. 'Yes', he said, 'I understand.' (I was very relieved to see that he did in fact grasp the point of my visit.) 'We'll assume that that will be the end of the story.' This was said with an upward glance at the chandelier, which was where we always assumed the bugs were.

Naturally, I have dined out on the Horst story over the years, and its ending may have got a bit neater in the process than it actually was. The way I tell the story, my ploy with Ian Fleming's brother-in-law was a brilliant success and I never heard from Horst again, presumably because the KGB called him off immediately. Certainly, Horst didn't call me in the next few days after our meeting, as he had said he would, but as I search my memory a dim recollection emerges that he may have rung a couple of weeks later, sounding a lot more tentative than the first time, and I said I was too busy to see him. Regardless of whether I was as clever as I thought

I was in dealing with this entrapment attempt, I was quite lucky to come out of it unscathed. A British scientist on the Academy of Sciences exchange had been sent home the previous autumn after being discovered having an affair with a Russian woman, and in my time in Moscow several students on the British Council exchange were sent home after successful entrapments. As for Horst, who knows what became of him, but he didn't become a Lunacharsky scholar.

Around the time of the Horst incident, I struck a road block with the State Archives. Whether there was any connection between the two, I don't know. I had been working away on my Narkompros protocols, reading them year by year, but when I reached 1924, they stopped bringing them. 'There are no more protocols', Natalia Dmitrievna said firmly, ignoring my protests that there *must* be more. Technically, as I later discovered, she was right: when the Soviet Union was formed in 1924, Narkompros was downgraded to a Russian republican institution, putting its files under the jurisdiction of a different archive, the State Archive of the Russian Republic of the USSR, as opposed to the State Archive of the USSR, which I was working in. Had she told me that the later protocols were in a different archive, I might have accepted it, legalist that I was, since I was not formally cleared to work in the State Archive of the Russian Republic because I hadn't known about its existence. But she stuck to the time-honoured Soviet tradition of unelaborated denial, and I stuck to my passionate conviction of entitlement.

I tried to get Ovcharenko to intervene on my behalf, but he was 'very evasive', as I wrote to my mother. Obviously he didn't feel like helping me any more with the archives, although he didn't say so outright. I kept citing his support regardless in putting my case to the State Archives people until somebody (Natalia Dmitrievna?) told me in an embarrassed whisper that I was wrong about having my supervisor's support, he had in fact privately told them *not* to give me any more material. It wasn't actually out of the question to bring materials from the State Archive of the Russian Republic to the State Archive of the USSR, as far as I could gather; the republican archive had only recently been spun off from its USSR parent, and it wasn't clear to what extent it really operated independently. But the message Natalia Dmitrievna brought from above was that for me they weren't going to do it.

My first idea was to pay an unauthorised visit to the State Archives of the Russian Republic and see what happened. Andrzej gave me the address and directions and I turned up and got an unexpectedly warm reception. The archivist who came out to talk to me 'knew at once who I must be and became quite excited', as I wrote to my mother. (In fact, my arrival was such a notable event that it went round the Moscow archivist grapevine, including the fact that the girl on the British exchange who showed up unexpectedly was actually Australian; when it finally reached an acquaintance of mine, not an archivist herself but a friend of one, she asked me if the bit about being Australian was true, as she hadn't known it.) Friendliness aside, however, the answer was negative: I was told that they had no reading room for foreigners and access to their materials was a matter that would have to be decided by the State Archives of the USSR. So I had to think of something else.

I consulted Andrzej, who advised buying a bottle of cognac at the foreign-currency store and taking it as a present to the archive director. I didn't think I could do that: Australians don't even know how to tip, let alone bribe, and I had the feeling that the present-giving conventions might be different for women than for men. But Andrzej told me the director's name and patronymic and where his office was—this was the kind of thing fraternal foreigners were allowed to know, but not capitalists—and I decided to try my luck.

Fortunately, the director's office was located on the only corridor I could use without escort, on the way to the women's lavatory. I went in and said my piece with my usual earnestness. It didn't seem to go down well: he wasn't friendly like the woman at the Russian Archive but seemed annoyed to be bothered. He looked me over—a small 25-year-old whom all Russians instinctively classified as a mere girl, ill at ease with the language, lacking either feminine charm or masculine authority—and said flatly, 'No'. To my humiliation, I burst into tears. If I'd only known, that was exactly the right thing to do. 'Grown-ups don't cry', he said, lingering over the words with a smile of infinite condescension. Not yet aware that I had accidentally played the right card, I was ready to concede defeat and slink away when he picked up the telephone. 'Give it to her', he said in a bored voice.

Later I worked out that arbitrarily breaking rules can be even more fun for bureaucrats than routine refusal, but at the time I was simply confused and could scarcely muster the Russian to get myself politely out of his office. I was so ashamed of crying that it took me a while to understand that the outcome seemed to be successful, and even then my dominant mood was anxiety rather than exultation. 'They are giving me something', I wrote to my mother, 'but what remains to be seen. Tomorrow is the day when they promised to give me more material. I am very apprehensive in case it goes wrong'.

Two days later I was able to report a qualified success. I had asked for Narkompros collegium protocols from 1925 to 1929, when Lunacharsky resigned. They now told me that the protocols for 1925 to 1927 would be sent from the Russian State Archive, but that those for 1928 had been lost and those for 1929 were being microfilmed. The three mid-twenties years duly arrived, though unfortunately it turned out that protocol keeping became skimpier as Stalinism took hold, and there was much less in them than in the earlier years. By the middle of the month, I had almost worked my way through the 1925–27 protocols. 'It was a famous victory', I wrote to my mother 'even if there was only four or five days' work in them'.

I wasn't sure if I believed that the 1928 protocols had been lost. The year 1928 had been full of incident for Narkompros, with the onset of the Cultural Revolution among other things, and this could well have left traces that the archivists deemed unsuitable for my eyes. Archivists were prone to tell you that material they didn't want to give you had perished during wartime evacuation, drowned in a barge that sunk on the Volga, and who knows if it was true, but it could have been. But I let that be and focused on the 1929 protocols. My strategy was to suggest to the archivists that I was going to cause them so much trouble, in a nice way, if they didn't produce these that they might as well give in. To save everyone trouble, I told Natalia Dmitrievna, it might be best if I simply ordered a copy of the microfilm, paid for it, and had it sent to me in Oxford when it was ready. This flummoxed poor Natalia Dmitrievna, as I clearly wasn't meant to be allowed to buy a copy of the microfilm, but she wasn't meant to tell me that. If that wasn't possible, I added, I could easily make an arrangement with the British Council to come back next year for a month, at a time convenient to the archive, for the specific purpose of working on the 1929 protocols. (This was drawing a long bow, as I had no idea if the British Council would sponsor an extra month, but when people keep telling elaborate lies to you, you start to tell lies back.) Natalia Dmitrievna 'looked rather taken aback', I wrote to my mother, 'and said perhaps after all I could have the 1929 protocols before I leave in July'. They did finally produce them, which was satisfying, especially because there was quite a lot in them. Since 1929 was another year full of incident for Narkompros, including the resignation of Lunacharsky and a number of his associates on a point of principle, this perhaps made more plausible the claim that the 1928 protocols were lying at the bottom of the Volga.

Everything becomes routine after a while, and my relationship with the State Archives was no exception. Over the years, I became a familiar presence in the foreigners reading room; and during *perestroika* we foreigners finally graduated to the main reading room and were allowed to consult inventories and eat in the cafeteria. No doubt nothing was ever as exciting as those first Narkompros protocols, but there were dramatic moments. In the early 1970s, when I was working on the topic of Soviet industrialisation, I got an incredible run of trade-union materials—minutes this time, even better than protocols—in which Stalin's No. 3 man, Lazar

Kaganovich, told the trade-unionists in his patented bullying manner that they should stop acting as if their job was to represent the interests of labour against management; in a Soviet proletarian state, these interests were identical. That Soviet trade unions were subordinate to the Soviet state wasn't news to Sovietologists, of course, but it was news that as of 1929 Kaganovich thought the unions were still defending labour interests, and that he should order them to stop in such unvarnished terms. I was so excited by my discovery that I took a cigarette break—you were allowed to smoke in a beautiful circular hall with no external windows just outside the reading room, an awful fire hazard—and, in English, told one of the American scholars all about it. I noticed that the woman on duty had come out for a smoke, too, but assumed she didn't know English, which was a rather elementary piece of carelessness. My run of trade-union minutes dried up immediately.

The archivists, it appeared, formed their own judgements about who was or was not a legitimate scholar, independently at least to some extent of the KGB. Their main criterion was hard work: if people regularly put in a lot of hours and kept their heads down, the archivists tended to think well of them, but if they made a big fuss about getting material but then left it untouched for days, they thought badly. Once, in the days when I was working on industry, I was given an extraordinary file on convict labour, an absolutely taboo subject. I hadn't ordered it and assumed it was simply a mistake, as the label didn't indicate the contents. Of course, I read it with great attention, took detailed notes, and unsuccessfully asked for further materials from the same set. After a while, I almost forgot about the incident. But during *perestroika*, I met a senior archivist from the

State Archives for the first time—they were now making themselves accessible to foreigners, unlike in former days—and she greeted me as an old friend. 'Weren't you pleased when you got that file on convict labour I sent you? It was my little gift to you, you were such a hard worker.' Perhaps the Stasi man's affection for his surveillance object in the film *The Lives of Others* wasn't so far-fetched after all.

You can get a taste for excitement. Spies have it, and journalists, but it's not something you expect of a historian. Perhaps in a scholar it is a kind of corruption. I became addicted to the thrill of the chase, the excitement of the game of matching my wits against that of Soviet officialdom. I thought it must be terribly boring to work, say, on British history, where you just went to the archives, checked the inventories, ordered some documents, and they brought them to you—fully predictable, no drama. What would be the fun of it? Knowledge, I came to feel, has to be fought for, torn 'with rough strife through the iron gates of life', as the English poet Andrew Marvell wrote about pleasure. I thought of myself as different from the general run of British and American Soviet scholars, with their Cold War agenda (as I saw it) of discrediting the Soviet Union rather than understanding it. But that didn't stop me getting my own kicks from finding out what the Soviets didn't want me to know. Best of all was to find out something the Soviets didn't want me to know and Western Cold Warriors didn't want to hear because it complicated the simple anti-Soviet story.

As I write this memoir, it's become increasingly clear to me that the Soviets were not totally stupid in thinking that historians like me were essentially spies. We were trying to get information they didn't want us to have, and we were prepared to use all sorts of ruses and stratagems to get it. It's true that we wanted the information for ourselves, not for a spymaster. On the other hand, 'ourselves' included a Western scholarly audience; it was not purely for our private satisfaction. If we found something explosive in the archives, we were going to use it in our work, without any sense of obligation to the archives, still less loyalty to the Soviet state.

There were basically two ways to control us. One was the threat of declaring us persona non grata and refusing visas, which for an archive-based historian was total disaster. This threat, though we didn't usually admit to it, was quite powerful. Backing it up were various administrative mechanisms that influenced the way we worked. If we wanted to keep going to the Soviet Union, we formulated our topics so that the Soviets would accept them. Sometimes that just meant translating a Western concept into SovietSpeak without changing its substance, as when I presented a research project on upward mobility into the elite as 'Formation of the new Soviet intelligentsia'. But there could be a substantive impact too. Suppose, for example, that my work on Lunacharsky had made me passionately interested in the oppositionist Bukharin. I still probably wouldn't have switched topics because I knew that on Bukharin I would get no archives, and indeed wouldn't be accepted on the exchange (probably not by the British, knowing the topic was hopeless in Soviet terms, but certainly not by the Soviets).

Our supervisors were there to keep us on the straight and narrow, along with the archivists and libraries who scrutinised our orders to see that we didn't get the wrong sort of information. Ovcharenko's initial adjustment of my topic, though it turned out greatly to my advantage, can be construed as an attempt to keep me off dangerous ground. But there is only so much influence a supervisor who isn't responsible for failing or passing your dissertation can have, and in the end I think Ovcharenko was more scared of what I might do, by way of publishing something back in England that would be judged anti-Soviet and reflect badly on him, than I was of anything he could do to me.

The other way of controlling us was through friendship. But this was a kind of control that was independent of the state, unless your supervisor or archival assistant happened to be or become a friend; and there was always a question, from the state point of view, of whether the friend's control was the kind the authorities wanted. Irina aspired to control my work, but her agenda was personal, and in any case she was only partly successful (instead of writing a biography of Lunacharsky that would fit her requirements, I gave up the idea altogether). Igor's control was ultimately far more effective because he had personal sway and intellectual influence as well—but probably not the right kind of intellectual influence, from the standpoint of the authorities.

Fear of damaging your friends by your actions and publications in the West was a major constraint. I didn't worry much about Irina (although I did turn down an invitation from the *Guardian* to write a piece on children of the Soviet political elite because the connection with her would have been so obvious), but I worried a lot about Igor. It wasn't very likely that he would be hauled over the coals for telling me things about Narkompros in the 1920s. The worry was almost all about the journal he worked for, *Novy mir*, because its fortunes were followed so eagerly not only in the Soviet intelligentsia but in Cold War centres of Sovietology like St Antony's. It wasn't just that I might look like a spy from a spy college who was pumping Igor for *Novy mir*'s secrets. Given that the 'not unknown' Max Hayward was a close follower of *Novy mir*'s affairs, I might look like a spy with a real-life spymaster: my Oxford supervisor.

6

Novy mir

Novy mir quickly became a central topic of discussion in my conversations with Igor—or rather, a subject of monologue on Igor's part, as all I could do was listen with fascination. I was very happy to do this as, like everyone else interested in Soviet affairs at this time, I considered *Novy mir*'s fortunes to be a key indicator in the hidden struggle between reform and conservative backsliding going on in Soviet politics. That's why *Novy mir*'s affairs, or what Igor told me about them, became a staple of my diary. I thought Lunacharsky was important to me, but *Novy mir* was important to the world.

I wasn't the only one keeping a record. Half a dozen people from the *Novy mir* circle were making daily entries on what was happening to the journal in the 1960s, judging by subsequent publications, and, at the height of *Novy mir*'s battles, practically everybody connected with it was ringing around and giving blow-by-blow reports to family and friends in Moscow. That's how important it seemed, not only to the people who worked for it but to a wider public who thought of it as 'the window through which the Russian reading public saw the pure light of day'. (That phrase, with its suggestion of Russia as a prison, is

Solzhenitsyn's, though he came to feel that the journal's moral reputation was exaggerated.) Of course, with all this note-taking, *Novy mir* leaked like a sieve. Or, to change the metaphor, its editorial office became an echo chamber. Most things that happened in that chamber were on the Moscow grapevine within days. That included things that were meant to be secret, like private conversations between Alexander Tvardovsky, the chief editor, and people from the Party Central Committee, or the fact that the censorship had forbidden publication of a particular work. Those forbidden works themselves, which were often already in galleys, circulated as well.

You would expect that if multiple people are taking notes of the same events, their accounts might be interestingly different. But in this case that wasn't really so. It's true that the writer Alexander Solzhenitsyn, who was one of the note-takers, came to disagree with the 'liberal' consensus that the journal represented light as against darkness, truth as against untruth; and there were other subterranean currents within *Novy mir*, including one hostile to Igor, of which I knew little. But what struck me overwhelmingly when I re-read my diary, along with other diaries being written at the time that have since been published, was how similar they all are. We were all telling the same story, in which *Novy mir* is the white knight fighting for truth against the forces of evil. Perversely, when I read the diaries *en masse*, I couldn't help wanting to hear something from the other side. What was the version of *Novy mir*'s opponents—those censors and officials from the Central Committee and the Writers' Union who regularly thwarted the journal's publication plans, the literary critics like Ovcharenko who disliked it and all it stood for, or the people from competing journals such as *Oktyabr'*, where my friend Alyosha's father worked, who both disagreed with *Novy mir*'s line and envied its success? Why didn't any of them keep diaries to tell the story from their point of view? It may be partly that *Novy mir*'s light-against-darkness frame, with its heroes, villains, martyrs and fighters for truth, still has broad currency, so that people thinking otherwise find it hard to get published in Russia or abroad. Or perhaps it was a matter of self-confidence: the *Novy mir* diary-keepers were impelled by a conviction of moral superiority, whereas the opponents—making no similar moral claim, but finding *Novy mir*'s pretensions annoying, naïve, grandstanding and so on—simply lacked the incentive to leave a record for posterity.

As far as I know, I was the only foreigner among the note-takers and diarists, and I was essentially acting as Igor's amanuensis. But I wasn't the only foreigner paying attention. *Novy mir* and its battles with the authorities were of tremendous interest to Western Sovietologists like Max Hayward. Thanks to the foreign correspondents, passing on what they could pick up about *Novy mir* on the Moscow grapevine, these battles, seen as a significant fulcrum of the Cold War, were as well known to ordinary readers of the *Guardian* or the *New York Times* as Soviet dissidents would be in the 1970s. In addition, Russian *émigré* journals were eagerly following events through their informants in Moscow. Sometimes they managed to publish articles or fiction whose publication in *Novy mir* the censor had knocked back even before *Novy mir* had given up trying to get the decision reversed.

The *Novy mir* editors always said they were not in the business of sending manuscripts and information abroad and routinely deplored such foreign publication. On the other hand, people close to them certainly did such things, Solzhenitsyn being a notable case in point. Manuscripts and information leaked regularly from *Novy mir* to the outside world, hidden in the luggage of journalists and exchange students or sent by embassy people via the diplomatic pouch. I was not one of those document smugglers, partly out of prudence (not wanting to be caught and become persona non grata in the future) and partly because I thought *Novy mir* and I were above such things. Igor once remarked that he would never ask me to take out a manuscript, because my connections with him, and thus to *Novy mir*, were too well known to the KGB. The implication that they sometimes *did* ask people to take out manuscripts didn't strike me at the time.

For me, *Novy mir* and Igor were inseparably linked. While I had separate external sources of information through reading *Survey* and *Encounter* and talking to Max Hayward, I had no other local source of inside information other than Igor. I was acquainted with a couple of the younger *Novy mir* people, Volodya Lakshin (one of the diarists) and Misha Khitrov, but I didn't know or meet them separately from Igor. I saw *Novy mir* from Igor's perspective, and he saw it from the perspective of Tvardovsky, the chief editor and his close friend—and perhaps sometimes from what he thought should have been Tvardovsky's perspective, as the nuances in Tvardovsky's (now published) diary sometimes differ from the account I heard from Igor. But there was no doubt that Igor was absolutely loyal to Tvardovsky: whenever there was an internal argument within the journal, let alone a clash with outsiders, Tvardovsky was in the right, in Igor's version. A popular poet of peasant origins and a legendary drinker, seven years younger than Igor, Tvardovsky had made his reputation in the 1930s but greatly enhanced it during World War II with his epic of the Schweik-like soldier, *Vasilii Terkin*, which was particularly beloved among frontline soldiers in the army. After the war, Tvardovsky became chief editor of *Novy mir* and in the first half of the 1950s turned it into the pace-setting journal, compulsory reading for the intelligentsia, that it would be for the next twenty years.

Tvardovsky had brought Igor into *Novy mir* during his first editorship in the early 1950s, a time when Igor—a trouble-maker, associated with the disgraced journal *Literaturnyi kritik*, and moreover a Jew, in a period of quasi-official anti-Semitism—seems to have been virtually unemployable. They were dismissed together from the journal in 1954, and then came back together in 1958, Igor working inconspicuously, as befitted a man whose reputation was still under a cloud, in the journal's department of criticism. In August 1965, against considerable opposition from superior authorities, Tvardovsky managed to bring Igor onto the editorial board.

Tvardovsky and Igor were friends and drinking companions. They socialised at Igor's flat, and less often at Tvardovsky's *dacha*, as well as going occasionally to restaurants with friends and seeing each other at the *Novy mir* office. Some felt Igor was a bad influence because of the drinking, and you can see from his diaries that the same thought sometimes occurred to Tvardovsky himself. But he had a great respect for Igor's erudition and judgement, enjoyed his company, and trusted him, while calling him somewhat ruefully a contrarian, and deploring Igor's almost total refusal to write, which he saw as a waste of his talents. 'How many times I have tried to drag him up to the surface', Lakshin recalls Tvardovsky saying, 'but he burrows down again into his underground kingdom'. I was surprised when I read that, as I hadn't seen Igor as a man from underground (or was I, with the other waifs, part of the underground kingdom?). But there was something about Igor's extreme grumpiness when forced to move in Soviet high society that did remind me of an animal dragged, blinking and unhappy, from its burrow.

I report Tvardovsky's attachment to Igor mainly at second hand, since I was kept out of his way by the other editorial board members, fearing adverse consequences from a foreigner's proximity, and even by Igor himself, in deference to this anxiety. Reading Tvardovsky's diaries when they were published in the 2000s, I almost got the impression that Tvardovsky and I were alternating presences in Igor's life in the late 1960s. When I was in England, entries like 'went round to Sats' place; drank (a little, a lot)' were frequent; when I was in Moscow, they seemed much rarer. This is probably a solipsistic reading. At any rate, I never encountered Tvardovsky at Igor's, though I was there a lot (and so, at other times, was he). But about Igor's loyalty, love and constant concern for Tvardovsky I know at first hand. He was always talking about him and worrying about his welfare; sometimes there was a hint of anxiety or competitiveness in his references to others who were also Tvardovsky intimates. I must have suspected that it was an unequal relationship, with Igor in the inferior position, since it was a distinct relief to me to read confirmation in Tvardovsky's and Lakshin's diaries of Tvardovsky's affection for Igor. (The relationship *was* somewhat unequal, all the same, but less than I had feared.)

One of the first things Igor impressed upon me about *Novy mir* was that the journal was not a 'liberal force' in the Soviet Union; rather, it stood, in the first place, for Communism (the right kind, of course, not the kind corrupted by time-servers), and in the second place, for critical intelligence. He needed to make this point forcibly—indeed, may have intended it as a message to Hayward and St Antony's—because virtually everybody outside of *Novy mir* disagreed with it. In the Soviet Union, to be sure, 'liberal' was still a pejorative, so only enemies would publicly describe *Novy mir* in such terms. But it was the journal's reform-minded stance and boldness in challenging regime pieties that appealed to Soviet admirers, not its Marxist or Communist commitments, however genuine they were. In the West, everyone saw *Novy mir* as a liberal journal, Communist and Marxist only as a matter of form, and that, of course, was why they liked it. As dissidents—outright challengers to the regime—emerged in the Soviet Union in the late 1960s, Western commentators saw them as part of a continuum with *Novy mir*, causing endless annoyance and embarrassment to the journal's editors. They objected both for prudential reason and on principle—at least this was how I understood it from Igor: no doubt there were others on the journal whose Marxist-Leninist enthusiasm and sense of Communist identity were less strong than his, an Old Bolshevik of Civil War vintage. *Novy mir* people were not dissidents, Igor never tired of repeating, but critics from within, critics who were themselves Communists but wanted a better Soviet Communist practice. A 'loyal opposition' was how I paraphrased this in my mind. Of course, such a stance had its problems in a country where opposition and loyalty were generally assumed to be incompatible.

In its approach to literature, *Novy mir* was in favour of the orthodox Soviet creed of 'socialist realism', that is, realism informed by a Marxist-Leninist world view. But they had their own version of what that was. Whereas the official version established in the late Stalin period tended to mean artistic representation that was prettied up to emphasise the positive, *Novy mir*'s version meant showing it like it was, no matter how ugly, in order to see what had to be done to improve it. *Novy mir*'s truth-telling was much appreciated by reform-minded Soviet readers, but the journal was often thought to be conservative in its insistence on realism as a *sine qua non* in the prose fiction and literary criticism it published. On this point, Igor was an ultra-conservative, even by *Novy mir* standards. Following his philosopher friend Mikhail Lifshits, a fellow disciple of Georg Lukaćs who had worked with them on the journal *Literaturnyi kritik*, he actively disliked artistic modernism for abandoning realistic representation.

In St Antony's circles, the general assumption was that people in the Soviet Union who were reform-minded about politics and social policy were also sympathetic to artistic innovation. This was true of a lot of people, but it certainly wasn't true of Igor. My diary for March 1967 records a walk Igor and I took round the Arbat, he holding my arm in the old-fashioned Russian manner (Irina did it too), and vigorously denouncing modern art. The cause of leftist art had become chic in the Soviet intelligentsia, he claimed; indeed, it had been taken up by 'pure Stalinists' among the literary critics (naturally, he named names). According to Igor, Beckett, Nabokov and even Picasso—generally lauded in the Soviet Union since the Thaw—had gone up a blind alley; he criticised them for narrowness, irrelevance, and lack of specificity and a sense of purpose.

Later, when he presented me with a copy of Lifshits's provocative book *Crisis of Ugliness*, a root-and-branch attack on modernism in the visual arts that linked its rise in Europe with fascism, I understood more where Igor was coming from, though Lifshits's arguments left me unconvinced. I seem to have reacted to Igor's fervour on the question with some amusement, while not dismissing it outright. In my Western persona, I was an admirer of Beckett and Brecht (another wrong path, in Igor's view), and liked Nabokov and his formal experimentation too. As I recorded in my diary early in April, Igor and I 'had an argument last week about Samuel Beckett, in which I didn't feel at all embarrassed at disagreeing with him'. A few weeks later, I saw an avant-garde theatre production which I described to my mother as 'quite entertaining, and probably quite in the Meyerhold tradition' (the reference being to the famous avant-garde director of the 1920s, a victim of the Great Purges, whose name was revered by most forward-looking Soviet intellectuals since his resurrection during the Thaw—but not, of course, by Igor). Still, I continued, obviously a bit tongue in cheek, 'it is not the sort of thing Igor Alexandrovich and I approve of (in fact the number of things we approve of is rather small, especially as I have to stop liking Brecht and Beckett for the time being)'. No doubt Igor discerned that I was not a whole-hearted convert to anti-modernism, but he kept trying anyway. Writing to me in Oxford in 1968, he urged me to read Lifshits's recent article on 'Liberalism and democracy' since 'it is very important for your work and in general', the first an implausible claim. 'You know how I respect MA Lifshits', he continued, and I imagined him sticking out his bottom lip as he wrote it. 'After all, I am not a liberal.'

Tvardovsky and others on the *Novy mir* editorial board found it hard not to rise to Igor's bait. There had been a fight about it in 1963 (recorded in Lakshin's diary), when Igor had included an anti-modernist diatribe in an article on Lunacharsky's views on art. According to Lakshin, he and Tvardovsky were the only people who supported Igor on this: 'of course, Igor Alexandrovich is harsh and one-sided in his judgements of painting', Lakshin commented, 'and in general he is a contrarian, but how can we not let him say what he wants to say?' Still, Tvardovsky called Igor a dogmatist in his hostility to modernism, and they quarrelled again about the issue in 1967 and 1968.

Even for Igor, however, modernism was a side issue. The thing that was really important was bringing back a true spirit of criticism, which in Igor's interpretation meant launching vigorous polemics against accepted pieties in the Criticism section of the journal. Very early in our acquaintance, Igor sat me down to read the pieces that had appeared in *Novy mir* under his sponsorship of which he was particularly proud. They included polemical articles by Lakshin, Lifshits and Mark Shcheglov, all brilliantly taking the mickey out of pompous, highly praised Soviet literary figures who were mocked for servility, blandness, mendaciousness and ignorance of whatever aspects of Soviet life they were writing about. The insistence on telling the truth in literature was a staple of *Novy mir*, but the gleeful skewering of the mighty and self-satisfied was very much Igor, characteristic of his own conversational style (though not his written style, whose flatness was a matter of regret to him and puzzlement to me). Shcheglov and Lakshin had both been his protégés in their twenties, in relationships that were almost filial (Igor was still mourning Shcheglov's untimely death when I met him a decade later), and they had surely absorbed some of his iconoclasm and talent for one-liners, as well as learning how to extend the meticulous and mercilessly sarcastic polemical analyses over dozens of pages, a stylistic characteristic well developed in Igor's personal favourite polemicists, Marx and Lenin. Igor's instruction of me was so similar to what Lakshin described of his instruction of Lakshin ten years earlier that I have to think that at some unconscious level he was training me, too, to be a *Novy mir* polemicist. What a pity the world wasn't arranged in such a way that that could happen. It would have been right up my alley.

Interestingly enough, Igor was quite uninterested in claiming credit for the most famous of the reform articles published on his watch, Vladimir Pomerantsev's 'On sincerity in literature', which came out in the *Novy mir* Criticism section at the end of 1953. Igor had just been brought into the journal at this point, with a particular brief to keep an eye on the department of criticism while Tvardovsky was away on a long trip, and as a result, he was the man who edited the Pomerantsev article and shepherded it through to publication. But he never sat me down to read this article (which, as a good Western Sovietologist in training, I had read anyway) because he thought Pomerantsev 'hysterical' and intellectually confused. In a letter to a Western *Novy mir* scholar I'd put him in touch with in the 1970s, he emphasised that he hadn't commissioned this article and thought there were lots of things the journal published at that time that were more worthy of attention, although no doubt 'with all its failings the article played a certain beneficial role, awakening critical thought from slumber'.

This was ungrateful of Igor. Perhaps part of his reaction is to be explained by the fact that the Pomerantsev article was a smash hit, and Igor didn't like successes. After the Pomerantsev article, Lakshin recalled, 'people began to read the journal starting with the criticism department'. Of course, not everyone liked what they read. The objects of criticism and their admirers were appalled by the 'abusive, mocking remarks' about respected writers to be found there. There had been nothing like the ferocity of *Novy mir*'s criticism since the days of the Soviet Cultural Revolution, one victim complained. It was scarcely surprising that when the day of reckoning came in 1954, Igor should have been fired along with Tvardovsky. In fact, when Tvardovsky accepted full personal responsibility for the 'errors' of *Novy mir* at a Writers' Union meeting, a competing literary journal complained that 'he did not say a word about the weight and influence that I Sats, the former head of the department of criticism' had in the journal. Other Writers' Union members present remedied this omission, however, and 'correctly evaluated' Igor's contribution, raking him over the coals with a vengeance.

In the 1960s, in Tvardovsky's second period as editor, Solzhenitsyn was at the centre of *Novy mir*'s rows with the authorities. Already a larger-than-life figure in Western media, beloved of people like Hayward (his first English translator), Solzhenitsyn probably inspired something of a contrarian response in me. I wasn't overwhelmed by the literary merits of his Gulag novella, *One Day in the Life of*

Ivan Denisovich, which had caused a sensation inside and outside the Soviet Union when *Novy mir* published it in 1962. I liked *Cancer Ward* better—perhaps partly because I read it in *Novy mir* galley proofs, sitting in Igor's room—but still thought that he was stylistically pretty crude (the line that stays with me as an example of bathos is the one about the removal of a cancerous breast: 'Today, a marvel; tomorrow, into the rubbish bin'). Igor must have been aware of this, as in one of his late-1960s letters, reporting the latest Solzhenitsyn development, he asked: 'Am I right that to you he is not even particularly congenial as an artist?' Until I re-read that, I had forgotten about my reaction to the early work, having in the meantime come to admire Solzhenitsyn's literary style of mocking polemic (for example, in *Gulag Archipelago* and *Lenin in Zurich*), with its clear line of descent from the over-the-top invective of Marx, Lenin—and, indeed, the Criticism section of *Novy mir*. But it's true, now I come to look back, that in the 1960s and 1970s I was touchy about Solzhenitsyn. Part of it was a matter of partisanship in his developing battles with *Novy mir*, his initial sponsor. And part of it, as far as the 1970s were concerned, was personal in a rather embarrassing way: when Solzhenitsyn was expelled from the Soviet Union, a hero and martyr in the West, a journalist asked him what he would do now, and he said he wouldn't mind teaching Soviet history at somewhere like Columbia University in New York. As the precariously incumbent Soviet historian at Columbia at the time, I didn't appreciate that remark.

Igor himself was not an unqualified admirer of Solzhenitsyn, and Solzhenitsyn liked him no better. He knew Igor as one of the close circle of Tvardovsky's intimates, but he thought those intimates badly chosen: Igor was just 'a cloudy drinking companion' while Mikhail Lifshits was 'a dyed-in-the-wool Marxist dogmatist'. Probably Solzhenitsyn saw Igor and Lifshits as sinister Jewish manipulators behind the frank and open Russian lad, Tvardovsky, with whom he was initially great friends. And Igor, for his part, no doubt always suspected that Solzhenitsyn, in his heart of hearts, was more of a disloyal critic of the Soviet Union, hostile to Communism, than a loyal one. Tvardovsky, however, loved Solzhenitsyn for a number of years, so Igor kept any negative opinions more or less to himself.

The publication of *Ivan Denisovich* in *Novy mir* had required not only all Tvardovsky's pull and energy to get past the censors but also Khrushchev's personal intervention. Gulag remained a very delicate subject to discuss in print in the Soviet Union, even after Khrushchev's Secret Speech at the Twentieth Party Congress in 1956, and Solzhenitsyn's was the first eyewitness account (albeit in fictional form) to be published. *Novy mir* put all its prestige on the line for Solzhenitsyn. It nominated *Ivan Denisovich* (unsuccessfully) for a Lenin Prize. Lakshin's article 'Ivan Denisovich. His friends and enemies', published in *Novy mir*'s Criticism section (and approved by Igor with only one word changed), presented the work as an exemplar of the kind of truthful realism Soviet literature needed but often lacked: empirical, focused on social problems, and respectful of the dignity and freedom of the individual. This was an encapsulation of *Novy mir*'s program, and of course firmly identified the journal as foremost among Solzhenitsyn's friends.

Unfortunately, Solzhenitsyn had plenty of enemies as well. One group of them, regarded by *Novy mir* as Stalinists, was entrenched in the competing journal, *Oktyabr'*, edited by

Vsevolod Kochetov. My advisor, Alexander Ovcharenko, who disliked both Solzhenitsyn's *Ivan Denisovich* and Tvardovsky's *Novy mir*, was an enemy, too. Ovcharenko never talked about this with me, no doubt because, as a sophisticated man, he knew it wasn't what you said to a Westerner unless you wanted to look like a Party hack. But the dislike is visible in his writing on Solzhenitsyn in the mid 1960s (which, at the time, I hadn't read). Ovcharenko doesn't follow a crude anti-Solzhenitsyn line; his piece offers what is clearly meant to be the sophisticated anti-liberal critique. Ovcharenko had friends of his own, he wrote, who, like Solzhenitsyn, were Gulag returnees (this was a demonstration of his Thaw credentials). But, unlike Ivan Denisovich and presumably Solzhenitsyn, they knew they had been unjustly convicted, and 'the consciousness of their own innocence gave them the necessary strength to keep the beauty of their human souls in purity'. In other words, they were beings of a higher moral order. Solzhenitsyn, in Ovcharenko's view, wrote as if he didn't realise the profound difference between Gulag political prisoners who were innocent and had been wrongly arrested and those who were in fact guilty—real 'enemies of the people'—and deserved to be there. The reader was left to draw his own conclusions as to which category the real-life Gulag prisoner Solzhenitsyn belonged.

Solzhenitsyn was lionised in Moscow literary society in the mid 1960s, and there were people within the intelligentsia he trusted, such as future dissident Lev Kopelev, a friend from Gulag days and a *Novy mir* contributor, who had given the manuscript of *Ivan Denisovich* to Tvardovsky and thus launched Solzhenitsyn on his literary career. But generally speaking Solzhenitsyn retained a wary attitude to intellectuals, however fawning: his world was divided into those who had been in Gulag and those who hadn't, and the latter were not fully to be trusted. None of the *Novy mir* editorial board had been in Gulag (indeed, if they had been, they wouldn't have been on the editorial board). Tvardovsky, to be sure, came from a peasant family that was expropriated and deported as *kulak* (meaning peasant exploiter). This would have made him one of the victims, except that, unlike the rest of his family, he had escaped deportation by the fortunate accident of having already left home to make his fortune as a proletarian poet. He tried to keep this quiet, naturally but perhaps not heroically, but it still caused him career problems in the 1930s.

Solzhenitsyn was writing two autobiographical novels, *Cancer Ward* and *First Circle*, in the early 1960s, as well as more furtively gathering material and writing the book that became *Gulag Archipelago*. In August 1964, Tvardovsky announced that *Novy mir* would be publishing *First Circle*, and from the end of that year, the manuscript sat in the journal's safe, waiting for the right moment to submit it to the censor. But after Khrushchev's ouster in the autumn of that year, the times were no longer opportune, especially for a novel set in a *sharashka* (Gulag research station for prisoner-scientists) and featuring an evil Stalin as a character. In July 1966, a couple of months before I arrived in the Soviet Union, Solzhenitsyn delivered the first part of a second novel, *Cancer Ward*. This was potentially easier to publish as it wasn't set directly in Gulag and could even be read as upbeat, since the hero's cancer is successfully treated in a Soviet hospital. The second part was delivered in June 1967 and was in galleys by December. I must have read both parts in galleys at Igor's when I came back to Moscow in the spring of 1968. As for *First Circle*, I wish I could remember if I read the *Novy mir* manuscript at Igor's: it would have been very rash of him, but he did a lot of rash things. I don't know whether to read the absence of references in my diaries and letters to my mother as establishing that I didn't read it before its Western publication, or an indication that I considered it too sensitive a topic to mention.

I had only known Igor for a month when he gave me a detailed account of the house search of Solzhenitsyn that had just taken place. I recorded it in my diary, which perhaps wasn't the most prudent thing to do, despite my primitive attempt to conceal the identity of the subject. I just couldn't resist writing down this insider's account of something so newsworthy in the West, even if it was only for my own benefit:

> S[olzhenitsyn] has written two novels and some bad plays: one of the novels was taken from him (literally from the house of an old teacher of mathematics): they then rang up Tv[ardovsky] and Sim[onov; editor of *Novy mir* in the interim between Tvardovsky's first and second tenure] and asked them to read the anti-Soviet etc works of their protégés. Both refused (even the *khitreishii* [very cunning] Sim[onov].

Novy mir's epic battle to publish Solzhenitsyn raged for most of the three years that I was in Moscow for long periods of time as an exchange student. I followed it every step of the way, as, of course, did all the rest of the note-takers. Solzhenitsyn, Tvardovsky and Lakshin were all keeping diaries, as was at least one other member of the editorial board; Zhores Medvedev, a confidant of some of the editors, was taking notes; all the *Novy mir* editors and staffers were telling an array of friends and relatives, who subsequently told other friends and relatives, what was happening; and the foreign correspondents and embassy analysts in Moscow were picking up as much of the gossip as they could and disseminating it in the West. I thought at the time that I was one of a very few to have access to this information; now it seems that I was just one of the very few to keep my mouth shut. But I would have felt like a traitor to Igor passing it on, and in fact could have done him harm.

As the battle raged, Solzhenitsyn's and Tvardovsky's paths started to diverge. Solzhenitsyn thought Tvardovsky wasn't prepared to go the whole hog for him, if it meant destroying the journal; Tvardovsky was coming to suspect that Solzhenitsyn really was anti-Soviet and anti-Communist. I got regular reports from Igor, in person when in Moscow and by letter, deciphering his coded updates, when I was back in England. It was a cliff-hanger, not only because of the ever-changing balance of negotiation between the authorities and *Novy mir*, but also because of the larger-than-life characters involved, the Cold War context, and the sense of all concerned that incredibly weighty issues were at stake. No doubt, in the *longue durée*, it doesn't matter much whether *Cancer Ward* ever got published in *Novy mir*, but that's not how it seemed at the time. It was a life-and-death matter to Igor; and, in the West, Max Hayward and even *Time* magazine thought it was pretty important. I felt I had stumbled into the anteroom of the place where the fate of the world was being decided.

Solzhenitsyn was not *Novy mir*'s only *causus belli* with the authorities. The journal was constantly involved in multiple battles about particular writers and manuscripts, and periodically there were rumblings from above about changing the editorial board because the journal was so insubordinate. An internal report on censorship for 1966 found that *Novy mir* had given more trouble that year than any other journal, with twenty censorship interventions and rebukes. The report noted that *Novy mir* was obsessed with the subjects of repression, the Stalinist cult of personality and collectivisation (carried out so ruthlessly that it was a 'repression' subject too), and treated all of these in a partisan way—the last was an accusation that *Novy mir* would have vigorously rebutted, as they felt that the partisan distortion and whitewashing was all on the other side.

Novy mir was in constant negotiation with censorship officials, the Writers' Union (of which it was officially an organ), the Party Central Committee secretariat, and sometimes even individual Politburo members about what could be published in the journal. Some of the low-level negotiation was done by the secretary of the editorial board (Misha Khitrov, in my time), but a lot of it required Tvardovsky's personal involvement: there were endless telephone calls to higher-ups to be made, replies from higher-ups to be waited for, and summonses requiring instant responses for Tvardovsky to come round and discuss things in person with an important official. Tvardovsky's deputies (first Alexander Dementev, later Lakshin) were sometimes taken on these negotiating visits, but never Igor, since he could not be relied on to be polite in face-to-face encounters. The need for Tvardovsky personally to be present sometimes caused difficulties, given his habit of disappearing on drinking binges (sometimes with Igor): it was said that if he hadn't been drunk and unavailable when the Central Committee called him in to explain things in 1954, he might never have been sacked from the editorship. Another tense moment came in 1969, when Tvardovsky became tired of waiting for Brezhnev to return his call and went off for a drink with Igor and a couple of others; they had scarcely returned to the editorial office, somewhat the worse for wear, when Brezhnev actually *did* call back.

When I met Igor for the first time, two of his colleagues on the editorial board had just been removed as a warning to the rest. Naturally this was uppermost in his mind in the first months of our acquaintance. In March, I recorded a four-hour conversation with Igor about *Novy mir*. He said the position was now very bad, almost as bad as it had been in 1954 when he and Tvardovsky were sacked. This time, the authorities had been on the brink of dismissing the whole editorial board, but in the event settled on just two members (Dementev, an old personal friend of Tvardovsky's and his deputy, and the secretary of the editorial board, BG Zaks). *Novy mir* were expecting the axe to fall again the whole time I was in the Soviet Union—and, on the eve of my departure in 1970, it did.

'Things are bad with us (*Nashi dela plokhi*)', Igor would always say gloomily to me as a prelude to the latest update on the ongoing *Novy mir* drama. And things always were bad: the trajectory from 1966 to 1970 was all downhill to the final disaster, although the speed and the sense of an inevitable crash at the bottom increased after the Prague Spring in 1968. At the end of his daily commentary, Igor had a standard sign-off phrase, 'That's how things are with us (*Vot u nas takie dela*)', said with a kind of wry satisfaction. There was a formality about these reports, a set-piece quality, that reflects Igor's own sense that he was reporting not just to me but to History.

Novy mir's downward trajectory—as it now so clearly appears in retrospect—started with Khrushchev's ouster and the Sinyavsky-Daniel trial early in 1966. I knew a lot about the Sinyavsky-Daniel affair before I arrived in Moscow because it was so closely followed at St Antony's and in *Encounter* (which had published the novella *The Trial Begins*, written by Andrey Sinyavsky under the pseudonym Abram Tertz, back in 1960). I heard more about it from Igor, but at the time I didn't fully realise how close to *Novy mir* the Sinyavsky-Daniel affair had come. This was presumably either because Igor minimised the connections in talking to me, or because they belonged to another wing of *Novy mir*—less Marxist, less Party-minded, more sympathetic to artistic modernism, and closer to the dissidents—of which I had only a shadowy conception. Sinyavsky, in any case, had been a regular *Novy mir* contributor, and the journal had published some translations from the Czech by Yury Daniel just before his arrest. While none of the *Novy mir* editors signed the protest of sixty-two members of the Writers' Union in the spring of 1966, regular contributors like Lev Kopelev did. The whole affair was seriously compromising to the journal.

Almost as soon as I met him, Igor filled me in on the *Novy mir* perspective on the Sinyavsky-Daniel trial, which I described in my diary as 'very ambivalent'. Igor considered Sinyavsky's fiction (which I rather liked, especially *The Trial Begins*) a poor imitation of the modernists of the 1920s, who were themselves poor imitators of Silver Age symbolist writers like Andrey Bely ('Sats on the warpath against modernism again', was my comment in the diary). Igor considered Sinyavsky a gifted critic, however, both in his writings under his own name (in the literary criticism published in *Novy mir*, all of which must have had Igor's imprimatur) and in publications abroad, including the devastating dissection of Soviet clichés of *On Socialist Realism*). The fact of publication abroad Igor considered 'dishonest but not criminal', deserving 'a slap in the face but not prison'. According to Igor, Sinyavsky was currently sitting in his prison cell working on a book on Daniel Defoe; and Igor, like many others, anticipated that he would be released in a few months in the amnesty expected in connection with the fiftieth anniversary of the Revolution in November 1967. (In fact, Sinyavsky served almost his full sentence, being released only in 1971 and then allowed to emigrate to Paris in 1973.) Meanwhile, he had 'got everyone else into a nasty position', particularly *Novy mir*. The position was nasty not only because of the journal's links with Sinyavsky and Daniel, but also because of the wave of indignation in the West against Soviet repression and loudly expressed sympathy with its victims—including *Novy mir*. With friends like these, *Novy mir* often thought, it didn't need enemies, even though it had domestic ones in abundance.

Novy mir got into trouble not just for literature and literary criticism but for historical revisionism, too. This wasn't usually written by historians—a timorous lot, with a few exceptions, in Igor's opinion. On collectivisation, one of *Novy mir*'s favourite topics, revisionism came in a variety of genres: fiction, criticism, *publitsistika* (dissemination to a general audience), even poetry. I read Yevgeny Gerasimov's 'Journey to Spas na Peskakh', published in *Novy mir* at the end of 1967, in Igor's study. As a young journalist, Gerasimov (now a *Novy mir* staffer) had been sent out to report on collectivisation in the village of Spas, of which his newspaper had become a sponsor, and 'Journey' described a return visit in the mid 1960s. Who knows what he wrote or was able to publish in 1930, but the local collectivisation process as it appeared in vignettes in Gerasimov's 1967 article was a mixture of farce and tragedy, full of extraordinary idiosyncratic stories like that of the peasant who fled the village for work in town, leaving his wife to bear the brunt of collectivisation. Thirty years later, without so much as a letter in the meantime, he showed up again, and neighbours heard sounds of an epic fight between husband and wife in the *izba* (family hut). But the next day, it was over: the prodigal husband had been taken back. As I was a Lunacharsky scholar when I read this first, collectivisation was only a side interest for me. But a quarter of a century later, I wrote a book on it—and lots of Gerasimov's insights found their way into *Stalin's Peasants*.

It might seem difficult to squeeze historical revisionism into the literary criticism section of a journal, but Igor and Lakshin managed it. 'Legends and facts', an article by a little-known writer and critic (V Kardin), cut down to size one of the beloved myths of the Revolution—the key role of the battleship *Aurora* in the Bolshevik seizure of power in Petrograd in October 1917. The article showed in relentless detail the accretion of colourful embellishments that were appropriate to the Grand Narrative of the Revolution but took the story further and further from anything that participants would have recognised or archival documents supported. Surprisingly, 'Legends and facts' got past the censor and appeared in the February 1966 issue, but there was a terrible row afterwards about lack of respect for things Soviet citizens should hold sacred, with condemnatory articles in *Pravda* and *Izvestiya* and a lot of 'comradely criticism' in the Writers' Union. The censor got back into the act by refusing to pass an editorial in *Novy mir* defending Kardin in the April issue. Nevertheless, Igor the iconoclast was still gloating over this whole episode when I got to know him a year later; naturally it was one of the back issues of the journal that I was soon given to read in his study.

Kardin's article was a straightforward debunking piece that didn't need decoding. But some of *Novy mir*'s publications did, since they used the techniques of Aesopian language. This has a long history in Russia, going back at least to Alexander Herzen's *Kolokol* in the 1860s. An Aesopian point is made not directly but by analogy, as in Aesop's fables: the author writes, for example, of racial prejudice in the US, but in such a way that a Soviet audience will understand that reference is being made to ethnic conflicts within the Soviet Union. A public well schooled in Aesopian communication learns to understand and savour such references; it may even develop Aesopian readings of its own, which author and/or publisher may not have thought of. In a widespread Aesopian reading of Solzhenitsyn's *Cancer Ward*, the ward stands for Soviet society, riddled by disease. Solzhenitsyn may have intended this reading, but *Novy mir*—or at any rate Igor, in his commentary to me—didn't.

Igor was my first instructor in Aesopian reading, an important skill in the Soviet Union of the 1960s, creating a special, almost conspiratorial, bond among those who practised it. In a society with strict censorship, one of the advantages of Aesopian language is that the author and publisher can always deny that any analogy was intended.

Novy mir exploited this to the full in its protracted censorship fights over an article called 'Criminal No. 1: Adolf Hitler and his bosses' by Daniil Melnikov, which I read in galleys at Igor's. This was a brilliant exercise in Aesopian communication: a research-based historical article about Nazi Germany as a totalitarian state, written by a real German expert, a friend of Heinrich Böll, with nary a word about the Soviet Union in it—yet instantly recognisable to the Soviet reader in the know, which is to say every Soviet reader, as an exposé of Stalinism. It actually got past the censor initially, for, as Igor happily remarked, what censor would have the nerve to say that Nazi Germany reminded him of the Soviet Union? But then the Central Committee stepped in and forbade its publication. Although *Novy mir* kept up the tease for several months, resubmitting it repeatedly for publication and demanding a written explanation of the reasons for the refusal, the article never made it into print in the journal.

Once I was safely back to Oxford in 1967, I wrote a letter to my mother summarising highlights of my stay that I had glossed over in the letters going through Soviet censorship in the open post. One of them was the astonishing fact that Igor should have decided to make me his confidant about the very sensitive goings-on at *Novy mir*. 'I can remember him telling me one story', I wrote, 'and then saying sadly that it would get round because one of the other editors was a fool and would tell his wife'. And he was telling a foreigner! Moreover one whose Oxford advisor was one of the main *antisovetchiki* following Soviet literature, particularly the ups and downs of *Novy mir*. No wonder the other editors of the journal, even Lakshin, who quite liked me, were worried about his friendship with me.

The sympathetic attention of the West to its fights with the authorities was an extremely sore point with *Novy mir*. There was always a steady leak of information and manuscripts from the journal to the West, but it all escalated at the end of the 1960s, as Solzhenitsyn started sending his manuscripts abroad but not telling *Novy mir* he was doing it. The KGB got into the act as well, sending manuscripts for publication abroad—Solzhenitsyn's *Cancer Ward*, Svetlana Alliluyeva's *Twenty Letters to a Friend*, Tvardovsky's poem *By Right of Memory* among them—with the apparent intent of discrediting their authors in the eyes of the Soviet public. The Munich *émigré* journals had such good pipelines to Russia that their issues were full of manuscripts identified as 'rejected for publication in *Novy mir*', along with the texts of controversial unpublished lectures and open letters of protest; how they obtained these was never indicated, but regardless of whether it was the author or someone else who sent it, the author was likely to get into trouble back home.

Western intermediaries and messengers were crucial in these complicated games. I looked like one of them, although I did not so regard myself; and was always half prepared for an exposé article to appear about the Western female spy who had wormed her way into the confidence of *Novy mir* through the gullibility of IA Sats. There were ample precedents: the French Russianist Hélène Zamoyska, for example, was an old friend of Sinyavsky's from student days who, at his trial, was named as the person who had illegally smuggled out his manuscripts. It was easy to see myself being cast in the Zamoyska role if *Novy mir* ever ended up on trial; I wasn't sure that *not* smuggling manuscripts was adequate protection. Even closer to home than Zamoyska was Patricia Blake, Max Hayward's friend whom I had met in St Antony's, the subject of a savage lampoon in a novel by *Oktyabr*"s editor, Vsevolod Kochetov. The Blake character was portrayed as a beautiful spy from the CIA's '*Encounter* team' who slept round in the Soviet literary world, was sexually humiliated by the latest lover, and ended up receiving her just deserts—a smack on the bottom from a Kochetov-like figure goaded beyond endurance by her slanders.

Igor never asked me not to publish what he told me about *Novy mir* in the West, though he made it clear how damaging he thought it was when too many crocodile tears (as he saw it) were shed in the West. This omission puzzled me, and I occasionally tried to assure him that I would respect his confidences, but he always waved me off. Just before I left Moscow for the first time, he gave me a copy (which I still possess) of *Novy mir*'s in-house directory, with personnel listed by section and telephone number. It seemed just the kind of information a spy might want; there was no way of pretending it was related to my work on Lunacharsky, and Igor would have got into big trouble if he were known to have given it to me. I imagined trying to explain to the customs people, if they found it, that Igor had given it to me as a memento of our conversations, a sentimental gesture because both I and the journal were dear to him. But Igor didn't seem to be worried about such things. When I wrote to him from Oxford asking if I could quote him on something in my dissertation in a letter from Oxford, he just made a joke of it: 'My dear, my beloved Sheila! Quote me, for God's sake, however and wherever you want to, because I trust you like God'. But being trusted like God could be a burden, especially when

I got back to Oxford and had Max Hayward and his keen professional interest in *Novy mir* to contend with.

I thought I was being maximally careful about respecting Igor's confidences. Yet at the same time I kept a diary that first year in the Soviet Union, writing down a lot of what Igor told me, including at least one summary of an explicitly 'secret' document (a discussion on *Novy mir* at the Secretariat of the Writers' Union), together with Igor's commentary, which was often quite libellous of august persons. Some things I kept out of the diary for security reasons, such as the manuscript of Solzhenitsyn's *First Circle* (which is why I now don't know if Igor simply told me about it, or actually abstracted it from the *Novy mir* safe for me to read in his study), but this was the exception rather than the rule. I never left the diary in my dorm room at the university when I was out, keeping it in my briefcase at all times. But now I come to think of it, this protected it only against room searches. The KGB could easily have sent someone to the Lenin Library to get it out of my briefcase in the cloakroom while I was working upstairs; the cloakroom attendant would have fetched it in a moment. I had to leave the briefcase there because of the strict rule that all you could take into the library was paper to write on and a cardboard folder. I wouldn't have risked putting my thickish black diary into the folder because it might have attracted the attention of the guards (polite young men who weren't stupid, unlike the *babushki* in the cloakroom), who checked you on your way out.

Re-reading my letters to my mother, I see that I was sometimes careful and sometimes not. The same applied to conversations with friends and acquaintances. I wouldn't have talked to Valery or Galya, still less to Horst Bott, about Igor and *Novy mir*, but I certainly did to my friends at the Foreign Language Institute, as I remember asking why Igor, despite being so friendly, always used the polite form in addressing me. (*Of course* he uses the polite form, was the answer; given the difference of age and sex, a cultured man like him has no choice. This must have been an early stage of my Russian, as well as my acquaintance with Igor.) Undoubtedly I said enough about Igor to my Polish archival friend Andrzej, as well as to my Russian boyfriend Sasha (of whom more later), to have made it clear to them, and to the KGB if they passed it on, that Igor was talking to me much more freely than he ought to have done. I would put the inconsistency in my security precautions down to a foreigner's inexperience, were it not that all the Russians I knew except perhaps Irina seemed to be equally inconsistent.

I didn't see a great deal of Igor's colleagues at *Novy mir*, and even less of the writers he worked with. I think most of his work with contributors was done at the *Novy mir* office, or at home at times I wasn't around. The one exception was Nikolay Pavlovich Voronov, and I don't know if this was just happenstance or if Igor arranged it on purpose. Conceivably it was the latter, because Voronov was a rare bird in the Moscow literary world, a working-class writer from the provinces who had stayed working class, not in a performative way but out of modesty. Igor believed in the value of his work, but as an editor, it was a struggle: large-scale composition was not Nikolay Pavlovich's strong suit, he wrote to me. 'And it's his first attempt at such a grandiose genre'.

The genre was fictionalised autobiography, and what made Voronov's novella, *Youth in Zheleznodolsk*, so interesting were the circumstances of his early life. Born into a peasant family that broke apart during collectivisation, Voronov was brought up in the steel city of Magnitogorsk ('Zheleznodol'sk') in the 1930s. But it wasn't the Magnitogorsk famed in Soviet legend as the socialist city heroically built from scratch by enthusiastic volunteers. Voronov's Magnitogorsk was a frontier town with a rowdy, untrained workforce, housed in crowded barracks, with free labourers mingling with prisoners and deported *kulaks*. Food was scarce, violence common, families fragmented, and kids tough, streetwise and liable to be in trouble with the police. This was classic *Novy mir* material—authentic, eyewitness stuff, challenging to Soviet myth—and, as such, it caused trouble when the journal published it. Critics felt it diminished the stature of this heroic epoch in Soviet industrialisation, and in addition, the city fathers of present-day Magnitogorsk were offended. Voronov bore this manfully, Igor wrote, being 'a cheerful man, a believer in Communism'.

I had the impression that I was the only foreigner that Nikolay Pavlovich had ever met, and that I wasn't quite what he expected: not the sophisticated seductress of Soviet spy stories, but just a rather shy young girl. Igor also sometimes saw me like that—'I keep forgetting that you are grown up now', he would say, as if he had known me forever—but Nikolay Pavlovich carried it further, bringing me sweets and oranges as if I really were a child. I don't remember meeting him anywhere but at Igor's. But apparently the three of us once went together for a meal at the Vostok cafe (why should this have been edited out of my memory?), an occasion so memorable to Nikolay Pavlovich, or so Igor claimed in a letter, that when his novella was attacked in the press, he comforted himself by recalling it.

Nikolay Pavlovich was living in Kaluga, about a hundred miles from Moscow. Like all provincial towns, Kaluga had chronic shortages of basic foodstuffs, including sausage, so his regular trips to Moscow were not only for professional consultation with Igor but also for provisions. It was the same with Solzhenitsyn in his years of residence in Ryazan, another provincial town not much further away than Kaluga. In *The Calf and the Oak*, chronicling his friendship and battles with Tvardovsky, he recalls the day when he telephoned from the railway station, ready to board the train, and loaded down with provisions that were unobtainable outside the capital, and Tvardovsky told him that the latest crisis absolutely required his immediate presence at the *Novy mir* office. Solzhenitsyn brusquely refused to take a taxi to *Novy mir* from the station, unwilling to appear like a peasant with his bags of eggs and sausage over his shoulder, and also a bit resentful of the privileged life that protected Tvardovsky and other Moscow intellectuals from such problems.

In his first letter to me after I left Moscow in 1967, Igor wrote:

> Believe me, I value your interest in all the events and people which make up the greater part of my life now and in the past. And it is clear to me that ... you try to understand, and in many respects have already understood, things that we participants in these events, people of definite views, understand only with difficulty and far from completely ... You have the capacity to look at things with open eyes, not to let your view be dimmed with preconceived opinions.

The formal language sounds like a testimonial, and probably it was meant that way, as something I could use ('quote me, dear Sheila, whenever you want to') as a recommendation for my Lunacharsky work. But I also sense a certain wistfulness. One-sided though our early conversations were, enough of me must have come through for Igor to know more or less whom he was dealing with—not a person of his own 'definite views' on politics, but a sceptically inclined Westerner, whose ultimate goal was not only to understand how participants in Soviet events saw things but also, using my non-participant's detachment, to see things the participants couldn't see. To look with open eyes was certainly a quality Igor and *Novy mir* valued. But, as Igor once wrote to me, he was also 'a political man', and the journal had a political position and played a role in Soviet politics. *Novy mir*'s ideal reader was not just open-eyed but Party-minded, someone who knew which side they were on.

It was my aim not to be on anybody's side. But this was complicated for me in these years both because of my personal loyalty to Igor and because of the enormous intellectual effort I was putting into learning to see the world through his eyes. That meant also the eyes of *Novy mir*, which I internalised in the same way as Max Hayward and many others internalised the dissidents. One thing we all learned from our Soviet friends was the meaning of *svoi*—the thing or person that is ours, belonging to our group or tribe, not someone else's. For me, the loyalty question in a Soviet context was quite simple. *Novy mir* was *svoi*. I was on its side, not that of *Oktyabr'* or Ovcharenko.

Of course, I saw *Novy mir* through my own prism as well. Back in Australia, I had been brought up in a left-wing family where to be 'agin the government' was a mark of moral superiority. *Novy mir* wouldn't admit to being agin the Soviet government, but there were certainly a lot of similarities; my Soviet milieu of Igor and *Novy mir* didn't feel as unfamiliar to me as it might seem at first glance. My father's sardonic commentary on the absurdities of, say, the Australian Royal Commission against Espionage, and Igor's on those of the Writers' Union were essentially the same genre. My father was proud of being a brawler and disrespecter of persons; so was Igor. They were even sentimental in the same way. Lakshin recalls a private reading by Tvardovsky of his poem *Terkin in the Other World* that made Igor cry, something I never saw him do, drunk or sober: it was the moment when Terkin, having died and gone to heaven, decides to come back to earth because 'anyone who can help even just a little bit' is needed there. My father might have wept at that, too. Still, there was an important difference. My father was almost totally a mocker, iconoclast, gadfly and sceptical relativist. Igor and *Novy mir* were mockers and iconoclasts up to a point, but they also believed in the existence of a truth that it was their duty to proclaim. I was astonished when I first realised this: how could someone as sophisticated, shrewd and even cynical as Igor think truth was something unambiguous that could be discovered and made manifest? A truth every thinking person instinctively knew, were they only brave enough to say it? Of course, Igor could be a bit flippant about this view of truth: if you caught him out in a contradiction, or he caught himself out, there would be a mischievous smile and gesture of the hands as he exclaimed '*Dialektika!*'—the Marxist way of dealing with ambiguity, meaning *I may have contradicted myself, but everything contains its opposite*. But Igor was a believer in a way my father was not. He and *Novy mir* believed that truth was discoverable, non-relative, and communicable as long as its communication was not blocked.

I was very struck by this truth-telling mission. Truth seemed so easy to know, in a Soviet context: it was simply what the regime was trying to hide. That simplicity, for all my bumptiousness about my ability to 'get Soviet history right', went against the grain with me; it was so absolute, whereas I assumed that there was always a certain relativity—I see the truth from where I stand, not the truth as God might be able to see it. The odd thing was that the simple approach to truth seemed to work in a Soviet context; and when I was with Igor, I would more or less believe it. Along with the journal's multitude of readers, I would read *Novy mir*'s truth-telling articles and stories and think, yes, that's how it must be, and feel enormous gratitude that finally someone came out and said it. There must have been something about the very process of state suppression of information that created this sense of an unambiguous truth, available to those who could discover and publish what had been suppressed. In any case, *Novy mir*'s editing process was not about making truth clearer—it was always clear—but working out how much of it you could get away with telling at any given moment.

While *Novy mir*'s mission was truth telling, this had to happen in a real-life context. The moment was not always right for telling the truth, and there were questions of how much of the truth could or should be told at a particular moment. There were also questions of how it could be told—straightforwardly as non-fiction, with or without detailed supporting evidence, semi-disguised as prose fiction (or even poetry), further concealed by the use of Aesopian language, and so on. Listening to Igor talk, I was fascinated by the lines he and *Novy mir* were always drawing in the sand. These lines, indicating the parameters of what a decent (*poryadochnyi*) person must do, taking into account the current political configuration (*kon"yunktura*), were constantly shifting and endlessly contested. It was over the drawing of such lines that Tvardovsky and *Novy mir* parted company with Solzhenitsyn.

Some people thought it was the responsibility of all 'decent' people to sign open letters of protest against regime actions, like the latest condemnation of Solzhenitsyn or the Soviet invasion of Czechoslovakia. But the *Novy mir* editors did not sign such letters, even if they agreed with their content, on the grounds that to do so offered unnecessary provocation to the authorities and put the journal's survival at risk. This became a key issue between *Novy mir* and Solzhenitsyn, who in the late 1960s was moving towards a maximalist position of 'Live not by the lie', which involved taking every occasion to denounce everything false in Soviet life, regardless of *kon"yunktura* or consequences. Consequences were often part of *Novy mir*'s calculation about where to draw the line. Sometimes it was a matter of consequences to the journal, but it could also be international consequences in the Cold War context—not damaging the Soviet Union by a publication that could lend support to *émigré* and anti-Soviet forces in the West.

Novy mir was not the only one drawing lines in the sand. *Oktyabr'* and other journals had their own ideas of 'so far and no further', and so did newspapers like *Pravda, Izvestiya,* and *Sovetskaya Rossiya*. Lines were drawn, monitored and redrawn. They were the subject of heated dispute among the journals, as well as between individual journals and the authorities and among the authorities (Writers' Union, Party Central Committee, the censorship) themselves. There were bitter subterranean fights over line drawing, complete with slanderous rumours and denunciations. The reading public got involved too, via approving or disapproving letters to the editor, of which *Novy mir* received thousands. Individual readers also wrote denunciations to the authorities when they thought lines had been drawn wrong; and, judging by the novel in which Kochetov pilloried a fictionalised Patricia Blake, they also resorted to personal harassment. In one episode, the wife of the Kochetov figure pleads with intelligentsia 'liberals' to stop their campaign of accusatory letters and telephone calls at home, which were poisoning her life as well as her husband's. I never heard from Igor of *Novy mir* personnel suffering in this way: can liberals really have been more inclined to such tactics then Stalinists? It's counter-intuitive but not impossible: it was the liberal side that had the overwhelming sense of righteousness and moral entitlement, not the Stalinists, who in the 1960s were often just cautious conservatives with a dash of Russian nationalism and anti-Semitism.

No doubt having such simple access to truth is one of the advantages of living under a repressive government—not the seriously repressive Stalinist type, when doubting official precepts was too much of a luxury for most to indulge in, but the mildly repressive regime of the Khrushchev or Brezhnev years, when there was enough scope for independent thinking to make challenging orthodoxy a feasible proposition. Truth was the opposite of the untruths (whitewashing, evasions, comforting legends, pious verities, outright lies) that the regime and its acolytes put out: for example, that collectivisation was a glorious success, save for a few over-enthusiastic excesses; that the collective farms were prosperous and happy; that only criminals were sent to Gulag, where the best of them could be 'reforged' and returned to society as new men; that all Soviet citizens were assured of all the civil rights guaranteed by the Constitution; that Soviet society was equal and without a privileged class; that the Soviet Union was a true participatory, multinational democracy, without ethnic tensions or discrimination; that there were no alienated young people or poverty-stricken old ones; that in general everything was getting better and better in the best of all possible worlds. In this context, it was comparatively easy to tell the truth simply by gathering some empirical data to show that the bland generalisations didn't fit, and that was *Novy mir*'s stock in trade.

You might say that in the same way as I rather teasingly accepted Igor's anti-modernism for the duration, so also did I accept the *Novy mir* view of truth, acknowledging its appropriateness for the Soviet context but not seeing it as a possible export commodity. That's correct up to a point: no doubt I was still basically as sceptical a relativist when I returned from the Soviet Union as I had been when I went there. But the *Novy mir* immersion left its traces; I had ceased to be an unconditional believer in sceptical relativism. I had also acquired a kind of nostalgia for a context in which there was just one truth, and knowing it was easy, even if telling it was hard. My Moscow life left me with the conviction that the Soviet Union was the most inconvenient, uncomfortable place in the world to live. But in another way (*dialektika!*), my *Novy mir* experience told me, it was also the easiest, because the moral issues were all so straightforward. In later years, my lost Soviet Eden was the *Novy mir* world of certainties about the truth and companionable solidarity in proclaiming it.

7

Between Two Worlds

Svetlana Alliluyeva, Stalin's daughter, defected to the West in March 1967. It was a moment of great drama in East–West relations, exciting without being scary like the Cuban Missile Crisis, and we all enjoyed it. Except perhaps poor Svetlana, launched on the erratic course that would have her shuttling between continents and even briefly re-defecting to the Soviet Union for the next two decades. Foreigners with access to Western information sources knew about the defection before the Soviet press broke the story, and so did many Soviet citizens, because they heard her radio broadcast over Voice of America. By late May, as I wrote to my mother, we were all waiting for a *Pravda* explosion about Svetlana. It finally came, in a series of long vitriolic articles denouncing her as a traitor and a dupe of the CIA. They also attacked the Western Sovietological community, particularly the select group of scholars that was said to be coaching Svetlana in her public statements and helping her write her memoirs. My heart sank a little at that. If there were potentially bestselling, anti-Soviet memoirs in the works, Max Hayward was likely to be somewhere in the picture—another black mark.

Igor, as usual, was a fount of information; the whole affair was doubly exciting because I was getting the inside scoop from someone who actually knew Svetlana and could relate all the complex details of her marriages and affairs. He was quite sympathetic to Svetlana as a person, I wrote to my mother, saying that no-one deserved the kind of life she had had and describing her as 'a broken woman' (the fact that I sent this report through the open post indicates that I was not always as discreet and protective of Igor's reputation as I imagined). He knew about the defection very early on, but this didn't surprise me, as I assumed it had gone out on 'white TASS', the insiders' closed-circulation news bulletin, and that Tvardovsky had passed it on. It turns out, however, that Tvardovsky heard about it from Igor rather than the other way round: he says in his diary that Igor had got the news that Svetlana was writing her memoirs from Irina Lunacharskaya. Perhaps that came from the Novosti press agency where Irina worked. It wasn't information that Irina had shared with me, which was further confirmation that she knew how to hold her tongue with foreigners, even those who were friends.

The Svetlana affair was the signal for a new campaign against spying by Westerners, including exchange students. It was mainly focused on Americans and the CIA, although *Pravda* added the not particularly reassuring caveat that 'of course, far from all American scholars and students who come to the Soviet Union are professional agents of US intelligence or "volunteers" who take up espionage activities'. One story made it clear that the Soviets regarded the final reports that all exchange students had to write when they got home—that *I* would have to write in a few months—essentially as intelligence reports. In an article headed 'History and its falsifiers', *Pravda* told its readers about the 'special well-subsidised research centres' in major capitalist countries—read St Antony's and its like—that sponsor the study of Soviet history and, at the behest of their imperialist bosses, 'publish works that discredit—directly and in a veiled form—the struggles of the peoples of the USSR to build a socialist and communist society'. To combat this ideological sabotage from abroad, *Pravda* called for regular critical scrutiny of the journals that published such disinformation. Obviously *Soviet Studies*, where I had published my first article, was on that list.

There was plenty to worry about on the Cold War political scene in those last months of my first year in Moscow. But I was taking a break from worrying. Life was good, from my point of view. I had found Igor and Irina, got into the archives and made great strides with my research. I had stopped being depressed, lost weight and acquired quite good Russian. Even my asthma was better, as it was always to be in Moscow, though why this should be so, given the city's high levels of industrial pollution, was a mystery. I felt like a different person from the lonely girl making solitary trips round Moscow with a guidebook back in the autumn. Now Moscow was my town; I had a book full of telephone numbers, and friends who worried if I didn't ring.

Tomiko and I went off to do research in Leningrad for ten days in May and cemented our friendship, despite the bedbugs in the dorm and the rare appearance of hot water. Having become in my own mind a Muscovite, I was now fairly blasé about Leningrad's charms and decided that Moscow had turned out to be a better assignment than Leningrad would have been. Almost as soon as we got back to Moscow, I was off again, this time on the British Council students' end-of-year trip around the Soviet Union. This was a much cherished bonus of three weeks' free travel, with an itinerary including Kazan and Volgograd on the Volga; Tashkent, Samarkand and Bukhara in Central Asia; and Yerevan and Tbilisi in the Caucasus. Reflecting my changed state of mind, I now found the British Council students nice and the stories of their eight months in Moscow interesting. I particular got to like one of them, Ann Barlow, whom I had for some reason taken against back in September and lost sight of in between. Ann was studying Nikolay Fedorov, a Russian Orthodox philosopher of the early twentieth century interested in physical resurrection of the dead, though she surely had some other topic as a cover. Like me, she had been adopted by a Russian family, in her case via the more common route of an affair with a son of the family, an artist.

We had guides at various stops along the way, but our grand tour was remarkably unsupervised. Perhaps we had some Soviet watchdog along with us, but if so, I have no memory of it and didn't report it in my letter to my mother. We were housed in Soviet tourist hostels, not in hotels for foreigners, which was uncomfortable but worth it for the experience. To be sure, this may not always have been clear to us at the time: at one of our Central Asian stops, where our hostel had outdoor latrines and no water except on the ground floor, a group of us went to the local Intourist hotel and tried unsuccessfully to persuade them to let us have a bath and access to flush lavatories for foreign currency. The further we got from Moscow, the warmer it got and the brighter and livelier life became. There was an abundance of fruit in the markets, women in bright colours on the streets, and men placidly drinking tea in tea houses.

Tashkent was recovering from a major earthquake the year before, and a large area in the centre of the city was still flattened, so we were lucky to be allowed to go there. I liked the local modern architecture better than that of Moscow, and found the traditional Uzbek house—white mud-brick with a central courtyard with fruit trees and vines—very appealing. 'I don't think the Uzbeks will like living in progressive Soviet flats, even if they do have running water', I told my mother. It was a relief to find that there were parts of the country that hadn't succumbed to the drabness and austerity of Soviet standardisation, and surprising to find that, as far as everyday life was concerned, the non-Russian republics felt a lot more relaxed and liveable than Moscow.

One day in Tashkent, Ann, Michael (the group leader) and I ran away from an annoying guide and decided to make our own way to the Tashkent Lake, which the guide claimed was flooded. We got there somehow (could we have hitchhiked?), 'very impressed by the attractive and prosperous appearance of the villages along the road', as I told my mother, and discovered an idyllic scene with no signs of flooding.

> We took a boat and rowed, then came back and had a meal at a cafe beside the lake. This may sound a simple pleasure, but in the USSR it is almost a miracle to find not only a lake but boats for hire and a place to eat where you want it which hasn't run out of food and drink. It even had cigarettes. We were extraordinarily pleased with ourselves.

The next day Michael and I absconded again in search of a collective farm. Michael was an economist with a professional interest in agriculture, suspicious that the authorities' unwillingness to take us to a farm indicated that they had something to hide. We saw a bus with 'VI Lenin kolkhoz' as its destination and hopped on. Ironically, the *kolkhoz* (collective farm) seemed to be flourishing, unlike any counterparts we had seen in Russia. Buildings were solid, paint was fresh and the administrative building was so brightly decorated with Leninist slogans that if Intourist had taken us there we would have thought it was a put-up job.

Life seemed to be even more cheerful in Georgia. In fact, the mores in Tbilisi were almost too relaxed for us. There were a lot of cafes, I wrote to my mother, and hundreds of men lounging around on the streets doing nothing. Women couldn't walk down the street without being followed, whistled at, and 'simply pestered until they are forced to go home', which cramped our style quite considerably and led me to tell my mother that the Georgians were an unattractive lot, and moreover 'even more conspicuously drunk than the Russians'. This bad impression was slightly modified later in our visit, when we met some young people who took us for a (free) ride around the city in an open car, a very old Mercedes Benz. In Russia, you just didn't meet light-hearted young people with vintage Western cars at their disposal.

We took a bus to Gori, Stalin's birthplace, and saw the museum, established in 1955 and 'very lavishly set-up'. This was a change from Moscow, where public traces of Stalin had all been expunged after Khrushchev's condemnation of the Stalin cult. It hadn't occurred to us before that the Georgians might so openly follow their own path with regard to the most famous of their sons. We saw a number of wayside shrines to Stalin beside the roads and busts of him in public places. The manager of a bustling cafe we visited in Tbilisi had a portrait of Stalin in his office.

I found this all very intriguing, and wrote to my mother, a little tongue in cheek, that I was quite in favour of a Stalin museum, which at least made a change from the ubiquity of memorials to Lenin in Russia: 'the predominance of Leniniana can be oppressive—Staliniana gives almost an impression of pluralism'.

The prosperity of the place, particularly the countryside, impressed us.

> In the countryside there were lots of very attractive villages, especially in the wine-growing area—separate, quite substantial brick houses with roses and vines and verandas. People were always giving us roses (about a rouble per flower in Moscow), which was pleasant, although the people who gave were often not. It seems that all Georgian drunks carry roses in case they meet a girl: one even gave one rose each to Ann and me, and then two to our male companion 'because he has such a lovely face'.

The other thing that impressed us was the prevalence of private enterprise, openly practised. On one of our trips in Georgia, we were travelling around in a bus owned by the university with a cheerful 78-year-old bus driver who, as soon as we got out of the city,

> operated it like a passenger bus, charging fares by agreement with people he picked up (we went free). He picked up two drunken peasants, or tramps, who made a terrible noise and forgot their blankets when they got out. 'Absolutely drunk', the bus-driver said cheerfully. But he sent someone after them.

By the time we got back to Moscow, we too had loosened up and absorbed some of the Georgian insouciance.

We had to make our own way home from the airport (another indication of how unscripted this whole trip was), and a group of us did it by private enterprise.

> When we got back to Moscow airport, a man came up and said 'Taxi'. We went with him, but it was not a taxi but his own car marked 'Communications'. Either it was his day off or else work was slack. He charged us four roubles (without a meter) but we only paid three.

'Soviet car drivers are very willing to give lifts in general', I informed my mother, 'but you have to pay'. Up to now, however, that had been theoretical knowledge as far as I was concerned. I knew other students flagged down private cars, but I had never done it before.

I must have still been in holiday mood when I got back, because I took a Russian lover. This was quite a startling departure in my life. It wasn't just that I had made a conscious decision to avoid any sexual entanglements in the Soviet Union, for fear of getting into trouble and being thrown out; it also meant abandoning the 'no boyfriends' rule I had imposed on myself when I left Australia three years earlier, in reaction against the boyfriend messes I had got into in my last years in Melbourne. It meant being unfaithful to Alex, too, though somehow our marriage still seemed so tentative and unreal that that wasn't uppermost in my mind. I had already let my guard down with Igor as far as intimacy was concerned but had drawn the line at sex. That's when Sasha came along.

Sasha was an active Young Communist in his fourth year in the PhilFac of Moscow University who hailed from the closed city of Gorky on the Volga. The son of dockworkers, he was a beneficiary of Khrushchev's affirmative action program, so at least I wasn't breaking my rule by sleeping with the intelligentsia. He was serious, sweet natured and orthodox in his thinking, with no pretensions to sophistication. Moscow was exotic from his point of view, let alone the West, about which he knew very little. I met him when he came to my dorm room as student monitor of the eighth floor, and then he came round again and it went on from there. He was thin, medium height but athletic in build, with light-brown hair. For some reason, although he was quite good-looking, he had a low opinion of his looks, especially his facial bones: 'I'll be an ugly old man', he said, and I remember being surprised that such a thought might occur to anyone, let alone somebody apparently without vanity like Sasha. Getting to Moscow University had been more or less the sum of Sasha's ambitions, and he expected to go back to Gorky when he graduated the next year (Soviet university courses were five years). His chosen field was Soviet literature, which set him apart from the Moscow sophisticates like Valery among the students. Perhaps this was why he was without a girlfriend: the girls at the PhilFac often had elite or at least intelligentsia backgrounds and would have seen him as lower-class, while for the provincials, looking for a way to stay in Moscow after graduation, he lacked the essential husband qualification of a Moscow residence permit.

I'm not sure how I fitted Sasha in, given my intensive schedule with Igor Alexandrovich. It helped that I had finished my work in the archives, and I more or less gave up library work for the last month too. It was such a hot summer, and so pleasant to wander around Moscow River, whose grassy surrounds were full of people, alone or in couples or groups, who had stripped down to get the sun on their skin, women, regardless of age or fatness, lolling unselfconsciously in bras and underpants. This was an out-of-doors, simple-life Moscow quite unlike any I had previously encountered, with small pleasures that were to be had only at that season, like stalls selling Czech beer. Sasha particularly relished the beer, a deficit commodity; and when I went to a reception at the British Embassy, he made me list all the kinds of drink that were on offer so that he could rejoice on my behalf at the unbelievable luxury. 'I'm not a match for you', he would say gloomily; and he spoke of Alex, the absent husband who presumably was a match, with respect and deference. But in another mood, thinking of my reliance on his practical skills and Soviet know-how, he would say, 'You'll be lost without me'.

I didn't think Sasha had been sent by the KGB, on the Valery and Misha model. I suppose I could have been wrong, but it quickly became irrelevant anyway, since Sasha fell in love with me, and that certainly wouldn't have been on the KGB's agenda. Since I didn't think he was KGB, I used to tease him by calling him a *provokator* (literally, one who provokes; in common usage, a spy trying to entrap someone). He always objected to this, though he did confide that once back in Gorky he had 'infiltrated' a Baptist group, not for the KGB, but because he was curious to see what went on there. I was struck by his use of the word 'infiltrate', a very Soviet way of describing joining a society. My Russian improved by leaps and bounds with Sasha, creating a problem for me in later life when graduate students would ask how to achieve this. Judging by my experience and that of other exchange students, having an affair with a Russian is the way.

My visa was due to expire on 15 July. Out of the blue came a letter from Alex, thitherto a very unreliable correspondent, saying that he had made friends with one of the Russian exchange students in Japan, who said he could organise him a fortnight in Moscow without paying Intourist rates. This sounded highly implausible, but the additional catch was that Alex was proposing to leave Japan on 11 August, almost a month after my visa expired. I felt there was very little chance of getting a six-week extension—lots of exchange students had tried in the past, but there were no reports of success—but felt bound to apply. 'All my plans are upset', I wrote grumpily to my mother, 'and as I won't know about my visa for ages I won't be able to arrange anything at all', which meant there might be no seats left on the train. It irritated me that Alex should be so insouciant and assume that he could break the rules in the Soviet Union, not having any idea how inflexible they were, or that his rule-breaking might be counted against me. Anyway, why couldn't he leave Japan earlier? I spent two weeks battling for the visa extension, but unsuccessfully. In the end, predictably, Alex's plans for an illegal stay in Moscow fell through. He did touch down in Moscow on his Aeroflot flight from Tokyo to London later in the summer, however, a landing notable for the fact that fire broke out on the plane and the passengers had to slide down the escape chutes. Ignoring instructions to the contrary, Alex took his hand luggage with him down the chute and emerged unscathed.

The exit formalities from the Soviet Union were nightmarish. In addition to the visa you had come in with, which was valid only up to a certain date, you also had to apply for an exit visa, without which they wouldn't let you depart. The nightmare was that your original visa might expire before the dilatory Soviet authorities produced the exit visa, making it illegal for you to go or stay. When I say nightmare, I mean that literally, because the experience of that first departure from Moscow left a lifelong mark on me in the form of a recurrent nightmare in which I am trying to leave Moscow but for bureaucratic and practical reasons can't get myself to the airport and onto the plane. In the real-life 1967 departure, my luggage included a trunk that was too heavy for me to carry. A week or so before departure, we were supposed to take our trunks to some place in central Moscow where they would be inspected and sealed up with steel bands. Presumably this was to save Customs trouble at the airport, but what about our trouble? How did you get the trunk from the university to the centre and back when you couldn't call a taxi and they didn't cruise in the vicinity? The answer is lost to memory, but Sasha must have helped. Then, when I got to the airport for departure, Customs ordered me to open the trunk, despite the fact that it had been sealed by their own agents and that I was not carrying any tools for undoing steel bands.

'I was very sad to leave Moscow', I wrote to my mother after my return to Oxford. But I didn't think I had left it for good. Igor had suggested I should try to come back the next year in May, as I wrote to my mother; his idea was that I should persuade Alex to come with me for the whole year. I didn't think a whole year would work, but I went off to the embassy to apply for an extra two months on my British Council award the following spring, April to June 1968. I hadn't consulted Alex about this plan, judging by my slightly anxious comment to my mother that 'I don't know what Alex will think'. The embassy man I talked to, the same one with whom I had the Horst Bott conversation, whom I liked and regarded as an ally, was 'rather grumpy' about my request because he said they already had a bunch of short-term extensions and I might do someone out of a long-term place, but he promised to recommend me nonetheless. As of mid June, I hadn't heard definitely from the British Council about my application but was assuming, based on past practice, that it would go through.

I didn't want to leave Moscow and was scared about going back to Oxford, where I had been so unhappy, and apprehensive about how things would go with Alex. Yet, as the British Airways plane took off, I had the instinctive feeling of relief we always had in those years—relief at having made it out safely, without being prevented from boarding, taken into custody, having research notes confiscated, or any of the other possible last-minute catastrophes. Everyone on the plane had the same reaction: in the 1960s, the sighs of relief at lift-off were more or less silent, but in later decades they sometimes became quite audible, even accompanied by clapping. With the Sasha affair, as well as the whole days I had been spending with Igor, I felt that for the past month or so I had been living dangerously as far as the KGB was concerned, and was glad to have got away with it. I felt uneasy about the Sasha affair, which, surprisingly, I had reported in only slightly bowdlerised version to my mother. It 'may have been rash of me', I wrote to my mother in July from Oxford, 'because if Sasha is not trustworthy I told him too much' about Igor—not specific *Novy mir* secrets, though I knew some, but enough to make it clear that Igor was speaking very freely to me. 'But I think Sasha is alright', I concluded, 'and he is fond of me. I do think he will be questioned about me, because Galya will inform, but that is nothing'.

'Did you see Philby in Moscow?' That was one of the first questions asked of me by a St Antony's Fellow after my return, and my heart sank. If I had caught sight of Philby in Moscow, I would have run as fast as I could in the opposite direction—the same reaction I had to Victor Louis and other notorious spies. But it wasn't possible at St Antony's to avoid the spy connection. Max Hayward had recently been named in a Soviet weekly as a CIA agent, and it turned out, as I had feared, that he had been working with Svetlana Allilyuyeva on her memoirs, although he wasn't the formal translator. In October, as I wrote to my mother, St Antony's was in the newspapers again, this time as a training ground for MI6. The *Observer* had even (tongue in cheek?) proposed Deakin, the warden, for the position of head of British Security (of which MI6 was the foreign espionage division). The papers were in one of their periodic frenzies about intelligence matters, with the names of the present heads of MI5 and MI6 published for the first time and endless stories about the Cambridge spies Burgess, Maclean and Philby. 'I think to have come back to Oxford at all is perhaps a mistake', I wrote to my mother, 'in view of the dubiousness of its Sovietologists and their uselessness to me, but what else could I have done?'

There was a personal dimension to this, too, of course: Alex and I had met up in Oxford, after various hitches, but it wasn't a success. He didn't like the first flat I chose;

I didn't like the second; and it took a few months before a St Antony's flat that we both found tolerable became available. His thoughts were on Tokyo, mine on Moscow. I was tormented by asthma in the damp autumn and back in my familiar Oxford mood of demoralisation. As of December, I still didn't have formal approval from the British Council for a spring trip, but I was obviously determined to go, regardless. 'If the British Council won't pay', I told my mother, 'I may be able to get a grant from St Antony's. I have bought a fur coat and £10 of blackmarket roubles from a Pole to buy a Russian typewriter in preparation for going to Moscow'.

It was intellectually disorienting being back in St Antony's after a year in Russia. I could see things through both Soviet and British eyes, but I was confused about my own perspective. 'Sats' teaching was very successful', I wrote to my mother. 'You may not have noticed, but in many ways I came out of Moscow a real little fellow-traveller, even quite well-disposed to Marxist explanations and sometimes—odder still—Soviet ones.' I was mulling over what I had learnt from Igor and trying to fit it in with the rest of what I knew, or thought I knew. I had been sceptical about some of the things Igor told me, and was now reading up on various topics 'for the main purpose of informing myself for further arguments' with Igor. But 'I see that he was usually more right than I'. Exactly what all these topics were I don't remember, but international affairs and European politics were among them. Igor had told me, for example, that when the writer George Bernard Shaw came to the Soviet Union in 1931, Lady Astor, who was also along on the trip, was his watchdog for British intelligence. I thought this implausible, a Soviet mirror-image notion, and, as I wrote to my mother, had been meaning to tell the story to my friend Ross McKibbin, a British historian, as an amusing misconception on Igor's part,

> but have not, because he might say it might have been true. I sometimes get a disconcerting feeling that I do not understand where the boundaries of probability lie, even in relation to British affairs and much less to Soviet.

I felt uncharacteristically at sea, hampered by an inadequate base of knowledge and, as I told my mother, 'the lack of commonsense I have always felt'. I suppose I did feel lacking in commonsense as I was growing up—certainly I felt my mother thought I lacked it—but I hadn't really felt this as a lack in Moscow, and it was unlike me to be oppressed by ignorance.

I'd left Moscow in July, but the first letter from Igor came in December. He had been writing, but the letters weren't getting through. Mine to him were also being held up, though the success rate was higher. Letters from Irina, Sasha and Elena Borisovna arrived without problems. I had some indirect news of Igor, however, via a friend of mine on the exchange who had hand delivered a package with a letter for Igor, medical supplies for Raisa Isaevna, and some contemporary music scores (Webern and Schoenberg) for Sasha Sats. When a letter from Igor finally arrived, it was gloomy: he complained of missing me and of being bored and ill. His old Civil War wounds were playing up and, although only sixty-four, he already felt that he hadn't long to live. 'Come! ... Don't tempt fate!' he wrote. 'After all I am quite old and have not lived peacefully ... Don't put it off.' He sent some news about *Novy mir* and the world of Lunacharsky studies. Elkin had published his biography of Lunacharsky (the one my chance acquaintance had mentioned in spring 1966) and got hammered by reviewers. 'He's a queer fish', Igor said (I had met him only in passing, I think at Irina's). 'I reviewed the manuscript and advised him not to publish without basic reworking, but he didn't believe me, and now look what is landing on his poor head.' Ovcharenko had made an annoying speech at the annual anniversary meeting in the Lunacharsky Museum, but as Igor had boycotted the occasion, which he subsequently regretted, he wasn't there to rebut it. Despite the problems with Alex and the marriage, I must have asked Igor to find a way of getting Alex invited to Moscow when I went back in the spring, as he wrote, 'I'll try to find out about Alex and his invitation. But I don't even know his last name or where he studies—I only know that he is your husband. I envy him that because I love you'.

The big task in Oxford was to write my dissertation. My aim was to have a draft ready to take to Moscow with me in April, and after a month or so to catch my breath and order my notes, I plunged in. I had a little study in one of the St Antony's buildings where I spent a lot of time, poring over my archive and library notes, smoking and typing until the early hours of the morning. The writing went quickly, as I meticulously informed my mother in my letters: 4000 words down by late October, 14 000 by mid December, 60 000 by the end of February, and 70 000 (200 foolscap pages) a month later. That was a complete draft of all but two chapters. Surprisingly, I even found time to check out archival possibilities for an article on 'Lunacharsky and Britain' for possible publication, on Igor's suggestion, in *Novy mir*—an exciting possibility at the time, though it never came to anything.

Hayward was 'very impressed' by my report on my work in Russia, I told my mother, 'which flattered me but made me wonder if I should have said less'. I was determined to 'keep my mouth shut here and not boast that I know all about *Novy mir*'. I kept to this vow of caution, which must have been irritating for Hayward. He 'has become quite interested in me', I wrote to my mother in November,

> and comes along with bits of [Soviet literary] gossip to see if I have picked up confirmation or denial in Moscow: this is quite an interesting game which I do not really approve of. It is only vanity that makes me respond, and on a few occasions (when I almost positively knew that the gossip was wrong or misleading) concern for the truth.

In the same spirit of caution, I declined Hayward's request to give a seminar at St Antony's on the current literary scene in Moscow, and also refused an invitation to write something for *Survey* on my Soviet impressions. I was more forthcoming in public about my archival work on Narkompros, giving a seminar at the London School of Economics that went down well with Leonard Schapiro and other Sovietologists.

Still doing his best to be friendly, Hayward took me and Alex out to lunch. It was a comparative success, since he got on more easily with Alex than with me, they both being English working-class lads, though he was from the south and Alex from the north. Or perhaps it was just because Alex was more relaxed and friendly in his presence than I was. Judging by my letters to my mother, I seem to have been even warier of Hayward than before, and my comments to Igor must have been still less flattering than those to my mother, as he wrote, tongue in cheek, 'As far as your scholarly advisors are concerned, taking into account everything I know about your English mentor, I assure you as a patriot that your advisor in Moscow [Ovcharenko] is absolutely on the same level'—in other words, both useless. (I thought I had used a version of this barb myself a few years later in the acknowledgements in my dissertation book, *The Commissariat of Enlightenment,* but it turns out that wiser thoughts prevailed: I simply thanked them both politely, if a little less warmly than Schapiro and EH Carr, and dedicated my book to Igor.)

After reading two finished sections of the dissertation, Hayward said 'in a rather flat voice' (as I reported to my mother) that it was 'splendid, original, exciting, fascinating, and of wide significance for our understanding of the formative years of the Soviet government'. Poor Hayward, nothing but praise, but all he got from me was dissatisfaction with his 'flat voice'. I admitted to my mother that in writing the dissertation, I had been trying to avoid giving 'unnecessary offence' to Hayward as well as to Igor. 'Perhaps this is wrong of me', I acknowledged. But it did have the advantage of encouraging me 'to cut out passages of obvious emotional identification' with Lunacharsky and his Revolution that would have jarred on Hayward, as well as inhibiting my tendency to malice and mockery out of respect for Igor. Evidently both those impulses were still active, pushing my text in opposite directions. Still, in a choice between Hayward and Igor, it's clear whose side I was on when the chips were down.

By February 1968, I had been accepted for the exchange by both the British Council and the Soviet authorities, and was set to leave London by train on 4 April,with a copy of my dissertation for Igor to 'tear to pieces', as I told my mother.

Letters to and from Moscow were now getting through, so I felt I was probably off the KGB's close-surveillance list, at least for the time being. Igor sent one of his letters by hand via a foreign scholar—strictly speaking, this was illegal, though everybody did it when the opportunity arose—but even after poring over its content I couldn't see why he hadn't sent it by open post, as it seemed quite innocuous. Evidently I had not yet internalised the Soviet instinct that said whenever you could send a letter abroad by hand, you did. Writing through the open post, he expressed joy at the prospect of my return, warning me, however, that his English was getting worse, not better, so he would need lots of help reading the dissertation. 'So be prepared to allocate a lot of time for it. I will feed you—breakfast, dinner, supper, *lunch* [the last written in English]—and if Alex comes, him too.'

I was 'very excited about going back', I told my mother, 'only don't want to dwell on it for fear of anti-climax'. The excitement was mainly about seeing Igor, but Sasha was also in the picture (Alex having decided against the trip): he was doing practice teaching in a school and promised to take me to see it. I had prudently resolved that I must try to recover Ovcharenko's confidence because I thought this would improve my chances of getting back to the Soviet Union in the future (Igor, I considered, would understand this strategy, though I had doubts about Irina). I had had enough of St Antony's and its Congress for Cultural Freedom politics, I wrote to my mother. Still, I wasn't exactly lily white myself. Were the rumours true, I asked her, that *Dissent* (the Melbourne journal in which I had published my first article on Soviet literature back in 1964) had admitted accepting CIA money? 'It sounds plausible', I commented; and it was, in fact, true. Nothing was simple, including Hayward's request that I give his greetings to Tvardovsky, if I had occasion to see him alone. What was the purpose of these greetings? It was the first I had heard of Hayward's having a personal connection with Tvardovsky, and I couldn't imagine why else Tvardovsky would be glad to hear from Hayward. Were they friends, unknown to Igor? Or was something other than greetings being conveyed?

Moscow was different when I arrived back in the spring of 1968. For one thing, I was stepping back into a world to which I already belonged, complete with family (Igor and Irina) and lover (Sasha). For another, although Moscow had only the usual muddy mess left by melting snow, the political 'Prague spring' was in full bloom, constituting a background, uneasy or hopeful depending on your interpretation, to everything that went on in Moscow. Alexander Dubcek had become First Secretary of the Czechoslovak Communist Party in January and was busy introducing 'socialism with a human face', cheered on by his compatriots and quietly applauded by many Soviet intellectuals, but watched with great suspicion by the Soviet leaders, who wondered if this was another Hungary 1956 in the making. The *Novy mir* people were sympathetic to the Czech reformers but feared that it would all end badly.

For *Novy mir*, the political weather was blustery and uncertain. A few days after I arrived, the editors received a telegram from an *émigré* journal in Munich saying they were about to publish Solzhenitsyn's *Cancer Ward*. The manuscript they were using was not the one *Novy mir* had painstakingly edited but an unedited version seized by the KGB in a house search; the go-between Victor Louis had delivered it to the journal. The purpose of this KGB action, it was assumed, was to prevent *Novy mir* from publishing the novel, but it also succeeded in driving a wedge between Solzhenitsyn and the journal. While *Novy mir* was outraged by the whole operation, Solzhenitsyn's attitude was more ambiguous, since he wanted the novel in print, and *Novy mir* had not been able to achieve that. Tvardovsky finally managed to convince Solzhenitsyn that he needed to write a statement deploring foreign publication without his approval and saying he had not authorised it or sent out the manuscript, but it was a struggle, leaving both men resentful.

Novy mir's issues were still running way behind schedule because of censorship trouble, and the sniping by other journals and newspapers continued. One of the competitors—'the most reactionary', is how I described it to my mother, so I suppose it was *Oktyabr'*—published an article that the *Novy mir* people considered a manifesto for the return of Stalinism in literature. I was at Igor's one day when his sister Tanya (whose husband had been killed in the Great Purges of the late 1930s) came round and we talked about this article. Tanya remarked that it was so ludicrous and stupid, one couldn't take it seriously. 'That's what you said then, too', Igor replied sadly. The sense of foreboding was such that the referent of 'then' was self-explanatory.

I sensed a difference in Igor's attitude to dissidents in 1968. The previous year he had been very emphatic that, whatever people thought in the West, *Novy mir* had nothing in common with dissidents: they were putting themselves outside the system, while *Novy mir* supported reform from within. Looking back, I wonder if he hadn't been laying this on a bit thick, perhaps to drive home the point to me, but perhaps also to send a message to Hayward and other Western *Novy mir* watchers. In 1968, in any case, he wasn't emphasising the gulf between *Novy mir* and dissidents so much, and he was more likely to mention news items that had come via the BBC, Voice of America or Radio Liberty from Munich (officially regarded as anti-Soviet and jammed, but not consistently). According to Solzhenitsyn, it was around this time that Tvardovsky started listening regularly to foreign broadcasts and keeping up with *samizdat*; and I think Igor did too, though never in my presence, and with a preference for the BBC over the more propagandistic Voice of America or Radio Liberty. Igor also surprised me by revealing that he and Tvardovsky had at least a passing acquaintance with a cynical and amusing BBC Overseas Service staffer, an *émigré* from the 1940s, Efim Izrailovich Shapiro, whom I sometimes saw in London. But then Efim Izrailovich—surely a prime *antisovetchik* in Soviet eyes—had also surprised me by being able to travel to the Soviet Union, and moreover still somehow having access to the old house in Moscow in which he used to live. Just when you thought you understood Soviet rules, you'd stumble on some gross exception.

This time around, I was much more one of the Sats family than before. I got to know Tanya for the first time and liked her; according to a letter to my mother, I even invited her over to visit me in my Moscow University dormitory and she came with Igor. I have no memory of this occasion and can't imagine how I managed this, given that all visitors had to have passes. (Could Sasha, with his official position as floor monitor, have been able to fix it?)

On one occasion, I even met Igor's famous niece, Natalia Ilinichna Sats, who established the Moscow Children's Theatre when she was still a teenager back in the 1920s, and became one of the most glamorous members of the Soviet elite, along with her husband, Trade Minister Israel Veitser. Both of them were arrested in the Great Purges, and Veitser was shot. But Natalia Ilinichna survived a Gulag stay, made it back to Moscow in the late 1950s, founded a new musical theatre for children and, with her talent for publicity, managed to re-establish herself as a minor celebrity until her death at ninety in 1993. Igor was not a great admirer of his niece, regarding her as too worldly, ambitious and vain, but she was someone to be reckoned with, a kind of supercharged Irina (who was quite highly charged herself). She brought some young man along to Igor's, who chatted me up but was cold-shouldered as a probable informer by the others present, Igor being particularly rude to him.

Raisa Isaevna was in better shape than the previous year, not always in bed or in hospital and sometimes able to join the company. This may explain the sudden frequency of family gatherings at Igor's place. She was up and about the first day after my arrival, when I went over to see Igor and found him, to my surprise, ready with vodka to celebrate my arrival and the departure of an engineer who was off to build railways in Siberia. It was the first time Igor had ever produced vodka in my presence, and my first face-to-face encounter with him as a drinker, though I had heard tell of it from Irina—and, for that matter, from Igor himself, who unabashedly treated drinking as one of life's pleasures. Throughout the evening, Igor 'sat holding my hand and staring fixedly at me, not listening to what anyone said', while the engineer conducted a monologue on railways,

I wrote to my mother. Igor and the engineer quickly got drunk, so after a while I left. Sasha Sats, to whom I had sent the Webern and Schoenberg, was there too, very pale and seemingly overworked, but 'amused' by his father's besotted behaviour towards me, or so I claimed in my letter. That sounds a bit unlikely, but in any case he insisted on escorting me part of the way home, which I took to be motivated both by gratitude for the music and boredom with the company. In a small Moscow flat, there's really no place to hide when there's a drinking party going on.

Igor was in poor health, in constant pain from his back, where metal from his Civil War injury was still lodged. 'I don't think he is seriously on the point of death', I wrote to my mother rather heartlessly (or simply with relief?). 'I think this was just a way of getting me to come.' Still, a couple of months earlier, he had spent ten days in bed, which he would have done only in extremis. In addition to the pain, he was depressed by the death of one of his oldest friends, probably an old lover as well, Elena Usievich, who had worked with him at *Literaturnyi kritik* before the war.

I had brought two copies of the draft of my dissertation to Moscow. One I gave to Igor to read, the other to Irina. Igor struggled because it was in English (he never ceased to regret the fact that my language wasn't German) but got through it, and both he and Irina approved. I told my mother that Igor thought it should be published in Russian because no Soviet scholar had done anything comparable. That was pleasing, even if in the present political atmosphere there was next to no chance of Russian publication. Despite my good resolutions about mending fences with Ovcharenko, I didn't bring him a copy, no doubt because I wasn't prepared to make changes that he might suggest, though I would have got one for him if he'd asked. From Igor, I was prepared to accept correction; from Irina, less so—but at least she accepted that on matters not directly concerned with Lunacharsky, Igor had the final word.

As in the previous year, I had to write a scholarly Plan for the university, listing the sources I proposed to use. Ovcharenko signed off on it, including the archives I had listed (State and Literary, not Party), without protest; but I sensed some lack of enthusiasm and thought he just wanted to avoid having an argument with me about it. Perhaps he conveyed his lack of enthusiasm to the State Archives; in any case, I had some trouble getting back in. I finally sorted that out, but as I didn't get a lot of useful materials in the archive this trip, I ended up spending most of my time either with Igor or with Sasha, with visits to Irina on a less regular basis. I even took Sasha to meet Igor, perhaps partly because Sasha's final-year diploma thesis was on a novel about the Civil War that *Novy mir* had recently published. The meeting was not a great success. Igor was polite at the time, if a bit bristly, but later, when drunk, referred to Sasha as an idiot. Sasha, trying to be polite about my friend, described him as 'a nice man, although a Jew'. At least he said 'Jew' (*evrei*) rather than 'Yid' (*zhid*). The ethnic slur reflected Sasha's Russian lower-class origins, of course, but I think his reaction was based more on provincial working-class resentment of the privileged Moscow intelligentsia than anti-Semitism (for ordinary Russians, 'intelligentsia' and 'Jewish' were closely related concepts). As for Igor, it was probably mainly jealousy, with a bit of class prejudice thrown in.

Towards the end of my visit, the KGB became interested in me again in connection with Sasha. An alien cigarette butt on the window ledge indicated that someone had searched my room in my absence, but there was nothing incriminating in the room to find. Not even a diary, as I had stopped keeping one a month or so before leaving at the end of the first year; diary-keeping was evidently something I associated with being in a strange situation, and I no longer felt a stranger in Moscow. Sasha's academic supervisor liked him and his work and had been talking about finding a Moscow Institute placement for him after graduation, but now he called him in and said, without explaining what he meant but evidently regretting a blighted future,'What a shame; such a talented person'. Shortly afterwards it was revealed that Sasha was going to get an inferior placement outside Moscow, and in fact he ended up being sent to a primary school in his native Gorky region. By the end of my 1968 trip, I had a guilty sense that I had messed up Sasha's life in multiple ways, and that's how it looks in retrospect too, but I never knew for certain since he disappeared from Moscow that summer and out of all contact with me shortly after. 'The woman who sailed away', was how one English friend of mine described my role in this affair (he knew about it through his Moscow-resident wife, through whom I sent a few letters to Sasha before deciding that she was showing them to the KGB). He probably meant it as a compliment, more or less, but I didn't feel proud of myself.

The coda to my trip was an infuriating confusion about my stipend and exit visa. My visa expired on 6 June, but I had applied to extend it for a month. However, approval didn't come through until 10 June, meaning that my June stipend wasn't paid (you collected them at a set time once a month, from a surly woman behind one of those windows that could be slammed down). The result was that I ran out of money, including the money to book my train ticket home. I borrowed thirty roubles from Igor, something I no doubt wouldn't have done had I realised that he was in debt to the tune of thousands of roubles because of expenses for Raisa's illness (mainly medicines that had to be bought on the black market). Irina was quite annoyed when she found out, saying I should have got the money from her. Her assumption that she, as a friend, would naturally have given me whatever money I needed was typically Soviet: within your small circle of friends and family, you borrowed money (the Russian word was 'take', dismissing the question of repayment as insignificant) just as you would borrow a book or an umbrella. I picked Igor to 'take' from because he was closest, and also because he had repeatedly offered it—opening his desk drawer to show notes and coins scattered higgledy-piggledy in proof of his statement that he had lots on hand. Money, I decided, wasn't sacred in the Soviet Union the way it was with us; it was like any other commodity. When the June stipend finally came, I repaid Igor but couldn't spend the rest in the few days that remained, so I gave it to Sasha, who was on a very small stipend and was always short of money. My rational Western idea was that he could then give up his part-time job as a loader at the Moscow Film Studios near the university. His gallant or quixotic Soviet idea was that he should blow it all on lottery tickets, 'so that I will have a car to drive you round when you come back'. He didn't win the lottery.

The summer in Oxford after my return was even worse than the year before. Alex and I had had a row about

Sasha, and he took off for Europe, where he remained incommunicado for several months—having an interesting time in Paris during the student revolts, as it later turned out. None of my friends was in town, either in Oxford or London. It was 'pretty grim being on your own in Oxford in August', I wrote to my mother. The thesis was essentially done, and the final stretch of cleaning up, correcting, and checking footnotes didn't have much appeal. There was the question of what next. I hadn't applied again to the British Council, perhaps thinking I wouldn't get it for a third time once I was doctorate in hand, and was very depressed at the thought of being cut off from Moscow and my friends there indefinitely. Igor wrote, trying to keep up my spirits, but he wasn't too happy himself, and he had been sick again. The thing I should have been thinking about was jobs, but my approach to this was strangely lackadaisical. I had persuaded the Commonwealth Scholarships (who had sent me to England in the first place) to delay my fare-paid return to Australia for another two years; and a throwaway line in a letter to my mother indicates that I had had two approaches from Australian universities, of which I now have no recollection. At that point, it might have made sense for me and Alex as a couple (if we remained one) to return to Australia to live, although Alex, British by nationality and upbringing, had spent less than a decade in Australia; but it seems that this possibility remained quite abstract and unengrossing for me. It wasn't so much that I wanted to stay in England as that England was closer than Australia to Moscow.

For the time being, I was focused on the short term, to the extent that I was focused at all. I informed my mother that both the University of Birmingham and the London

School of Slavonic Studies had offered me 'good jobs', a term I used rather loosely to include fellowships. I owed the London prospect to Leonard Schapiro, I told my mother, since he had made them hold the job open until I came back from Moscow and could be interviewed. Later, after I got more career-minded, I looked back on my behaviour in that interview with astonishment. The school had two positions open for a Soviet historian, one a teaching position with prospects of permanency, the other a one-year, possibly renewable, research fellowship without teaching obligations; and when they asked me which I would prefer, I picked the fellowship, because I wanted to be free to continue fulltime research. Looking back, it's hard to imagine how I could have been so stupid. To be sure, I had answered the selectors' questions about teaching so absentmindedly and indifferently, despite Schapiro's prompting, that it would have been strange of them to offer me the regular job even if that had been my preference. In any case, they gave me the fellowship: £1260 a year plus a £60 living allowance for London, all of which I considered perfectly satisfactory. I would have to get a room in London and spend several days a week there, I wrote to my mother in late July; it would be useful for Alex, too, as he, like me, had a lot of work to do in the British Museum. This was putting a brave face on it, as Alex had temporarily vanished and I really had no idea if the marriage was still a going concern.

The Soviet invasion of Czechoslovakia on 21 August 1968 was a tremendous shock. In these years of self-preoccupation, it's the only external event that really got through to me. I was listening to every news broadcast because of Czechoslovakia, I wrote to my mother.

> I suppose I never expected the Czechs to get away with, or manage to invent, Communism without witch-hunts and police, but I didn't expect the Russians to move in. I thought it was all bluffing, those troops on the frontiers. I thought they would not risk acting without a shadow of support from Romania, Yugoslavia and European Communist Parties, or at least without staging a convincing counter-revolution. And Dubcek and Svoboda were popular in Russia.

Different perspectives jostled each other on the page. There was the purely personal interest: 'Thank God I am not on the exchange this year: there seems a fair chance it will be cancelled'. There was the analytical, Sovietological approach: 'I suppose everything will get more repressive in Russia, even though the Czechs may end up à la Hungary with a relatively mild government'. And finally, probably the strongest reaction, was identification with Igor and my Soviet world: 'I wish I was in Russia in one way. Poor Igor Alexandrovich will take this very hard'. I felt the Soviet invasion as I imagined that they would be feeling it: a moral insult, as well as a terrible omen for the future.

There was one more blow in that miserable summer: my exposure as a quasi-spy in *Sovetskaya Rossiya*. The article had come out in mid June, but it wasn't until October that I heard about it. The author was identified as 'VGolant, PhD in History', and Max Hayward later told me that, although writing for the most reactionary and anti-Western paper in Moscow, he was actually something of a dissident and subsequently emigrated to Israel. In telling my mother about the episode, I gave her the most optimistic reading, namely that as no connection was made between Fitzpatrick the author and Bruce the exchange student 'it was not a KGB campaign against me, but just some PhD student earning his right to read anti-Soviet journals'. All the same, I was 'rather upset', surely an understatement, and commented plaintively that 'you get rather a battering in Soviet studies one way and the other'. This led directly into some free-floating anxiety about the KGB: 'I wonder what has happened to Sasha, of whom there is no news at all. I have got so angry with Soviet sabotaging of mail that I have started sending letters registered, parcels insured, and paying for notification of delivery, but there hasn't been time to see if it works yet'.

There was no joy in Moscow either. 'The end of the summer and autumn were very difficult', Igor wrote on 20 September. It was a terrible moment for the reform-minded intelligentsia, with disbelief, disappointment and fear jostling each other. Everyone was appalled by the invasion, but few were bold enough to protest. A handful of dissidents including Pavel Litvinov (grandson of Ivy, nephew of Tanya) staged a brief protest on Red Square before being carted off by the KGB. Yevtushenko wrote an impulsive letter of protest, and as a result suffered abrupt withdrawal of privileges and official ostracism for several years. From the extended *Novy mir* circle, Solzhenitsyn's friend Lev Kopelev wrote a letter of protest, but was expelled from the Writers' Union for his pains. Solzhenitsyn and the physicist Andrey Sakharov talked about organising a collective protest, but the draft failed to get support from the usual suspects in science and the arts and was never sent; it seemed pointless, as well as dangerous, to protest against a *fait accompli.* Mandatory meetings at workplaces and Party organisations produced almost uniformly unanimous resolutions in support of the Soviet government's actions.

For *Novy mir*, it was not the finest hour. The *Novy mir* people were all privately against the invasion. But when their local district Party committee demanded that they take a resolution supporting the invasion, everyone except one of the younger editors (who stayed away from the meeting) agreed in advance that it was *force majeure*, and went along. 'Even Sats, from whom you can expect anything', as one editorial diarist recorded. To refuse, they reasoned, would have meant the immediate dismissal of the editorial board and the end of the journal as a force for change. On the other hand, signing the resolution had costs as well, especially when it was published, without *Novy mir*'s foreknowledge and clearly maliciously, in one of the other literary journals. *Novy mir* lost prestige and its editors must have felt shamed. It wasn't something Igor chose to talk about when I came back more than a year later. To be sure, Tvardovsky had partially salvaged personal honour by refusing to sign a collective letter from the secretariat of the Writers' Union reproaching Czech writers for supporting 'counter-revolution' and thus helping to precipitate the Soviet intervention. That didn't help his reputation with those 'up there', but it wasn't enough to make reform-minded people forget that abject, tail-between-the-legs resolution approving the invasion. Solzhenitsyn reproached Tvardovsky and his journal for not standing up for their principles, and he wasn't the only one to see it like that.

I sent a carefully coded account of the *Sovetskaya Rossiya* article to Igor, saying I was afraid that this meant I was out of favour in the Soviet Union and might have difficulties getting a visa in the future, but he replied almost dismissively. He hadn't known about the article but promised to look it up—and meanwhile, I should look in the same newspaper to see what awful things it had recently published about *Novy mir* 'so that you will understand that all that is just idiocy (*odin chort*). And what other signs are there "that people don't like you"? In any case your Moscow friends love you loyally and forever'. I hoped his optimism—if that's what it was, and not just defiant denial—was justified. Igor's letters continued to be quite upbeat for the next few months. *Novy mir* had won two Lenin Prizes (one for the novel that was the subject of Sasha's diploma project), which was a boost. The annual anniversary meeting in the Lunacharsky Museum came round, and Igor boycotted it again because he didn't like the company, presumably including Ovcharenko ('Irina Anatolevna was there and had to take a tranquiliser', he wrote. 'She is too sensitive.').

I had got myself back to work, and polished off another article, commissioned by *Soviet Studies*, as a follow-up to my first, on the most recent Soviet publications on Lunacharsky. It should have been an interesting exercise, given that I now had an insider's knowledge of all the authors and publication squabbles I had written about in the first article, but it turned out that that just made it complicated. I couldn't reveal some of my knowledge, and the fact that all the authors were known to me, and many had given me presentation copies of their books in hopes of getting a review in the West, was awkward and inhibiting. 'I don't think I actually perjured myself', I wrote to my mother, 'although I suppose it is not a good advertisement for my scholarly integrity. But my thesis is full of integrity and scholarship. I hate writing reviews anyway'.

By January 1969, the dissertation was finished—all 95 000 words, or just under the mandated Oxford limit of 100 000. It covered only the first three years of Narkompros under Lunacharsky's leadership, up to 1921, the moment of sobering up from the utopian idealism of War Communism, marked by drastic budget cuts that seemed likely to destroy much of what Narkompros had created since the Revolution. I had researched the whole period of Lunacharsky's tenure in Narkompros up to 1929, and 1921 emerged as my end point mainly because I hit the word limit and ran out of time. That, at any rate, was the way I understood my decision to end in 1921: it was a surprise when, a few years later, a critical Soviet reviewer of my book said that I had chosen that end date to fit the story I wanted to tell, which started with revolutionary hope and ended in disappointment. The surprise was partly because I saw that in a way the reviewer was right—that *was* my story, the central illumination I wanted to convey about revolution, even if I thought I had chosen my cut-off point for purely opportunistic reasons.

Hayward liked the dissertation, including no doubt the trajectory from revolutionary hope to disappointment. He had a feeling for the pathos of things; it was something we had in common, though I would never admit this. He invited me to what was evidently meant as a celebratory lunch, to which I responded with my usual gracelessness. It was a very expensive lunch, I noted in a letter to my mother. He ate at this place (could it have been the Randolph Hotel?) every day but didn't seem to be on greeting terms with the waiters, as regular clients usually are. 'After three hours of formal and slightly interesting conversation about Russia, waiting for him to say whatever he wanted to say, [I] decided it was either goodwill or desire for company.' Poor Max—three hours, and not a friendly smile, even from the waiters. I'm depressed in retrospect by the callousness of my report. All I can say in extenuation is that when you're young, you don't always believe that your seniors are human.

My strong reaction to the Soviet invasion of Czechoslovakia was an exception to my general habit of indifference to events in the world around me. This was 1968, the year of student rebellion all over the globe, but I paid little attention to it. I remember reading stories in the Soviet press when I was in Moscow about student riots in Europe and the United States, and noting the irony of the intense Soviet disapproval of these challenges to constituted authority, but it all seemed very far away. Then came Paris 1968, but I wasn't there with Alex to observe it, and probably tended to push it out of mind for that reason. By early 1969, it was the turn of the London School of Economics. After my return from Moscow, Schapiro told me of his anguish when revolutionary students trashed his office, behaving as if it didn't matter that he was a liberal and not a reactionary, but I listened with only half an ear. My letters to my mother scarcely mention the turmoil in the universities, beyond a passing remark in mid February that the LSE 'had been closed because of student riots but was about to reopen'. I had started at the School of Slavonic Studies (just around the corner from the LSE), and had belatedly come to the conclusion that it hadn't been particularly clever to go for the fellowship rather than the proper job, which had been awarded to a young man who was one of the school's own graduates. I was inclined to despise him because he hadn't put in a research year in the Soviet Union, and he disliked me, as a mutual acquaintance reported, because 'Fitzpatrick is a typical St Antony's product, and St Antony's is full of fascists'.

In March, I had a shot in the arm in the form of an unexpected letter from the great EH Carr, a historian I had always admired, despite the bad repute in which he was held in Oxford, but had been too shy or too busy to contact. It was elegantly structured around a donnish joke—addressing me as Mrs Bruce, he asked if I realised that an S Fitzpatrick was also working on my topic—and invited me to visit him in Cambridge. We became friends, if such a relationship is possible between a humble graduate student and a godlike figure who, in my memory, sits enthroned in a corner of a high, remote office at the top of Trinity College where neither light nor sound from the outside seemed to penetrate. His intimates called him Ted, I believe, but I not only called him Mr Carr (as was the custom then) but even thought and spoke of him always as 'EH Carr'. He had a reputation for being fearsomely impersonal in human interactions, although he was also notorious for having run away with the wife of the professor of French at Aberystwyth at an earlier point in his career (he was now in his early seventies), and I found him, as predicted, very formal and correct. But he actually had a lively curiosity about people and the odd way they run their lives (as can be seen from one of his early works, *The Romantic Exiles*, which in its sober way is almost gossipy). Naturally I never said anything about my private life to him, any more than he spoke about his to me, though both were fairly tumultuous at the time. We fell out of touch for six or seven months, during which time

I broke up with Alex and moved in with a new boyfriend, and he made contact again by writing to me *care of this boyfriend* at the London newspaper where he worked—another little Carr tease, like the initial letter to Mrs Bruce about her rival S Fitzpatrick—and inviting us both up to Cambridge for tea at his home. That was my first and only meeting with his comparatively new third wife, Betty Behrens, who demonstrated her status as a female don by pretending she didn't know how to pour out the tea. I didn't like her, and felt justified in this when, after his death in 1982 (by which time they were separated), she viciously denounced him.

Carr couldn't stand my London patron, Leonard Schapiro, and the feeling was mutual. Their hostility apparently dated back to the early 1950s, when Schapiro was just making his translation from the Bar to academia, and Carr successfully blocked publication by Chatham House of his first book, saying it lacked scholarly objectivity because of his anti-Soviet bias. Carr saw Schapiro as an *émigré* Cold Warrior, and perhaps also held his British intelligence connections against him, while Schapiro saw Carr as a pro-Soviet appeaser, too close to Isaac Deutscher and the New Left. An additional factor was that Schapiro had been a childhood friend in Riga of the Oxford philosopher Isaiah Berlin, who had his own running polemic against Carr's view that making moral judgements was not the historian's job. Schapiro and Carr both knew that I went to see the other, and each regularly reminded me of the other's political and intellectual deficiencies and (Schapiro on Carr) messy marital history. I cheerfully ignored the warnings, making no bones about the continuing contact in either case, which now strikes me as a more honourable and independent stance than might have been expected. I liked them both. Schapiro, a lover of music and Turgenev, was a very civilised man, but passionate in a civilised way about his opinions, which included a revulsion against Soviet tyranny. He must have noticed that on the question of moral judgement, I was more on Carr's side, but I don't remember that ever causing problems until my D.Phil. viva (final oral examination) in April 1969.

As was the Oxford custom, my supervisor wasn't present at the viva. The two examiners were Harry Shukman, a young Fellow from St Antony's who was in full academic regalia, and Schapiro, dressed in his usual gentlemanly grey three-piece suit (he had no higher degree, being a late arrival on the academic scene). By this time, I was used to universal approval of my work, and no doubt expected lavish praise on this occasion, too. In fact, the official record suggests that that's what I got. Max was sent the written report afterwards, and (against the rules) showed it to me: in summarising it to my mother, I wrote that 'I suppose if I had been writing a good report on myself I would have done it in much the same terms; one could hardly imagine that anyone could say more'. But actually I wasn't happy about the viva. 'I don't think Schapiro and Shukman liked the thesis very much', I wrote to my mother immediately after the event.

> They seemed to think it was written from too Soviet a position, although this was not said in so many words. Schapiro thought the Party should have been interfering more in Narkompros: he seemed not sure whether it was me or the Narkompros situation itself that was wrong, but either way he didn't like it ... I am sorry to lose (I think) Schapiro's goodwill, but I had often wondered if it was based on a misunderstanding of what I was doing.

I hadn't in fact lost Schapiro's goodwill at that point, as he went straight off after the viva and recommended the dissertation to a publisher. But I was right about the uneasiness. At the time of the viva, Schapiro was really shaken up by the student revolts at the LSE; it was hard for him to think of Lunacharsky without having all his disgust at mob rule rise up. 'Look where your Lunacharsky has led us', or words to that effect, is what I remember him saying to me at the end of the viva. I should have sympathised, if I hadn't been so wrapped up in my own concerns. In fact, I seem to have been quite critical of student revolution myself, at least in its Australian and American context, when I got round to noticing it. It was just gilded youth being childish, I wrote to my mother in October 1970. To be sure, this was immediately followed by a bit of self-mockery: 'Notice how I have been made reactionary by studying administration, i.e. my commissariat. I look at everything from point of view of those in charge because of Lunacharsky; I often feel I will grow up to be Dame Charles Snow' (the reference is to CP Snow, British establishment author of *The Corridors of Power*). This may have been a joke, but in retrospect I think it's not completely wrong: my 1967 immersion in Soviet bureaucratic archives was so total that it must have left its mark on me as a person as well as a historian.

Much later, Schapiro, having loyally acted as my patron throughout my English career, came to have reservations about my work; and in the early 1980s, after I had gone to America, he wrote a sharp criticism of a later book of mine accusing me of coldness and moral relativism. This looks like a different criticism than seeing things too much from the Soviet standpoint, but it is really the same objection, characteristic of the Cold War times we lived in: he thought

I failed to obey the moral imperative of taking a clear anti-Soviet and anti-Communist stand.

I wrote to Igor after the viva. Exactly what was in the letter I don't know, as it is lost along with the rest of Igor's archive, but I probably both complained about Schapiro's response and tried to turn the complaint into a compliment to Igor by saying it showed how well I had absorbed his teaching. Igor's reply, full of passionate indignation about Schapiro, reminds me of one reason his friendship was so important to me: I could always rely on him to take my side.

> If my advice in any way influenced Schapiro not to like [the Russian word means either like or love] you, I'm sorry. But to tell the truth, the person who doesn't like you is a fool, even if his name is Schapiro and he was a professor twice over. It shows that for all his vaunted historian's objectivity, he has succumbed to a gust of political passion. I won't blame him for that—I am a political man myself. But you shouldn't be upset about Schapiro not liking you. So the renowned Schapiro doesn't like you, but the non-renowned Sats does, and who knows which is better for the future.

I had secured my doctorate and written a dissertation that was widely noticed and admired; with support from Schapiro and Hayward, I was a young scholar ready for launching on the academic career path. But there was a strange hesitancy in my approach to this, unlike the single-minded determination with which I had pursued my goals in Moscow. I was thinking in terms of a career in England, although I didn't like the country and had been consistently unhappy there. That implied a decision not to go back to Australia. But I never sat down and worked it all out in my mind, in contrast to my careful planning with regard to the Soviet Union. Evidently the England–Australia issue was too complicated and laden with emotion to be thought about systematically. There were professional considerations, tending to favour England as the better place to make a career as a Russianist; issues related to my marriage, which didn't point clearly in either direction (it wasn't certain that the marriage would last, anyway); and, complicating it all, my irrational feeling that after my father's death I couldn't return to Australia.

Perhaps most important of all, at this stage of my life, was being able to get to Moscow. Yet I never for a moment contemplated doing a Svetlana in reverse and taking up long- or medium-term residence in the Soviet Union. That was possible, though difficult and unusual, but it looked like a terrible life to me. I knew some foreigners who had got jobs as translators (often at the Novosti agency where Irina worked, and usually because they had fallen in love with a Russian), and they were in general a miserable group: treated as pariahs by their own embassies, closely supervised by the KGB and forced to inform on other foreigners, and always liable to come under Soviet pressure to give up their British and American passports and become Soviet citizens. I was always extremely conscious of how important it was in the Soviet Union to have a passport that would get you out. My dilemma was that Moscow was the place in which I had put down tentative roots, but I could neither live there nor bear the thought of pulling up those roots and re-rooting myself elsewhere.

Complicating everything was that I didn't know what the impact of the *Sovetskaya Rossiya* article might be on my prospects of returning to Moscow. Igor didn't seem to take it too seriously, and neither did the people at St Antony's, but the KGB might when it came to issuing visas. The increased tensions associated with the Soviet invasion of Czechoslovakia put everything in jeopardy, conceivably even the exchanges themselves. I was between worlds, but I didn't know in which direction I was moving, or even if I was moving at all; I felt unexpectedly becalmed, in a condition of uneasy statis. Then, in November, everything changed.

8

Last Call for Moscow

I had had no concrete plans for returning to the Soviet Union, and perhaps considered it temporarily ruled out as atonement for the affair with Sasha. But in November, Alex's supervisor at St Antony's unexpectedly offered him the chance to go to Japan, doing a quick tour of Far Eastern departments of American universities on the way. That meant he would be away from England for six months. We were both pleased, and my first reaction was that perhaps I could tag along on the US part of the trip. 'I have not been to America', I wrote to my mother, 'but would like to go'. (This curious phrasing, as if my mother might not remember whether I had been to America or not, makes me wonder about the spirit in which I wrote these letters: were they a record as much as a family duty?) However, my mother soon resumes her place as addressee, since I followed this up immediately with an alternative plan, noting in a parenthesis surely intended for my mother rather than posterity, that 'this is written in a very small voice'. The plan that I thus diffidently presented was that while Alex was away, 'I might go to Moscow if the British Council would send me, and Bolsover [George Bolsover, director of the London School of Slavonic Studies, where I had a fellowship] would permit. Just for six months. Alex is not against'. Clearly I felt that going back to Moscow was something my mother would disapprove of. I reassured her that Sasha wouldn't be in Moscow, since he had graduated and lacked the residence permit necessary to remain in the city.

Early in the New Year (1969), I flung myself into action with my usual energy where Moscow was concerned. Bolsover not only agreed to my going but was 'surprisingly pleasant' about it (I was even warier of Bolsover, another British Russianist thought to have longstanding intelligence connections, than of Hayward), and also made some helpful suggestions. I could make a late application for the student exchange that I'd been on before, although the deadline had passed, but he would also sponsor a late application from me for the academic exchange for university teachers. I considered this an inferior option but better than nothing. 'Bolsover is on both selection boards, which might help.'

I said six months to my mother, but it turns out that I actually applied for another ten-month trip. This was perhaps because, as Alex prepared for his own trip and his thoughts turned back to Japan (about which he was as obsessed as I was about Moscow), we had amicably decided to call it quits on the marriage, or at least to consider ourselves separated. We gave up the Oxford flat, and I moved fulltime to London, living with my friend Ann. As I wrote to my mother in April, I wasn't the only one preoccupied with getting back to Moscow but apprehensive at the same time. Ann was trying to decide whether to apply for another tourist visa to Moscow, but she was afraid of being refused again. I was afraid both of not getting on the exchange and of being refused a visa. A London friend who valued his Russian connections was afraid of being molested by the

KGB if he went back to Moscow because they had searched him on the way out last time. Another friend, already awarded a place on the British Council exchange, was afraid both of KGB entrapment and of losing her husband if she left him on his own. 'But all of us are desperately anxious to go to Moscow, like soldiers wanting to get back to the front.' Despite Bolsover's support, it took a few months for my late applications to be sorted out, but late in April I finally got confirmation that I had a ten-month place on the student exchange.

By that time, there had been some changes in my personal situation. Here I have to say that re-reading my letters to my mother was quite a shock. I remembered the (non-Moscow) part of my life in these years as pretty much a desert of loneliness and misery, exacerbated by my mother's increasingly critical attitude and lack of sympathy for my various efforts to get my life on an even keel. When I re-read our correspondence, however, I found myself almost completely on her side. First I marry Alex, she thought for the wrong reasons; then I go to Moscow and start writing in exalted terms about a strange relationship with a man old enough to be my father; then I have an affair with some young Russian (my comparative frankness on this surprises me in retrospect) whom I am not really serious about, despite telling her that students could get blackmailed by the KGB for such things; then I say perhaps Alex and I are divorcing; and then, just a few months later, I say I have met an Englishman whom I plan to marry and we are going to buy a house, using my savings as the down payment—but I'm still going to Moscow for six months. Rex, the Englishman, was a successful journalist in his mid thirties who wanted to settle down. He spoke Russian, and I met him through a common friend who was a Russophile. Our relationship didn't last, and, if I had been my mother reading my letters, I wouldn't have expected it to. At the time, it represented both my acute need for some kind of anchor in the world outside Moscow and a decision to make my life in England rather than going back to Australia.

In addition to her dismay at the latest personal developments, my mother couldn't see why I wanted to go back to Moscow, since in the aftermath of the 1968 invasion of Czechoslovakia it seemed such an unpleasant place. But I wanted to see for myself what it was like now; I almost seem to have wanted it to be really bad, so that I could find out how that felt. The sense of confusion about what I thought of the Soviet Union, evident in my letters of the summer of 1968, surfaces occasionally in the 1969 letters; I wrote that 'I still can't quite reconcile what I see there with what I read about. I mean it never sounds quite like the same place'. But in general, my self-confidence increased along with the prospects of returning to Moscow. Regardless of what I thought of the Soviet Union, I could handle it, which was a source of pride.

The news from Moscow, not surprisingly, was bad. *Novy mir* was forbidden to publish Tvardovsky's latest poem, the anti-Stalinist *By Right of Memory*, and the refusal was repeated when they put it up again for publication in subsequent issues. In March, *Pravda* said that *Novy mir* remained stubborn in its mistakes, and that 'organizational conclusions', meaning changes in the editorial board, were inevitable. The campaign against *Novy mir* was taken up by various competing journals and (as Igor had told me) the newspaper *Sovetskaya Rossiya*, which had published the attack on me. High officials suggested to Tvardovsky first that he should get rid of some of the editorial board and second that he should resign, but he refused on both counts. The pressure on him was intense and unremitting, and in July he was hospitalised after a fall at the dacha and remained there for some months. To top it all off, *By Right of Memory* found its way abroad and was published in the autumn in one of the *émigré* journals. Tvardovsky wrote the kind of statement he had urged Solzhenitsyn to write when the same thing happened to *Cancer Ward* the previous year, asserting that he had not sent his poem abroad and deploring its unauthorised publication. But this time there was a new wrinkle: the Soviet press wouldn't publish his statement, presumably because of an injunction from on high, making Tvardovsky appear a willing party to the *émigré* publication.

Igor was delighted to hear I was coming back, and there was even a friendly note from Raisa Isaevna enclosed in his letter, thanking me for the medical supplies I had been sending through informal channels and 'hoping to be in better form and get to know you better when you come'. But anxiety and gloom predominated in Igor's letters in the late spring and summer. By now, he was convinced that *Novy mir*'s days were numbered and that he would soon be out of a job. Don't wait too long before coming, he wrote at the end of March. 'Actually I have so noticeably aged that it will be completely boring for you.' A month or so later: 'Dear Sheila, what a long time until September ... Although I am now convinced that by the time you come I will have more free time than before and we can work together well'. 'More free time than before' meant that he expected to be unemployed and, being in political disgrace and in any case past retirement age, unemployable. What a pleasure it would be to get back to writing a long-planned book about Lunacharsky, he wrote—but of course neither he nor any of his friends expected that that book would ever be written. He didn't pretend it wouldn't be hard to 'change my way of life' and become a pensioner. In May came a letter full of wistful regret and impossible fantasies: couldn't I come, after all, in the summer? (The British Council never sent people in the summer.) 'July–August would have been best of all; everyone goes away. You could have lived at our place.' (No, I couldn't; it was strictly forbidden for a foreigner to stay overnight in a Russian apartment.) 'So many questions to ask you. So many things for you to tell me about. And thinking together. I do so much like thinking together with you. Perhaps all the same you could come earlier?'

Soviet newspapers were upping their published attacks on Western Sovietologists, and there were rumours that the Russians had sent a couple more British exchange students back from Moscow, both sexual frame-ups. It puzzled me that they took the trouble to stage such entrapments when there was no shortage of real affairs (like mine with Sasha) going on. 'Why they frame the innocent, or more or less innocent, rather than just photographing the guilty is hard to understand', I commented to my mother. Adding a little Australian colour, I passed on Hayward's report (source unknown) that the poet Yevtushenko, recently under attack in Britain from conservatives such as Kingsley Amis after being nominated for the Oxford professorship of poetry, was 'almost as angry with Frank Hardy [the Communist writer who had recently fallen out with the Party and publicly denounced the invasion of Czechoslovakia], because of Hardy's articles about their friendship, as with Kingsley Amis'. Yevtushenko, himself under heavy attack in the Soviet Union after protesting the invasion of Czechoslovakia, had been sacked from the editorial board of the literary youth journal, I reported, 'so heads are falling on every side. I hope I can manage to keep mine'.

Igor took the news about the new man in my life more sympathetically than my mother, sending greetings and asking me, for some reason, to warn Rex 'that he shouldn't be shocked when we meet that my room is in disorder and I don't know how to wear my clothes well'. (This strange comment must have been provoked by my writing that Rex was an elegant dresser, neater in his habits than I was used to, and that I was a bit intimidated by living in his flat, which was elegant, too. But is it possible that Igor, at some distant point in the past, might have aspired to sartorial distinction?) He hoped Rex was a drinking man (he wasn't).

Even without the hints in Igor's letters, I would have known that the writing was on the wall for *Novy mir*. In fact, I didn't even need to rely on St Antony's as a source of information: the *Novy mir* saga was considered of such general interest that you could follow it just by reading the daily newspapers. In late May, British papers reported that Tvardovsky had been asked to resign as editor of *Novy mir*, which, as I told my mother, almost certainly meant Igor would go too and everything in Moscow would tighten up.

Tvardovsky was still in hospital in August, and Igor went with Volodya Lakshin to visit him. Igor didn't tell me about this visit, but it is recorded in Tvardovsky's diary. They came after visiting hours, were made to wait humiliatingly at the gate, and were admitted only after Tvardovsky made an angry scene. He found Igor 'sad, sober, his face ravaged, almost indifferent to everything—he's had enough of it all, poor man'. By 'sober,' he meant that Igor hadn't been drinking and didn't bring a bottle of vodka with him to share with the patient, a common Soviet practice that Igor normally followed. Igor's drinking habits were a puzzle, if you were used to Western patterns. He was more likely to drink because things were good than because they were bad. When he didn't drink at all, as I was to find in later years, he was giving up hope.

'It is a great shame in a way to have to go to Russia just at this particular time', I wrote to my mother. The juxtaposition of 'great shame' and 'in a way' gave off oddly mixed resonances; perhaps it was only from some points of view that it was a great shame, and mine not one of them? But that is probably refining too much: we were instinctive qualifiers of definitive statements, my mother and I. Rex had just bought a rather upmarket house (my down payment, his mortgage, ownership in his name) in London, complete with garden, music room and future nursery, and we were preparing to redecorate and then move in. The question of my giving up the Moscow trip had been raised, but I was against it, and Rex, perhaps not very happily, agreed. I say 'perhaps' because I can't remember, which suggests that I regarded it as a non-negotiable issue. All the same, you might expect that, if I had had any excuse to cancel the Moscow trip without hurting Igor's feelings too much, I would have taken it. Not so: the Soviets turned me down at the last minute, but instead of accepting this involuntary solution with relief, I immediately jumped into action to get the decision reversed.

The problem was not with my visa, which had been issued, but with my placement at Moscow University, which had been refused. That was very unusual and the British Council found it hard to interpret. But it was clear that both visa and placement were required, so when the SS *Maria Ulyanova* (named for Lenin's sister) sailed early in September, it sailed without me, just as the *Baltika* had done in 1965. Perhaps it was that memory that made it so intolerable to accept refusal, but more likely it was because Moscow was still the centre of my life and I wanted to go there no matter what. The British Council knew of no precedent for getting such a decision reversed, but I was determined to set one. I reasoned that, if it were the KGB blacklisting me, they would have blocked me from getting a visa, or stopped the British Council nomination at an earlier stage. Since the problem came from Moscow University, it was probably Ovcharenko who was at the bottom of it. I assumed that he was worried that, in the worsening political climate, he might get into trouble when my dissertation was published, since he had been my official supervisor, and that blocking my return was both a pre-emptive strike and a way of dissociating himself from me. So I just needed to make Ovcharenko change his mind by showing him that dissociation wouldn't work. The way that I decided to do this was by a kind of blackmail, and one can see from my letter to my mother that I was very pleased with myself for thinking it up. I feel, looking back, that this deserves some moral condemnation, but actually I'm quite pleased with myself even now. It was sneaky but clever.

I wrote a businesslike but friendly letter to Ovcharenko, addressed to him at Moscow University, with copies to every Soviet official body I could think of punctiliously listed at the bottom, telling him that there had been a regrettable hitch in my plans to return to Moscow for further research on Lunacharsky, but I counted on him to get the mistake corrected, given that he had read and approved all my work so far. This was a total lie, as I hadn't even tried to show the dissertation to Ovcharenko; it was Igor, Ovcharenko's enemy, who had read and approved it all. But he couldn't very well deny it—after all, as my official advisor, he *should* have wanted to read the dissertation and made sure I showed it to him on my previous visit—and I thought that, once he realised that he was tarred by association with me and my book regardless, he would just shrug and give in.

Remarkably, this is apparently what happened. After about a fortnight, the British Council was informed that Moscow University had withdrawn its opposition and was prepared to let me come—not, to be sure, for the full ten months, but for five, with the possibility of negotiating for an extension once I got to Moscow. A total success; I was exultant. 'It was a very odd and uncharacteristic thing for Moscow to do', I boasted to my mother, 'and everybody is rather puzzled and impressed; but I think it just illustrates that unto him that hath shall be given'. That, of course, is a reference to my future happy life with Rex. I wasn't sure about applying for the extension after five months, I continued, 'because I am sure they would give it to me, and it would be rather miserable for Rex living in that large house in Muswell Hill by himself'. Well, that's as may be. I'm sure I was keeping an open mind about the extension. But I get a fleeting glimpse of an unfamiliar self here, someone who thinks the world is her oyster. She doesn't reappear in the correspondence.

I left on 5 October, with a visa valid for five months and placement at Moscow University for the same period. This time the British Council sent me by air, and I arrived at Sheremetyevo Airport to find Igor awaiting me—something he had never done before—in a van labelled 'Produce'. It was fairly standard Moscow practice to flag down any vehicle on the road, commercial or private, and ask them to take you somewhere, trusting that the lure of extra income would encourage them to take a break from work, but it wasn't my practice or Igor's, so I was stunned by the magnificence of the gesture.

In the Moscow University dorm, things were much as before, except that I was two floors lower and had a new neighbour. Lida was a great improvement on my previous neighbours—'intelligent, friendly but not inquisitive, clean', as I wrote to my mother. She was a final-year student from Stavropol in the south of Russia (Gorbachev's town, but who had heard of Gorbachev then?) and, as graduation drew near, she was thinking about the future, namely finding someone with a Moscow residence permit whom she could marry. *Perspektivnyi*—a good prospect—was a word whose colloquial use I learnt from her: it was applied to situations and jobs but particularly to men. Rex was *perspektivnyi*. I never saw any of Lida's boyfriends because they didn't live in the dorm, and I don't know if she ever got her Moscow man. I hope so. She used to practise fortune-telling from tea leaves, and speak wryly about the various prospects: 'it's not a Great Love, of course' was a phrase I heard many times from her, followed inevitably by 'but' as she weighed the advantages. I assumed that, being my neighbour, she would have to report on me, but we came to an agreement (I wish I could remember how unspoken it was) that I would make some interesting parts of my life available to her, and she, in return, would say nice things about me in her reports and indicate that I was totally harmless and innocent. For some reason, this felt like a necessary deception, as if I hadn't actually been innocent, but that's how things were in the Soviet Union. Lida's good-natured cynicism and eye on the main chance suited me very well. I liked her, though we didn't keep in touch after I left. I trusted her not to pull any nasty tricks on me, as Galya had done in the Horst Bott episode, and she never did.

I enjoyed my first meeting with Ovcharenko, partly because of my sense of triumph and partly because he responded so beautifully. Modestly accepting my thanks for having intervened on my behalf and saved the day, he told me that as soon as he got my letter he had rushed to the authorities at Moscow University to defend my nomination. Imagine his surprise when he learned from them that the real opposition to my trip to Moscow came from *the British Council itself,* which in a typically corrupt capitalist manoeuvre was pretending to support me while trying to get me blocked by the Soviets. But his intervention had foiled the plot. Ovcharenko was the kind of rogue who could tell an outright and implausible lie like that without blushing (though given my own lie about him reading the manuscript, perhaps I can't claim to have taken the moral high road). I thanked him warmly for his quick thinking, saying I knew I could rely on him. Ovcharenko didn't make any reference to the article about me in *Sovetskaya Rossiya.* (Nobody did. The only sign I ever had that anyone other than St Antony's intelligence gatherers had read it was a rather mystifying letter that arrived that autumn, out of the blue at my seldom-used Moscow University address, from the rector of Saratov University, who happened to be a Lunacharsky scholar. He offered some mild criticisms of my work, including what appeared to be an oblique reference to the *Sovetskaya Rossiya* article, but also expressed appreciation and a desire for contact.) As he had done the previous year, Ovcharenko signed off on my Plan, including State and Literary Archives but not Party Archives, without objections; but the results were much the same—delays in giving permission, and only slim pickings when I did get in.

Igor had his own back story on the saga of my acceptance. When the British Council's nomination of me was under consideration (probably in the summer, before the Moscow University placement issue came up), he had been called into the Party Central Committee. This was in effect a summons by the KGB, he said, the locale being a tribute to his status as an Old Bolshevik. They told him that if I were allowed to come, it would be on his head: was he prepared to take personal responsibility if I put a foot wrong? He said yes. The conversation was strictly confidential, he was told; under no circumstances should I know of it. Igor, of course, passed it on with relish. But now that we had been given notice that I was being watched, he gave me his own instructions: no socialising outside my established circle of friends; any new acquaintance who seemed to want to make friends was to be cleared with Igor. I accepted these conditions without hesitation. In a way, they weren't that different from the normal conventions of Moscow friendship, which assumed faithfulness to the family circle you had first entered and treated excursions outside of it, even of the most harmless social sort, rather like promiscuity.

As it happened, Rex had his own objections to my making new friends, fearing that I would fall back into my old Australian bohemian habits. According to my memory of things, I accepted this unreservedly too, because I had made a firm decision to change my life, become a new woman under his guidance, and follow his lead in everything, with the expectation of living happily ever after as an English suburban wife and mother. This doesn't exactly square with my determination to put off Muswell Hill and go to Moscow, of course, and I was further surprised to find that the tone of my letters to him (which he kindly returned for the purposes of this memoir) lack the submissive quality I had expected. Shortly after my arrival in Moscow, for example, I reported having made a new friend—Margot Light, one of the British exchange students, who, as a woman, should be acceptable—and added rather acidly, 'After all I must have some friends in Moscow, and between you and Igor Alexandrovich I feel rather limited in my choice ... Thank God I brought my violin', meaning it would be something to do in the lonely evenings. Actually I never played the violin on this trip, and very rarely on my previous long-term one, and am surprised I bothered to take it. There weren't any lonely evenings, as it turned out, because I quickly got into the habit of spending time with Margot, a linguist (later an international relations specialist) from South Africa who has been a friend ever since.

Igor was very insistent on his prohibition about my meeting new people. I wrote to Rex (partly in Russian, for some reason: was I worried about the *British* reading my letters?) passing on Igor's 'extremely stern warning' not to widen the circle of my acquaintances because this would be dangerous both to me and to them, especially if they came from the liberal intelligentsia. That was fine with me, I wrote—'I never have mixed with [Soviet] liberals and don't feel any particular need to'—but I added my own warning: 'do observe the letter of every possible law when you come'. Rex was planning a two-week trip in the second half of December, and this, although welcome, made life considerably more complicated. He was a journalist with a leading financial newspaper in London, as capitalist as you could get from the Soviet standpoint, and, to make matters worse, not only had he been sent off to learn Russian during his National Service (clearly an intelligence assignment) but he also had his own contacts with the kinds of Soviet liberal intellectuals who knew foreigners. 'What are we going to do about celebrating New Year?' I wrote anxiously. We had been invited to the dacha of one of these liberals that Igor was worried about. It was awkward, in light of Igor's prohibition, which obviously in practice had to more or less cover Rex as well; and in addition, dachas were often outside the forty-kilometre limit, so in theory (though the rule was being flouted more and more often) out of bounds.

There were signs of KGB attention, as I intimated in a roundabout way in my letters. In one incident, a youngish man in a belted raincoat lurking in the stairwell of Igor's building accosted me as I came out late one evening. I was quite relieved that it was not a drunk or would-be rapist but only a KGB man, something I knew instantly because of his well-groomed appearance and polite manners and the fact that he immediately started talking about Middle Eastern politics. I assured him that I had no interest in the Middle East or any other kind of politics, but would appreciate it if he would escort me across the slightly sinister square outside Kiev railway station on the way to my bus. He did, and when my bus came, we said polite farewells, and that was the last I ever saw of him. Unlike previous accosters, he didn't give a name or any personal details; there was no attempt to disguise, but rather a clear message that I was under observation.

I dutifully reported to Igor on every new Russian acquaintance, and after a while I noticed a pattern. If the acquaintance was a woman, there was no problem. If it was a man, he invariably told me not to see him again. I realised that something more than security considerations was involved from Igor's standpoint, but I was more touched than annoyed—whatever I thought at the time, I was definitely more amenable to Igor's control than Rex's. But even with Igor I could be a bit skittish. I didn't tell him about the new acquaintance who invited me home and cooked the only fresh fish I ever had in Moscow until *after* the fact, although surely it should have been before by the terms of our agreement. It was a pleasant dinner *à deux*, and not just because the fish was delicious. The man was nice, and didn't make a pass at me, but told me rather sadly that his father was a biggish man in the KGB, so I probably wouldn't want to see him again. I would normally have been a sucker for that kind of line—*how can I punish this poor man for his parents, rejecting him by association without even getting to know him*—but it didn't impress Igor, who told me not to see him again, and I didn't. Another reject was the son of Jewish intellectuals whom I met through British friends, though Igor knew the family quite well himself and had sometimes talked about them to me: the father had been a victim of the anti-Semitism of Stalin's last years. I asked if the son was on the banned list, and Igor said firmly yes—but, as I wrote to Rex, he was quite drunk at the time and there seemed to be a distinct element of personal jealousy ('He wants to make love to you, of course', was his justification, which, apart from having no direct security relevance, happened to be untrue).

The drinking in my presence, which had been a new element in 1968, was even more prominent now, and so was the jealousy. I wrote to Rex about a terrible evening when I went round with my book manuscript to Igor's, 'with purely scholarly intentions', but found when I arrived that Igor and a number of his *Novy mir* colleagues (not including Tvardovsky) were having 'a private celebration, or a wake' and were all very drunk.

> Not that I wasn't welcome, on the contrary ... [Igor] kept talking about me in connection with you and others and worst of all himself, and in general behaved like Yeats of the later poems [that is, an old man lusting after a young woman]. Raisa Isaevna was surprisingly enough present and bore it well, even the propositioning. One of the colleagues, on being told that my work was better than anyone else's in the field said 'I know you are very fond of her' [*ia znaiu, chto vy ee ochen' liubite*—in Russian in the letter], which was also unpleasant although he was otherwise rather kind. I was most uncomfortable. Added to this there was one of the anti-foreigners being anti-foreign. Awful.

I think this 'otherwise kind' person was probably Volodya Lakshin, who shared what I took to be the general feeling among the *Novy mir* group that Igor's infatuation with me, a foreigner with who knows what baggage, was putting the whole group at risk. They were very careful to keep me away from Tvardovsky, hustling me out into an anteroom once when he showed up unexpectedly at *Novy mir*; and even Igor implicitly recognised that it was better not to have me round when Tvardovsky was. So I never got to deliver Max's message to him, not that I would have anyway.

This evening must have particularly bothered me, because I returned to the subject in my next letter to Rex:

> I am tired of Russian drinking. I don't know why I was so offended, as there have been other similar occasions. [Igor] was very preoccupied by the idea of himself as your rival ... He said Alex was good-looking (he has a very good photograph of him, better than the original), and Sasha [my boyfriend, not his son] was an idiot. I feel very awkward about his loudly repeated invitations to stay the night, both in relation to him and to Raisa Isaevna and his Sasha. It is one thing to ignore unexplicit invitations and another thing to have to refuse [explicit ones].

Tired as I was of Igor's drinking, one episode left a memory I cherish. Igor was interested in my father and wanted to know more about him; he had even made a trip to the Lenin Library in my absence to check out his work, despite his poor English. He asked me to bring copies of my father's work, which I did (*Short History of the Australian Labor Party* and *The British Empire in Australia*); and he read through them with determination—evidently the struggle with my dissertation had improved his English. After that, he asked for a photograph of my father. He understood him to be a leftist and a quasi-Marxist historian, who, like himself, despised people with privilege and was instinctively inclined to challenge authority, often mockingly; and, on top of that, a drinking man. A fellow spirit, in short. And dead, which put him in the same category as all those friends of Igor's who had disappeared in the terror of the 1930s, leaving him *in loco parentis* to their orphaned children.

The result of all this thinking about my father and looking at his picture resulted in a curious leap of fantasy on Igor's part, under the influence of alcohol, of course. He started talking as if not only had he known my father in the flesh, but they had been close friends, comrades in arms. My father, in this drunken waking dream of Igor's, had fallen victim to the Great Purges, leaving me to Igor's care. I was greatly touched by this; it seemed the quintessential gesture of making me feel at home in Russia. I wished I could have told my father that, in an alternative universe, he had been an Old Bolshevik and fighter in the Civil War, struck down in 1937.

The great event of the autumn was my paper at the Lunacharsky memorial meeting. These meetings were held every year on the anniversary of Lunacharsky's death, and Irina, with her aspirations to control the whole field of *lunacharskovedy*, was a very active participant. Igor usually refused to attend, as he had done the past two years, and Irina more or less accepted this, as if he had shown up he would have been likely to be extremely rude to people like Ovcharenko. This year, the co-organiser with Irina was a literary scholar, Nikolay Trifonov, who was quite well disposed towards me; and so, now that I was a real scholar with a doctorate, I was invited to present a paper. Trifonov was to give the big paper on Lunacharsky's literary work, and I was to give a smaller one (up to thirty minutes) with the very Soviet title 'AV Lunacharsky—First Commissar of Enlightenment'. That title sounded more like a statement of fact than a topic for discussion, I joked to Rex, but then most Soviet scholarly papers were like that. Igor, who hated official occasions, initially said he wouldn't go, even if I was giving a paper, 'because of the people he might meet there'; but then he changed his mind. He was particularly truculent, at this time of troubles for *Novy mir*, in his dealings with people of authority and privilege, barely managing to exempt Irina from this category.

It was to be my first scholarly presentation in Russian (because of Ovcharenko's absence, I hadn't even had to present the normal oral report to the PhilFac at the end of my 1966–67 stay), and I took a lot of trouble with the paper. 'My Lunacharsky paper is writing itself very fluently in a stream of Soviet clichés', I wrote to Rex, my grammar reflecting the Russian immersion. 'It would be quite impossible to write in English and translate, I think, because in English one does not have Soviet ideas. I hope Igor A stays away.' A week later, I reported that 'Lida had spent hours editing [the paper] from a stylistic point of view; now Igor A is going to go through it from so to speak tactical point of view; and Irina says all I have to do is speak from the heart.' I think it also had to go through Trifonov's preliminary censorship. In the end, Igor showed up (proudly), as well as Irina and a large audience of interested people, including Lunacharsky scholars and former Narkompros workers. Ovcharenko was a notable absentee. I invited my neighbour Lida, both to give her something to write about in her KGB report and for her private entertainment.

The paper was a success—'well-delivered [and] had no loopholes for serious attack', as I assessed it in the account I gave Rex—and both Irina and Igor were very pleased. There was a wonderfully Soviet discussion afterwards, the kind that makes you throw up your hands at Western generalisations about unbreakable Soviet conformity. I had passionate supporters. 'Sheila [a daringly intimate formulation, but then as a foreigner I had no patronymic] is our miracle', said one old-timer from Lunacharsky's commissariat. Even one of the younger Lunacharsky scholars, who usually didn't much like me, got 'carried away by professional solidarity' and said the paper was brilliant. But there were critics, including one who made a long, rambling speech on the theme that I was young and inexperienced (Irina called out loudly 'A Doctor of Philosophy!' at this point), as well as being a protégée of Igor's, which spoke (negatively) for itself. An odd elderly man who had apparently worked for Lunacharsky as a financial and administrative assistant 'got up and said I should be careful not to fantasise. The chairman interrupted to say that the comment was uncalled for, and Irina muttered in a loud sotto voce that the man was a cretin'.

There always seemed to be somebody slightly crazy, or at least emotionally distressed, at Soviet meetings, and this one was no exception. An old man who had worked in Narkompros got up and made a long, excited speech, which I would have taken as hostile had I not seen from the faces that Irina was making that he was a friend and I should treat him kindly. He was trembling and gasping for breath at the end of his speech, and Lida, who was sitting near him, saw him take out a pill and swallow it. (Presumably it was heart trouble, very common among Soviet men of his age.) He sat down but then got up again to apologise for being incoherent (there were friendly cries of 'No, no').

After the formal discussion, everyone started milling around and things became a bit farcical. 'People kept coming up to shake my hand and asking how old I was ...

The Narkompros man came up shyly and shakily and muttered that "they said you wanted to come and see me".' (I did go and see him a few weeks later: he turned out to have been a Young Communist enthusiast in the 1920s, who thought that as a foreigner I didn't appreciate the excitement of those pioneering years.)

> While I was writing down his telephone number and wondering who 'they' were, the odd man who attacked me seized the pen and wrote his number as well. Then he went off and pushed Lida into a corner and told her he was the only real secretary of Lunacharsky and all the rest were frauds. Lida was very taken by the whole evening.

Meanwhile, back in London, Rex was preparing to move into our house in Muswell Hill. I had left in his charge all the worldly possessions I had other than those I had brought to Moscow, and in November he suggested that some of the clothes could be thrown away. He thought I dressed badly and needed to be made over in a more fashionable image; in general, the nature of our pact was that he was offering me a New Life, different in almost every respect from the old one; and I was so demoralised about my life (apart from the Moscow part of it) that I went along. I was appalled at the idea of throwing away my clothes, or anything that was evidence that I existed and had a history, but foolishly I didn't object outright (this *does* seem to be submissive behaviour). I gave two contradictory responses, first suggesting that Rex hang onto my things, at least until I came back ('I am not extraordinarily attached to my past self, but it is familiar'), and then backing off ('On second thoughts you can throw them away if you want to, as long as you remember that I am not elegant and won't be'). He threw them all away. I was shocked but tried to make light of it, writing that 'when I told people about your authoritarian personality they laughed. Even Igor Alexandrovich, who said you were a man of decision'. 'Well, OK', I concluded. 'But don't throw me away as well, please.' The last comment was quite prescient.

Rex arrived in mid December for two weeks on a tourist visa. They put him in Hotel Ukraina, which has had a repulsive aspect to me ever since (but, to be fair, perhaps before too; it's a monstrosity). I remember lots of trouble getting past the woman on duty on his floor, and of course he couldn't get into the Moscow University dorm without a pass. We didn't go out to the liberal intellectuals' dacha for New Year's Eve but celebrated it with them in Moscow—lots of people and drink, and a guitar poet who sang ballads. Casting around for the right kind of thing to say to Rex—that is, something conventional—I remarked how lovely it was to be together for the New Year, the first of many. It sounded completely phoney as I said it, which is not to say I didn't mean it, or at least mean to mean it. But he didn't pick up on the phoneyness; he just blanched. I was irritated by that, since this bourgeois marriage was, after all, his idea.

I took Rex to meet Igor and Irina. They were polite, but I had the impression they didn't much like him, and were not predisposed to do so. The fact that he spoke Russian should have been an advantage but didn't seem to be. Perhaps they hadn't thought the story about throwing away my clothes was so funny after all; perhaps they suspected him of having intelligence connections. Rex had brought along an expensive journalist's camera and took pictures of Igor and me, really good ones. I took a picture of him and Igor which was also good, in the sense of capturing the field of tension between them. I don't know why he didn't take pictures at Irina's. She, if I remember rightly, did the proper parental thing of asking him in detail about his prospects and material situation. I thought she would appreciate my presenting her with such a man of the world—after all, she was always pushing me to be more worldly—but that quality only seemed to make her suspicious. Or perhaps she was not convinced that, if it were 1937 in Russia and all my parents' friends were being arrested as enemies of the people, he would have done the Rafail Naumovich thing and stuck by me. Well, it wasn't 1937.

I had procured tickets for Rex and me to a fashionably daring play (in a Soviet context this, of course, means politically daring, not sexually), Mikhail Shatrov's *The Bolsheviks*. I can't say whether it was good or not because I never saw it to the end. Something happened to me that was like nothing experienced before or since. We were sitting waiting for the play to start, or perhaps it was already the second act, when an extremely strange and indescribable feeling came over me suddenly. I knew something bad was about to happen and I must get out of the theatre, so without a word I took off my glasses, put them in Rex's hand, got up and climbed out over the row of knees into the aisle. After a few steps up the aisle, I fainted, but I managed to get up, and I made it out the door before fainting again, this time remaining unconscious for more than five minutes. By the time I came to, an ambulance team had arrived, as well as Rex, and the team gave me a caffeine injection to get me on my feet; it was quite painful because the needle was so blunt. I assumed they would take me to a hospital, or at least drive me home, but they just told Rex to take me to the Metro and see I got home safely. When I asked what had happened, they said I had had a heart attack (*infarkt*). Since my Russian friends, particularly the men, were always talking about heart attacks they had had, I was already inclined to the theory that the word *infarkt*, although supposedly the same as heart attack in English, was actually used much more loosely. I used to tell that story for years as an example of how Russians overstate their medical conditions. Obviously the ambulance people couldn't have meant I had had a heart attack in English terms, or they wouldn't have sent me off to go home on the Metro. So it was a surprise, in the 2000s, to have an Australian doctor look at my ECG and find evidence of a heart attack long before: had there been some such event in the 1970s? I should have been more literal-minded that evening in Moscow. In any case, Rex took me back to the dormitory by Metro and bus, and when we got there, there was the inevitable argument with the person on duty, who wouldn't let someone without a pass in even if they were escorting a heart-attack victim. The next day, as far as I can remember, or at least the day after next, life went on as usual.

My dissertation had been accepted for publication by Cambridge University Press (it came out in the winter of 1970–71 as *The Commissariat of Enlightenment*), and was already in press during this Moscow visit, but it was still possible for me to revise the new introduction and first chapter I had written for the book in the summer. The new chapter contained snappy pen portraits of Lunacharsky and his associates (the style perhaps influenced by my association with a journalist), and the tone was to some degree a reversion to that of the first (unpublished) articles I had written on Lunacharsky at St Antony's, though with less mockery and more of a sense of the pathos of revolution, with its inevitably disappointed hopes. It was very important to me to convey that sense, but after much struggle I gave up the attempt to do so in my own words. I ended up quoting Thomas Carlyle's *French Revolution* on Robespierre, going to his execution in the sky-blue coat he had ordered for the revolutionary Festival of the Supreme Being: 'O Reader, can thy hard heart hold out against this?'

That was for Lunacharsky and the revolutionary idealism he personified. But there was another quotation from Carlyle, equally moving to me, that isn't in my *Commissariat*, though I could have sworn I put it in. This one is about the Abbé Sièyes, framer of the 1791 Constitution. Writing in 1834, Carlyle wondered how Sièyes looked back from the sober vantage point of old age, long after the revolution's collapse: 'Might we hope, still with the old irrefragable transcendentalism?' That was not so much my hope for Lunacharsky, who died at fifty-eight with the Revolution still (as he would have seen it) incomplete, but a kind of prayer for Igor, my own personal Old Bolshevik, who was still alive: please let him not end his life totally disappointed.

Igor didn't comment on the sky-blue coat in the introduction, but he had quite a few criticisms of the new material in the book. On a number of factual points, I made the corrections he suggested. I also adjusted the phrasing of some interpretive passages. My friend Margot thought this was too much of a sacrifice of scholarly integrity, but, reporting this in a letter to Rex, I disagreed: 'the truth of all these generalizations always seems to me highly relative, they are not susceptible of proof in any way that I understand, therefore one chooses them on emotional grounds'. An interesting point, and I suppose a kind of solution to my old difficulty of being able to see Soviet history from two incompatible perspectives and not knowing what to do about it.

The most serious issue was that Igor wanted the whole new chapter on Lunacharsky dropped, because he didn't like the tone ('Sovietology') and thought it liable to distortion by hostile critics. The tone was indeed a problem in a Soviet context: Soviet historians just did not write like this, and for that matter (*pace* Igor) neither did Sovietologists. I assumed, though he didn't say it, that he was worried that Irina would take offence at my description of Lunacharsky, which, while sympathetic, was not hagiography. 'He did his criticism very nicely', I wrote to Rex. 'Impossible to take offence. Possible and indeed necessary to argue, difficult to win argument. But I am not going to write another introduction, even if [the publisher] would let me. There are limits to self-censorship.'

Igor was also bothered by the new appendix, in which I gave potted biographies of the main characters in the Narkompros story. This was partly because of factual mistakes. It was extraordinarily difficult in those days to get accurate biographical information on the Soviet period, so errors had certainly crept in (a few remaining even after Igor's and Irina's corrections), but from my standpoint, the scarcity of the information only made the appendix more valuable for Western readers. The other problem was a peculiarly Soviet one: a large number of the subjects of these potted biographies had met untimely deaths in 1937–38, and in Soviet terms, publishing a 1937 death date was always a red flag to the censors. I dug in my heels on this one too, writing to Rex that 'I want to correct mistakes; but I think that is as far as I go on that line. It isn't my fault what happened to people [i.e. how many of my biographical subjects were Purge victims]. After all I am supposed to be a bourgeois objective historian'.

When I went back for a second round with Igor on the book manuscript, I found he had brought in reinforcements in the person of the brightest of the young Lunacharsky scholars, Artur Ermakov. 'IA read me an ideological lecture—although saying he thought my mistakes the result of ignorance, not ill intention—with E saying amen', I wrote to Rex. 'I didn't like it, but I saw the point of IA taking out some kind of insurance.' As I recount all this, I realise that it sounds like a turning point in my relations with Igor—the first time I had dug in my heels and set my judgement against his—but it wasn't. This suggests that, in a process imperfectly conveyed in my letters and memory, but accommodated without difficulty by Igor, I had been growing out of being Igor's little listener and becoming a person who made her own judgements. It helped, of course, that my Russian was now fluent enough for me to be able to express them. I perfectly understood Igor's objections; he was trying to edit my book for *Novy mir*, as it were, as well as disarm future Soviet criticism. But I was writing for a Western scholarly audience, a context I understood better than Igor did. If I had in fact been writing for *Novy mir*, I would have written it differently.

I took the book manuscript along to Ovcharenko, placing it visibly, but without comment, on the table so that he couldn't fail to notice it but could choose to ignore it. Ovcharenko had been drinking (he too? Obviously the atmosphere in Moscow was getting to everyone) and had that cunning look on his face that never boded any good. He said 'he had tried to help me write an objective book, without extremes', adding in a mutter that 'even in Moscow some people, for example Sats, have extreme views'. As for the manuscript lying on the table in front of him, he didn't ask to see it, so I took it away again, feeling I had done my duty.

I've kept the *Novy mir* story to the end because, for Igor and Tvardovsky, it was the last act. All through the autumn, Tvardovsky had been under pressure to resign as editor. *By Right of Memory* had appeared abroad, but the Soviet media still wouldn't publish his condemnation of this. An older controversial poem of his, *Terkin in the Other World* (a satirical continuation of his World War II success, *Vasily Terkin*), was removed from an edition of his works as it went to press. Rumours were afoot that the ninetieth anniversary of Stalin's birth in November 1969 would be marked by some kind of semi-rehabilitation of Stalin. *Novy mir* issues were still coming out late because of constant censorship trouble. By the late autumn, rumours were circulating that the plan 'up there' was to dismiss four members of *Novy mir*'s editorial board, including Igor and Lakshin, as a way of making Tvardovsky resign.

As predicted by the grapevine, Igor and three other editors were dismissed on 11 February 1970; the next day, Tvardovsky handed in his resignation. A new editorial board was appointed—including, of all people, my supervisor, Alexander Ovcharenko. Ovcharenko was, of course, an enemy of Igor's, but I hadn't realised that he was also regarded as a significant enemy of Tvardovsky and the journal. He had publicly criticised *Novy mir* several times over the past two years, particularly offending Tvardovsky by hinting that he had sent *By Right of Memory* abroad himself, and calling it (with reference to the deportation of Tvardovsky's peasant father in the 1930s) a 'kulak' poem. Shortly after the new *Novy mir* board took over, there was a fight at the editorial meeting after Ovcharenko linked Tvardovsky's name with Andrey Sinyavsky's (implying that he, too, was a traitor deserving imprisonment) and Misha Khitrov, a temporary holdover from the old board, called it slander and stormed out of the room. Later, when Solzhenitsyn reproached Tvardovsky for not hanging on as chief editor after Igor and the rest were dismissed, Tvardovsky said that he couldn't have worked with Ovcharenko under any circumstances. While the new editor, a comparative moderate, said Ovcharenko's accusations against Tvardovsky were 'tactless', Ovcharenko not only survived as an editor but remained on the *Novy mir* board for many years.

In the last days of the old *Novy mir*, Tvardovsky made one last desperate effort to get through to Brezhnev on the telephone and try to persuade him to rescue the journal by a personal intervention. Nothing came of this, but the story was still unfinished when I left the Soviet Union at the beginning of March, and Igor promised to let me know what happened. Since he would be writing by open post, he said he would use a code, substituting our friend Nikolay Pavlovich Voronov's name for Brezhnev's. He had never proposed anything so clandestine before. The letter duly arrived, and there was indeed news of Nikolay Pavlovich: he had come up from Kaluga to Moscow to buy sausage. In other words, it was the real Nikolay Pavlovich. Igor had forgotten about his code.

Igor was sixty-six at the time of his dismissal, so the question of finding him another job didn't arise. If he'd been younger, he probably wouldn't have been given a job anyway: of the two young members of the editorial board who were dismissed with him, Lakshin landed a job at another journal, but the other man was essentially unemployed for many years. Igor wasn't totally without occupation, since he continued to do literary editing for various publishing houses on a casual basis, but he was demoralised. Going round to see him in May (as his diary records), Tvardovsky found him 'limp, apologetic and indecisive', too exhausted even to be bothered drinking. I can't imagine that 'apologetic', unless it was a guilty feeling about Tvardovsky personally: that he should have kept him safe.

In July, Tvardovsky invited a group of friends, including Igor, to a party in a restaurant to mark his sixtieth birthday. Even in this select company, there was a hierarchy of closeness: most of the guests apparently paid for themselves, but Igor was one of Tvardovsky's special guests. Describing it to me in a letter, Igor remarked, 'How did it happen that you didn't once meet my comrades from the editorial board?' This wasn't strictly true, as I had met Lakshin and Khitrov often and most of the others occasionally; but he meant Tvardovsky, and the answer to his rhetorical question was that I would have been a security risk to him. Now that the old *Novy mir* was gone, of course, there would have been no problem about my meeting Tvardovsky; he had little left to lose. But Tvardovsky's health was rapidly declining. 'I am never free of worry for Alexander Trifonovich', Igor wrote me in June 1970. 'It's a kind of constraint.' Not long after, Tvardovsky had a stroke and was later diagnosed with lung cancer. His days were clearly numbered, and Igor wrote that 'even when you aren't thinking about it, it casts a shadow'.

The old *Novy mir* editorial board had agreed to gather every year on the anniversary of the journal's demise, but before the second of these reunions Tvardovsky was dead. He died in December 1971, and I was by chance in Moscow, back on a tourist visa for a short trip to see Igor. It was a sad meeting. Igor and Raisa Isaevna were, of course, going to the funeral, and they took me along to the Writers' House where Tvardovsky was laid out for viewing and leave-taking, in the Russian manner. The viewing was open to the public, and thousands came to pay their last respects. Ordinary members of the public had to keep their coats on and shuffle past the coffin and out the door. For members of the Writers' Union, there was a different procedure: they were allowed and indeed required to leave their coats in the cloakroom, and after making the circuit round the coffin with the public, they were let through the barrier to take their seats in the hall to await the speeches and formal farewell. I had come in with Union members, and we had immediately met up with others of the *Novy mir* group and gone to the cloakroom to leave our coats. I walked round past the coffin, coatless, with Igor and Raisa Isaevna, and then they were pulled out of the line to stand in a little huddle of intimate mourners, leaving me on my own. Immediately I saw that I was in for trouble: as an ordinary member of the public, I had to leave, but I couldn't leave because I didn't have my coat. *Where was the cloakroom?* I didn't know the building and couldn't remember even which direction it was in. *Who had the ticket for my coat?* I couldn't bring myself to push through the mourners to get to Igor and Raisa Isaevna, looking old and disoriented in that sad little group at the centre, and anyway, I didn't think either of them had the ticket. I ran around the building in a panic trying to find the cloakroom, all the time scared that someone in authority would challenge my presence in a members-only zone, and finally ran into Misha Khitrov, the young secretary of the editorial board, who by great good luck had the cloakroom ticket and retrieved my coat. I put it on and fled.

All around me at the Writers' House, if I had only known, other little dramas were being played out. I wasn't the only person to be disconcerted by the barrier separating sheep and goats. Solzhenitsyn, now expelled from the Union, faced them down at the barrier ('they didn't dare stop me') and took his seat in the hall; afterwards, officials tried to prevent him going to the grave and backed off only on the insistence of Tvardovsky's widow. Zhores Medvedev, not long out of a brief spell in a psychiatric hospital (his critical writings about the regime being taken as a sign of insanity), shuffled past the open coffin twice in his coat before coming across friends, presumably Union members, who helped him and his wife divest themselves of their coats, get past the barrier and sit down. Not allowed to go to the graveside on the buses laid on for Union members, Medvedev took the trolley bus to Novodevichy Cemetery but found it cordoned off by large squads of police. Rebuffed at the gate, along with many other Tvardovsky admirers without Union cards, he went round to another entrance and finally managed to get in with a group of schoolchildren. But by that time the ceremony was over, and the crush of people prevented him getting to the front to throw a handful of earth on the coffin, as is the Russian custom.

'The love affair is over', was one of Lida's favourite phrases. It didn't exactly fit, but still the phrase kept drumming in my head towards the end of my 1969–70 stay in Moscow. I loved Igor as before, and still thought of him and Irina as family. But it seemed so clearly to be an end. *Novy mir* was dead, my book was done, and I had more or less run out of archives. I didn't seek an extension on my five months on the exchange, which ran out in March 1970, the month after Igor's dismissal. It was time to go.

It was also time to start the New Life in London, postponed for the sake of Moscow. There was the house in Muswell Hill, not just the first house I had ever (semi-) owned but also the first whole house I had ever lived in, having grown up in a small flat in Australia and lived in college rooms, flats and digs since. There was the nursery, waiting for an occupant. I wasn't feeling up to par: there had been another near-fainting episode in Moscow in January, and when I got back to England I noticed that my face was unusually pale, with a yellowish tinge. It stayed like that for months, but I never went to a doctor about it or consulted anyone about that mysterious 'heart attack' diagnosis; after a year or so, my health went back to normal. My letters to my mother were full of rather unconvincingly bright chatter about my future with Rex. But it wasn't in a mood of ebullience that I returned to England.

This time, getting my stuff out of Russia wasn't as much of a problem as the first time round because I didn't have a trunk. All the same, the packing nightmare, which has stayed with me throughout my life, was already entrenched, for I wrote about it to Rex in January: 'I dreamt I was packing for somewhere in a completely disorganised way and the plane was about to go. You were there, fixing things that I broke, but also slightly disorganised'. That was undoubtedly an edited version. Rex may have been there fixing things in my dream, but I still couldn't catch the plane. In real life, however, I caught the plane and returned to England where, as usual at the end of a trip, I wrote my Final Report—that same mandatory submission that the Soviets regarded as an intelligence document—for the British Council. I happen to have kept a copy of this one, which is severely focused on archival and library access, with emphasis on the fruitfulness of my research despite the inevitable bureaucratic problems. No mention of *Novy mir* or Igor and Irina, of course; but in a few weeks Bolsover, director of my institute, took me out to lunch and tried to debrief me on those topics, or that's how I interpreted it. I stonewalled.

In deciding to marry Rex, I had opted to make England, not Australia, my home, but my letters to him convey a strong sense of unease about this. In October, I had brought him up sharply for a cliché to the effect that Russia was my second homeland:

> When you wrote about Russia as my second homeland, I was puzzled to know what you thought was my first. If you meant England, it was never my home until I came to London this summer; always before it was very alien.

Then in November, describing my archival battles in Moscow, I wrote that 'I am very much at home in this funny atmosphere. If I understood English mores better, I would be more ill at ease here'—a curious double negative that might be taken to imply that not only was Moscow more like home to me than England, but I wasn't sure I wanted that to change.

Those two letters were written at a time when my spirits were high. That was no longer the case in February, when I returned to the topic with a diatribe against the novelist Angus Wilson, a specialist in the dissection of English class distinctions. 'He makes me feel as if English society is made up of about twenty-five characters and you have to choose one, and then be pinned down and despised', I wrote to Rex. 'I am glad I am not English.' I was 'really frightened' about living in London, I went on; and indeed I must have been, as the tone of these comments on my future homeland was not only tactless, as directed to an English future husband, but also aggressive in a panicky way. 'Who is this person who is going to live with you in Muswell Hill?' I asked. 'Who do your friends think she is?' Who do *you* think? (This last question was not asked outright but hung in the air.) Is she a daughter of the Old Left? An Australian expatriate? A Sovietologist? A refugee from North Oxford? A messenger from Moscow? And then, a final wail (recognising that people living as man and wife in English suburbia were still expected to have the same surname): 'I don't even know what my name is.'

Postscript

My departure from Moscow in March 1970 wasn't completely the end of my Soviet life, of course, still less the end of the Soviet Union in my life. I became a Sovietologist, and after a while, once Soviet history was recognised as a legitimate field, a Soviet historian. With the collapse of the Soviet Union, the designation tended to shift to modern Russian history, but it was always the Soviet Union, not Russia, that was my subject. My personal ties with Igor and Irina lasted until their deaths. As far as my professional work on the Soviet Union is concerned, Igor's footprints are all over it, and will be forever. And I suppose, since I have had many students in the United States who themselves became Soviet historians, his footprints can be found in their work, albeit fainter and unrecognised by them.

In the early 1970s, I moved from England to America (another New Life!). For some years, I couldn't go to the Soviet Union except as a tourist because I wasn't eligible for anyone's exchange: not the British, because I was living in the United States and working at an American university, and not the American, because I didn't have American citizenship. Once I got a US passport, about the middle of the 1970s, I started to go to the Soviet Union regularly again for research, along with Jerry Hough, the American Sovietologist I had married, and resumed regular face-to-face contact with Igor and Irina. That visa was in the name of Khoff, if I remember rightly, though the name was variously transliterated into Russian as Khaff, Khog, Gog and Goff. I'm not sure if the KGB was really on top of this new name change; they were more interested in Jerry (as a political scientist and policy analyst) than me, so it's possible that the Bryus, Fitspatrik and Khoff files never got consolidated. S Fitzpatrick continued to publish, except that in America, following local convention, she became Sheila Fitzpatrick.

The focus of my work shifted in the course of the 1970s. I moved into social history, following a trail that started in Lunacharsky's Narkompros, where affirmative action on behalf of workers and poor peasants was a divisive issue in the 1920s. Stalin and the Party Central Committee, concerned about elite recruitment, wanted more of it; Lunacharsky, worried about educational standards, wanted less. The Party position prevailed for the years of Cultural Revolution at the end of the 1920s and the beginning of the 1930s, but then the Lunacharsky policy returned, though without Lunacharsky. My discovery was that those affirmative action people from the early 1930s formed the core of the new Communist elite consolidated after the Great Purges, and remained in the leadership up to Brezhnev's time. That argument got me into trouble in the United States, where it was felt that affirmative action and upward mobility were American, democratic inventions, and Igor didn't like it much either. He knew the affirmative action people as a type, of course, and he loathed them: they were the Stalinist bureaucrats, crude and half-educated, who thought the Revolution had done its job when it let people like them climb out of the gutter into the elite. That wasn't what Igor thought the Revolution was about. Unlike many American Sovietologists, he understood that I chose to study this group not because I admired them but because I thought they were historically significant. But that judgement itself caused him pain, even though he couldn't disagree with it. These were the people who had hijacked his Revolution, and now, in a way, they were hijacking me.

I've spelt this all out at greater length than Igor ever did: we knew each other, and he didn't have to. The strength of the personal tie between us was not affected, but its nature changed, no doubt inevitably, as I grew up and he grew old. America was further away than England, more alien from Igor's point of view. We saw each other less often and corresponded less frequently: reading Igor's letters of the 1970s, I notice that he often says he has nothing much to tell me because nothing has happened. Raisa Isaevna fought her way back to something like health and resumed work as a translator; their son Sasha persevered in his career as a pianist, though with a sense of grievance at constricted opportunities. Igor shrank over time, got a lot thinner, lost bounce; he no longer drank a lot, at least in my presence; girlfriends seemed to be a thing of the past. His intelligence and wit were unimpaired, but he was getting less fun out of life and his humour had darkened. He started to treat each meeting as the final one, saying he was going to die soon. The last time, feeling him so brittle in my hands as we kissed goodbye, I thought it was true.

Igor died in 1979 at the age of seventy-six. It was the Civil War wound in his back (unremoved shrapnel) that killed him, and I couldn't help thinking of the ballad in which Okudzhava imagines his own death on a Civil War battlefield, with commissars in greatcoats silently looking down at him. Perhaps Igor would have thought that sentimental; he wasn't really a man for the bards, preferring Liszt and Beethoven. Up to the end, he stuck to his position that one Party and one country was the hand he'd been dealt, but I think he was increasingly thinking it was a pretty lousy hand. He stayed in the Party, but his sense of allegiance grew weaker; he started socialising with dissidents, which he never would have done in the *Novy mir* days. When he died, Raisa Isaevna and Sasha sent a telegram to me in the US telling me of the death and inviting me to join the family mourning. They did it, no doubt, because they thought he would have wanted them to, but even so it warmed my heart to be counted as family. The Soviet Union survived Igor's death by twelve years. Its collapse wasn't a sight for Old Bolsheviks, and I was glad he didn't have to see it.

After Igor's death, I kept going round to the apartment to see Raisa Isaevna whenever I was in Moscow. At first these were courtesy calls; then we became friends. They had moved in 1974 to a new apartment with its own bathroom, 'organised' as they say in Russian by Irina. Igor never got used to it, but it made life much easier for Raisa. We used to sit together in the kitchen when Igor was still alive and in Raisa's room afterwards. Sasha, after a period away in a marriage that failed, had his own room with the grand piano and even a little space left over, but he was chafing at not being able to set up on his own. The apartment was a rectangular kind of place, dark and lacking the idiosyncrasy of the old one on Smolensk Square. It was in a late-Stalinist building almost opposite what was then the US Embassy, and Igor claimed that the devices by which the Soviets snooped on the embassy were on their roof. In the 1980s, when my work was mainly focused on everyday life, I used to ask Raisa Isaevna about the practical side of living in Moscow in the 1930s. Unlike Igor, Raisa was not a raconteur, but she was an exceptionally good informant, remembering details accurately and without embellishment. We talked about Igor, too. She said once that after all she was glad that it was me Igor had fallen in love with—there was always going to be someone, and luckily I was a decent person (and absent most of the time, though she didn't say that). In those unhappy years, it was a source of happiness for him, she added, after a pause. But this was more than a decade after Raisa's near-fatal illness and my first meeting with Igor; her anger against him had fallen away and just left the affection of a lifetime together.

I don't know if Raisa Isaevna was a member of the Communist Party, very likely yes, but she wasn't an Old Bolshevik in spirit like Igor. Still, I was distressed when I heard that shortly after the collapse of the Soviet Union, when Sasha got a job in Austria, she had emigrated with him (he died there in 2007, at the age of sixty-six; she, I suppose, must have died long before). It seemed so late in life for her to have to uproot herself, and her languages were French and Spanish, not German. In the process of their departure, which was evidently hasty, those of Igor's papers that remained in the apartment were lost. His other papers had been gathered in the 1980s by Volodya Lakshin, who was the literary executor appointed by the Writers' Union. According to Lakshin, there were lots of letters from me, for all that Igor was always complaining that I never wrote; in fact, he said, there was a special *opis'* (inventory) for my letters. I was very struck by being the subject of an *opis'*, as these were documents the archives would never give to us foreigners. But I never saw my *opis'*, so never found out how they had labelled it ('Letters to IA Sats from Sh Bruce, England'? 'From Sh Fitzpatrick'? or did they go the whole hog with 'Letters to IA Sats from Sh Bruce-Fitzpatrick-Hough, England-USA'?). The papers should have ended up in the State Literary Archive, but they haven't. I don't know how they came to disappear, and, as Volodya died unexpectedly at sixty in 1993, there is nobody left to ask.

Irina outlived Igor by more than a decade, dying in a car accident in London in 1991 shortly after the collapse of the Soviet Union. She was disappointed that I didn't write a Lunacharsky biography, but she accepted it; and our friendship actually became closer in the 1980s, despite the relatively infrequent meetings. Perhaps that was because, with Igor dead, Irina was the last of my Soviet family; or perhaps with the passage of time we had become more like contemporaries—twenty-five and forty-eight when we first met, fifty and seventy-three when she died. I didn't write to her often, but in the 1980s, with relations with my mother at a low ebb, I came to regard Irina as fulfilling at least one quasi-parental role, that of following my progress through life. Irina was often critical of my actions, and always inclined to cross-examine me about them, but (unlike my mother, or so I felt) she was basically on my side. She looked over the men in my life, usually somewhat disapprovingly. This had the advantage that when I broke up with them, it was always their fault, whereas my mother was inclined to assume the opposite. Irina wanted me to be a success in worldly terms (to which professional success was a stepping stone, though a good marriage would have served the same purpose), and warmly applauded whatever signs of success she could find, though she was disappointed that I never seemed to know the American ambassador. She even had time to meet my last husband, Michael Danos, a physicist, who impressed her by his good-humoured failure to be intimidated or let her patronise him. He took photographs of that meeting, Irina looking elegant as ever and even Rafail Naumovich quite benign. Irina might have preferred Misha to have a Nobel Prize, but the fact that he kept an apartment in Paris and spoke French as well as Russian was in his favour. And the fact that I was happy, which Irina would not have failed to notice; that mattered to Irina, though other things mattered, too.

Once, perhaps in 1989, I stayed the night at Irina's apartment in Gorky Street. That might seem unremarkable, but it came after all those years of being marked as a foreigner, hence not allowed to stay overnight with Soviet families. I remember Irina's look—a bit gleeful, a bit sly—when she said it's late, you'd better sleep here, and produced face cream and a nightgown. Nobody else was home, so it was a kind of girls' slumber party. We sat up late, and Irina started musing on how to survive in the old Soviet Union, how to make your way back if you had the misfortune to land in Gulag. You needed to get a boss out there, in Magadan or wherever, who would act as your patron and protector and help you get back to the centre. Later, I realised that she was in effect describing the strategy her aunt Natalia Ilinichna had followed in Kazakhstan after the camps, but what struck me at the time was that all the Soviet right-thinking that was normally so characteristic of Irina had suddenly been stripped away. She was just telling it like it was, or at least like she saw it, giving me an impromptu sociological analysis of Soviet behaviour that was amazingly sharp, clear-headed and full of insight. It was like seeing an alternative Irina, the person she might have been if she hadn't come to adulthood at the height of the Great Purges and had to learn self-protection. Next time I saw her, she was back to normal. Or rather, a new normal, as she was intent on building a new set of connections outside the Soviet Union, with my help and using the Lunacharsky secrets as a calling card. But that's not how I like to remember her. I'd rather see her with the face cream in her hand and an affectionate, slightly mischievous expression on her face.

I wasn't in Moscow in the short period between the Soviet Union's collapse and Irina's death, and her sons didn't send a telegram when she died. Not surprisingly, because everything was in turmoil. Irina's elder son, Sergey, a scientist without her worldly ambitions, came through the transition rather well: he was happy to be able to go and hear jazz in the evening when he felt like it, he told me when I saw him again in the 1990s, but otherwise he just went on with his work and trusted that sometime someone would pay his salary, which in the end they did. The younger son, Andrey, had a more spectacularly successful transition, but at a price. Trained as an economist, he became one of Russia's new rich—a businessman and market specialist who seemed weighed down by care when I caught up with him again. It was a dangerous world for businessmen—murders by rivals were common—and Andrey was responsible for keeping his extended family financially afloat. He said he would give me exclusive access to the Lunacharsky diaries but wouldn't put them into an archive. I was working on other things at the time and wasn't interested, but I was also rather indignant at his proposal. Perhaps it felt like another proposed deal, the one from Ovcharenko long ago. It felt like Irina, too, of course, with her entrepreneurial approach to controlling Lunacharsky scholarship. Andrey himself was not particularly interested in Lunacharsky, as far as I know, so I suppose he saw it as filial duty—or perhaps he shared Irina's hope that the Lunacharsky secrets would turn out to be marketable assets. Thanks to Andrey's connections in the new post-Soviet world—he really was a son for Irina to be proud of—he was able to pull strings in the Moscow mayor's office and keep the Lunacharsky Museum intact in the apartment (now very valuable real estate) where Irina had grown up and Igor had lived in the attic. But it was no longer open to the public, the question of legal ownership had not been resolved, and its purpose and future were uncertain.

Max Hayward and Ovcharenko vanished from my life after my move to the US, only to make one farewell appearance each before disappearing, this time for good. I met Max by chance in New York, sometime in the late 1970s, on the steps of the International Affairs building at Columbia University, where I then worked. He took me off to coffee at the swish Upper East Side apartment he was staying in, guest of rich American admirers interested in dissident Soviet literature, because he wanted to show it off. He was a different person in America, liberated from the constraints of trying to be the right class for Oxford, greeting me almost exuberantly (though he was quite sober) as another enterprising Brit who, like him, had managed to con the generous but innocent Americans into supporting me. (That's not what my American life was like, but it was a new and arresting image.) We talked as if we were old friends, though we never had been; and he told me what a nightmare it had been having me as a student in Oxford, how inadequate he felt when I talked about archives and sources, how he dreaded our formal conversations, expecting all the time to have his ignorance shown up, so stern a young judge did I seem to him. It was remarkable that I had become so different in his eyes. He was different in my eyes too—for one thing, comparatively young, almost a contemporary. We parted with great mutual goodwill. He died at fifty-four in 1979.

Ovcharenko continued active in Soviet literary studies and as an editor of the revamped *Novy mir*, but after 1970 I heard and saw nothing of him until sometime in the early 1980s, when I ran into him at a reception at the Kennan Institute in Washington. I was a year-long fellow there and he, thanks to détente, a short-term visitor. He was delighted to see me, greeted me warmly and even affectionately, and told everyone around that I had been his student way back when and what a pleasure it had been to see me come into my own as a historian. For all my loyalty to Igor's memory, I couldn't help smiling back. A rogue, but my rogue, part of my past. He didn't live to see the collapse of the Soviet Union, though it was a near thing. If he'd lived just a bit longer, I would have become an asset to him, since during *perestroika* foreign scholars morphed from being objects of suspicion to prize possessions: in the Institutes of History, the old Sections of Bourgeois Historiography redefined their mission from criticism of foreign scholars to acting as our publicists. That wouldn't have been beyond Ovcharenko; indeed, with his keen sense of the way the wind blows, he seemed half-prepared for it even in 1983. He died, however, in 1986 at the age of sixty-four.

The atmosphere in the Soviet Union was loosening up with détente; stories of attempted entrapment of students and scholars became rarer, and I never had any significant trouble with the KGB after my student years. When I worked at Columbia University in New York, there were lots of spies snooping around the Russian Institute, not just American and Soviet but also Israeli and who knows what else, but they didn't bother me. The FBI came round a couple of times, asking for information about students (I didn't give it), and I once had an entertaining visit from a hopeful Soviet spy, who wanted to stir up trouble between me and Zbigniew Brzezinski, a Cold War hawk in the political science department one floor up, with whom I was on perfectly good terms. I wasn't attacked in the Soviet Union as a 'bourgeois falsifier' of history, in fact they tended to put me in the 'so-called objective' category of Western historians (meaning historians who were as objective as they could be, given their basic category allegiance to capitalism), along with EH Carr. That was because I was what was called a 'revisionist' in the 1970s; that is, a social historian critical of the totalitarian model (which the Soviets also strongly disliked) who disputed the idea that all initiative in the Soviet Union came from the top. It was in the Soviet State Archives, working on Narkompros, that I had learnt scepticism on that score.

In the 1970s and early 1980s I had more political trouble in the US than I did in the Soviet Union. I was a newcomer to the American academic scene, and newcomers are natural objects of suspicion. Probably, the rumour went, I had got into Soviet archives because my father was a big Communist apparatchik in Australia; it could well be that I had come to Columbia as a KGB spy and married Jerry Hough with the intent of converting him to my left-wing world view (that was the implication of a very nasty piece in the right-wing weekly *Commentary*). So this was part two of my personal experience of the Cold War, and I didn't enjoy it. But it was a different experience from the Soviet one: I felt victimised and scared, but not in the least guilty. I wasn't half-prepared to think the charges were true, as I had been in the Soviet Union when I was called 'next thing to a spy' for the West. I was quite clear about not being a Soviet spy, or even pro-Soviet or Marxist. I felt innocent—perhaps even more innocent than I actually was, since anti-anti-Communism has its pitfalls—and thought the Americans, because of their exaggerated Cold War anxieties, had got me wrong. After a while, rather a long while, they thought so, too.

I never felt completely innocent in the Soviet Union. Part of this came, no doubt, from my private burden of guilt over my father's death and my estrangement from him. But it was something the Soviet Union generated as well. Soviet citizens hadn't forgotten the witch-hunt of the Great Purges, when you could suddenly be accused of being an enemy of the people and find no way of proving your innocence, even to yourself. This sense of being perpetually under suspicion is captured in Andrey Sinyavsky's *The Trial Begins* (translated by Max Hayward, published with CIA support, but a fine novella nonetheless). A young boy who organised a childish conspiratorial group has been arrested and is under interrogation at the Lubyanka. He objects to the interrogator's tone, saying that, while he may be on trial, he hasn't yet been condemned. His KGB interrogator takes him to the window and points to the crowds of non-arrested Muscovites in the street below, going about their daily business. 'That's where they are, the people who are on trial', the interrogator explains. 'You're different now, my boy. You're not on trial, you're condemned.'

I wasn't just one of the people on the street below who were on trial; I was a foreigner, which in itself put me midway on the continuum between being on trial and being condemned. Then, with the *Sovetskaya Rossiya* article, I moved further along, let's say seven-eighths of the way in the direction of being condemned: I wasn't quite a spy, but close to it. 'I turned out to be a terrorist', says one of Eugenia Ginzburg's companions on the train taking prisoners to Gulag, meaning that that is the charge on which she was condemned, but also suggesting that, regardless of the truth of the charge, that's who she is now. In the same way, I could have turned out to be a spy. It was unlikely, of course, but imagination isn't ruled by statistical probability. If I had turned out to be a spy, given the St Antony's connection, it would have had a certain plausibility.

Was I, in some sense, a spy? If the Soviets couldn't make up their minds, it's not surprising that I had trouble. I can certainly recognise some spy-like characteristics in myself, starting with my intention to find out everything about Soviet history, including the things that the Soviets wanted to keep hidden. If a spy is a chameleon who can speak two languages and doesn't know what his ultimate allegiance is, that partly fits. I could speak the two languages, both literally and metaphorically, and the question of my national identity was certainly moot at this point. As to my allegiance, it was neither to the Soviet Union nor Great Britain, because I didn't pose the question that way. I thought in terms of *Novy mir* versus St Antony's, and given that choice, my allegiance went to *Novy mir*. That was a Soviet allegiance, on the face of it, but a tremendously ambiguous one. *Novy mir* claimed to be a loyal Soviet journal, but the Soviet authorities were increasingly inclined to reject that claim, and it was also rejected by the journal's admirers at St Antony's. If it was a two-camp world, in other words, it was really unclear in which camp *Novy mir* belonged—and the same applied to me.

If you came down from the realm of abstraction to practicalities, on the other hand, there was no doubt which side I was on. I had a British passport, and nothing would have made me give it up, as far as my dealings with the Soviet Union were concerned. I would not for a moment have contemplated living in the Soviet Union, because if you lived there, you were trapped: the moment you lost the ability to leave at will (which I possessed, but not Igor and Irina or any other Soviet citizen), it became a prison. We all knew that, and that's why there was always that collective sigh of relief when the plane lifted off from Moscow. Our luck had held, we had made it out. Just as if we were spies going home from a mission, the whole plane-load of us.

Spies not only collect information, they give it to someone. I was wary about giving information to my most plausible spymasters, Max Hayward and George Bolsover. But that doesn't mean I wasn't passing on the information I had gathered in the Soviet Union. As I researched this memoir, I realised that the person to whom I was giving information was my mother. She was the person to whom I regularly sent detailed accounts of my experiences, including whatever political and social information on the Soviet Union I had gleaned; to avoid Soviet censorship, I would often save the best bits to tell her after my return to England. I can imagine her as a spymaster, sitting snugly in her flat in Melbourne as she received reports from her far-flung agents, pondering their reliability, wondering if they could still be trusted. That cold eye, that scepticism, that refusal of partisanship—she was well suited to the job. It's true that she was less interested in much of my data than MI6 or the CIA would have been. In fact, I suspect she often just skimmed the analytical and descriptive sections, reading the letters primarily as coded communications about my personal fortunes. She knew how to decode.

But there's the possibility that I wasn't writing my reports only to my mother but to something beyond her. That is the something, or somebody, that needed to be told that I had never been to America. 'Posterity', people often say in such cases, but I'm not sure that that fits. I wasn't so much trying to make myself look good in those letters (sometimes, reading them, you might conclude the opposite) but rather to clarify my impressions and approach understanding. The letters to my mother of 1966–67 are much closer to the diary I was keeping at the same time than you would expect; I kept some of the worries and confusions out, but often the letter is a second pass at a topic discussed more telegraphically in the diary. Rex took over for a few months in 1969–70 as my primary information recipient, and those letters have some special characteristics, including a greater dramatic flair, but as reports they differ little from those to my mother except in assuming greater knowledge of Soviet mores and familiarity with Russian. Taken together, the letters and diary look more like research notes than anything else, meaning that the researcher—and, more distantly, the scholarly community she belongs to—is the real addressee. That would make me both my own spymaster, which is a bit far-fetched, and an agent of myself, which I suppose is what we all hope to be.

The Puritan John Bunyan was much exercised in his book *Grace Abounding* about whether he had committed the sin against the Holy Ghost. It was the unpardonable sin; but, as he didn't know for sure what the unpardonable sin was, he could never be sure if he had committed it. That's rather how I felt about being a spy. Perhaps I was, perhaps I wasn't, but I hoped grace would abound and I would escape being cast into the pit. There was a kind of craziness abroad in the English Revolution of the seventeenth century that made people preoccupied with sins against the Holy Ghost. In the twentieth-century Soviet Union, the craziness was about spying, and it spread to the Westerners who studied the country. I'm not sure if I committed the Cold War equivalent of the sin against the Holy Ghost or, if I did, on behalf of which side. But how should I know, if even the Holy Ghost, known in the Soviet Union as the KGB, couldn't make up its mind?

Acknowledgements

My first statement of gratitude must go to Tara Zahra, my colleague at the University of Chicago, who suggested the title of this book. Bernard Wasserstein critiqued my original book proposal, and Barbara Gillam and Lynn Dalgarno acted as sounding boards as I wrote. I am grateful to Ross McKibbin, Katerina Clark, Margot Light and Robert Dessaix for discussing various points with me, and Rex Winsbury for letting me use my letters to him. Stephen Wheatcroft gave me a copy of the Leningrad KGB's 1972 booklet *Nauchnyi obmen i ideologicheskaia diversiya* (Scholarly exchange and ideological diversion) that I quote liberally throughout the book. Mark McKenna was kind enough to read and critique the whole manuscript. Ann Curthoys and other members of our Research Support Group at the School of Philosophical and Historical Inquiry, University of Sydney, provided very useful feedback on a draft of chapter 6, and the University of Sydney's History on Monday audience made helpful comments on chapter 5. I thank my publisher at Melbourne University Press, Sally Heath, for her help and support throughout the process and for reading several drafts.